Alex Atock is a graduate of the Veterinary College of Ireland. Following some years in general veterinary practice in Ireland and England, and resulting from his interest in racing, he was appointed veterinary officer at the Irish Turf Club (Jockey Club).

He next moved to become head of the Veterinary Department of the Federation Equestre Internationale (FEI), the ruling body of international equestrian sport, based in Switzerland.

Following an early retirement from the FEI, he moved on to the United Arab Emirates on his appointment as veterinary officer and consultant to the UAE Equestrian and Racing Federation, and finally to the British-based equine charity, World Horse Welfare, responsible for its international training programmes in developing countries.

He has a particular interest in facilitating the international movement of horses, doping and the control of medication in equestrian sport. He was past secretary/treasurer of the World Equine Veterinary Association.

He and his wife, Sherley, have three grown-up children and live in Herefordshire.

To Sherley, my wife of 58 years, children: Sandy, Martin and Philip, and grandchildren: Georgina, Alexandra and Charlie.

Alex Atock

MY FRIEND
THE HORSE

AUSTIN MACAULEY PUBLISHERS™
LONDON * CAMBRIDGE * NEW YORK * SHARJAH

A CIP catalogue record for this title is available from the British Library.

ISBN 9781786937933 (Paperback)
ISBN 9781786937940 (Hardback)
ISBN 9781786937957 (E-Book)

www.austinmacauley.com

First Published (2018)
Austin Macauley Publishers Ltd.
25 Canada Square
Canary Wharf
London
E14 5LQ

Acknowledgements

This book is essentially a personal account of my experiences as a veterinary surgeon. I accept that my recollection of events may have become hazy over the years, but regardless, the opinions expressed in it are my own, and I take full responsibility for any errors or misrepresentations.

My very grateful thanks go to H.R.H. Princess Haya Bint Al Hussein, for not only giving me the encouragement to produce this book in the first place but also for writing the most generous and kind foreword.

I am immensely grateful to Michael Slavin, who guided me through the early days of this book, to Andrew Higgins, Roly Owers and Emma Cook, who each proofread and made helpful suggestions to specific chapters. And to Tony Shaftain, who skilfully transferred my miscellaneous collection of photographs into digital format, and of course, to my publishers Austin Macauley and their team, notably my production coordinator, Connor Browne.

I would also like to thank many other individuals who assisted me during my travels through the equestrian world, some of whom are sadly no longer with us. In alphabetical order, these include, but are not limited to: Max E. Ammann, A. H. Billar, Andre Bubear, Mike and Henry Bullen, Thierry Chillaud, Gerry Cullen, Andrew Dalglish, Roland Devolz, Ingmar De Vos, Kevin Doyle, Richard Felton, Alf-Ekbert Fussel, Bernard van Goethem, Sabrina Ibáñez, Jeremy James, Ulrich Kihm, John Lengel, Amy Mann, Fiona McCormack, Brian Marchant, Keith Meldrum, Catrin Norinder, John Roche, Alaine Storme, B.L. Surendra Babu (Dr Bobby) and Andrew Turnbull.

In addition, there are many others who assisted me during my career. These include the key personnel and staff in a number of organisations for which I was privileged to work, or have connections with: Lewis Doyle, Tip Morgan and Alan Brown (veterinary practice); Denis Baggallay and Cahir O'Sullivan (chief executive officers, Irish Turf Club); the presidents of the FEI during my tenure: H.R.H. The Prince Philip, Duke of Edinburgh, H.R.H. The Princess Anne (now Princess Royal), S.A.R. L'Infante Dona Pilar de Borbon and their secretary generals: Fritz Widmer, Etienne Allard and Bo Helander (FEI); Jean Blajan and Jean Blancou (director generals, OIE – World Animal Health Organisation); Jean Romanet and Louis Romanet (International Federation of Racing Authorities); Faisal Seddiq M. Samea and Hussein Mohammed Hussein (secretary generals, UAE Equestrian and Racing Federation), and Douglas Munroe, Johnny McIrvine and John Smales (ceos World Horse Welfare).

Finally, I would like to thank the many colleagues, too numerous to mention individually, in the different organisations in which I worked, for their assistance, guidance and support throughout my career.

Contents

Acknowledgements..7

Foreword.. 13
H.R.H. Princess Haya Bint Al Hussein
President of FEI 2006–2014

Introduction/Prologue...15
A History of International Horse Welfare

Chapter 1 23
The Early Years
Ponies and Horses – School – Student Days – Race-Riding – the Bicester Horses
– Graduation

Chapter 2 37
Veterinary Practice and Racing
Veterinary Assistant in Ireland and England – Own Practice in Dublin –
Veterinary Officer Irish Turf Club – Presentation to International Conference of
Racing Analysts and Veterinarians (ICRAV)

Chapter 3 51
Introduction to FEI
Doping Control Dublin Horse Show – Acting as Foreign Official – Olympic
Games Moscow – World Cup Final Birmingham – Appointment to FEI

Chapter 4 61
History of Equestrian Sport
Changing Function of the Horse – Move to Bern – FEI Secretariat – Vet.
Committee and Regulations

Chapter 5 73
Controversy at Championship
Horse Inspections – Repercussions – Aftermath

Chapter 6 78

Drugs in Horse Sport
Conflicting Opinions – The Phenylbutazone Issue – Potential Consequences –
NSAID Conference

Chapter 7 88

Medication Control Programme
Historical Review – Comparison with Racing – Proposal to FEI – Introduction of
MCP

Chapter 8 99

International Movement of Horses
Global Disease Situation – Liaison with Official Authorities – Practices and
Problems

Chapter 9 117

Tackling Welfare
Ethics Committee – Negative Publicity – Welfare Joint Committee and Sub-
Committee

Chapter 10 129

Olympic Research
Heat and Humidity – Atlanta 1996 – Hong Kong 2008

Chapter 11 137

Back to the Office
Change of Guard at HQ – Dinner at the Palace – Secretariat Move – Australian
Tour – World Horse Welfare Petition – Retirement from FEI

Chapter 12 146

United Arab Emirates Equestrian AND Racing Federation
Official Veterinary Officer UAE Equestrian and Racing Federation – Endurance
in the Middle East – International Movement of Horses in the Region

Chapter 13 158

World Horse Welfare
History of the Charity – Appointment as Veterinary Consultant – Training in
Developing Countries

Chapter 14 ....**173**

Summing Up
    Review the Past and Look to the Future

Annex I **181**

Meetings/Conferences Attended

Annex II **183**

Code of Conduct for the Welfare of the Horse

Annex III **186**

Abbreviations/Glossary

Foreword

H.R.H. PRINCESS HAYA BINT AL HUSSEIN

President of FEI 2006–2014

I have always thought of horsemanship and the evolution of horse sport as a golden thread that reaches back into the history of mankind. It is a single strand consisting of multiple interwoven fibres; a strand which weakens in places but which has never been broken. The many people who have loved horses throughout history, and those who have found roles, positions, functions and an identity alongside these beautiful animals, are themselves small fibres within the thread; integral parts of the story of the majestic animals and the sport.

Some fibres belong to those who mastered the art of riding so that they could deliver messages across Europe in times gone by. Others belong to those who truly had inquisitive and curious minds, that loved horses, always seeking to understand them better; those who allowed horses to fulfil their potential, even as the human story twisted and turned, faithfully unrolling itself alongside the thread of horses. And on the other end of the spectrum, fibres belong to the Kings of territories and peoples, the heads of industries, and all of those who love to possess horses of great bloodlines for the status that they represent, or the powerful poignant moments of human enrichment that they provide.

The storied histories that make up the golden thread that unites all people of the horse are as endless as the sea is deep. And perhaps everyone who has contributed to that historic thread has cared about horse welfare in their own way, for their own reasons; in my experience, everyone involved with horses believes themselves to love them.

Of course, it goes without saying that the interpretation of love differs wherever you go in the world, and depends on what period in time you have lived.

But, I have seen that even the poorest families, those who have to struggle to farm for food, give what meagre offerings they have to all the mouths that are hungry, including the horse. Of course, sometimes a horse represents a livelihood, or more basically, a means to survival, and as such, it is loved for that reason as much as any other.

I met Alex Atock when I was a teenager. At the time, he was the Head of the FEI Veterinary Department. He was a man who was then – as he is now – greatly respected. Alex was known, among other things, for his ability to troubleshoot, so it does not surprise me, reading his book, to learn that his ancestors were railway engineers and historians; people who looked to the past but used their todays to build paths to the future.

Alex was and is widely respected for his dedication, innovation and pragmatism; he is loved for his Irish twinkle. Alex never missed the chance to see the humour in any situation as he faithfully built the foundations of what is now one of the strongest and most important fibres in the modern story of horse sport: that of equine welfare.

It is not an overstatement to say that Alex Atock is a man who has contributed to the golden thread of horse sport in many different and remarkable ways. Thankfully, he has also documented the extraordinary times within which he has lived and worked; perhaps the most tumultuous period in equine history. As a witness to the direction that the thread of horse sport has taken, Alex shares with us in his book many lenses and perspectives from all over the world.

I greatly enjoyed reading the journey of Alex's family and of Alex himself, and seeing through his eyes the good in many horses, and even more people. The chapters of this book are alive with descriptions of great people who played a part in making horse sport what it is today. We are indebted to Alex for committing to paper descriptions of the traditions and lifestyles that form the foundations of values that we should honour and celebrate far into the future. Those values are the essence of the fibres that will ensure the golden thread of horse sport endures into the future.

Thank you, Alex.

Introduction/Prologue

A HISTORY OF
INTERNATIONAL HORSE WELFARE

I had often wondered what my ancestors really did, but it was not until I retired that I had a chance to commence the relevant research.

I discovered that I came from a long line of railway engineers, although I broke with tradition to become a veterinary surgeon. At about the same time as I was looking into my past, Ernie Shepherd, an Irish railway historian, was also researching my family tree. He made contact with me in 2004, and this liaison resulted in a book—*The Atock/Attock Family, a Worldwide Railway Dynasty.*

From this book, I discovered that 13 members of my family over four generations, covering 130 years, had been involved in the railways, not only in Great Britain and Ireland, but also in Australia, Burma, Ceylon, Cuba, Egypt, Malaya, New Zealand, Sudan and Venezuela. I am proud that my grandfather, Tom, had travelled on the footplate of the engine, which took the Prince of Wales, who later became King George V, from Dublin to the West of Ireland, and back, in 1903.

In addition, my maternal grandfather, Alexander Strain, features in a chapter, *Profile of a Builder* in Ruth McManus's book, *Dublin, 1910–1940, Shaping the City and Suburbs.* This chapter describes his contribution to much of the development of the North Dublin suburbs with high quality but affordable housing in the 1920s.

Now that I knew what my ancestors had done, I was determined to keep the momentum going and to produce a record, mainly for my family, of my own modest achievements after I left veterinary practice and branched into veterinary administration of national and international equestrian sports.

Those who have read James Herriot's book *All Creatures Great and Small*, or seen the TV series, probably know all they need to know about the life of a veterinary surgeon in a mixed veterinary practice.

Hence, I do not intend to dwell on some 12 years of veterinary work both in England and Ireland during the 1960s – the stories are very much the same. However, there are alternative ways for a veterinarian to earn a living, and this book will take you through some of the options that opened up for me during an interesting life, largely dedicated to horses and their welfare.

Horses were always my raison d'etre for becoming a veterinary surgeon. But first there were the practice years, initially in farm work, with a few horses included, followed by companion animals; dogs and cats and a miscellaneous collection of other small animals, often presented in cardboard boxes. How do you tell which is Bonnie and which is Clyde when presented with two hamsters only a few days old by a six year old child, to which the answer is vitally important?

Eventually, brucellosis, a disease which causes abortion in cattle, and which is transmissible to humans, and was the bane of many farmers and veterinarians at the time, terminated my years in veterinary practice.

However, when one door closes another invariably opens and out of the blue, I was offered the post of stewards secretary (veterinary), effectively veterinary officer, to the Irish Turf Club. This involved being paid to go racing, virtually on a daily basis, to take care of the relevant administrative veterinary duties: medication (doping) control, identification of horses, examining horses after racing at the request of the stewards to determine reasons behind a poor performance and collaboration, or otherwise, the trainer's excuses and generally to advise on what was necessary to care for the racehorses' health and welfare.

The racecourse veterinarian, employed by the individual track, cared for accidents and injuries during racing. To go racing on a regular basis was my idea of ecstasy. Gradually, an increasing attendance at relevant international conferences, initially with the racing authorities of the UK and France and then expanding to Germany, Italy and Spain and finally to Australia, the USA and other countries, was required. The subjects covered ranged from the control of medication and forensic analyses, to horse-related health issues, the rapidly expanding international movement of horses and more, but always with the health and welfare of horses being paramount.

In the mid-1970s, I was asked to set-up the first medication control procedures for the international competitions at the Dublin Horse Show, which is held at the Royal Dublin Society show grounds in August each year.

This was due to my so-called 'expertise' in this field. I was told that medication control was being introduced to international equestrian sport by its governing body, the International Equestrian Federation, known by its French abbreviation—FEI—and that this was the first time it would be applied in Dublin. The Turf Club generously gave me leave of absence from my racing responsibilities to carry out these duties.

Eventually, having tended to the needs of the RDS for several years, in addition to racing, another door opened. And, having officiated a number of international events, including the 1980 Moscow Olympic Games, and the Volvo World Cup (show jumping) Final in Birmingham the following year, I was offered the post of Head of the Veterinary Department of the FEI, based then in Bern, Switzerland.

I commenced this role in January 1982 and it quickly broadened my horizons in the top-level of horse sport with all its ramifications. At the time, the FEI was the sole authority for international events in dressage, jumping, eventing, driving and special disciplines; the latter of which included endurance riding, vaulting, tent pegging and pony riders. There were 70 member National Equestrian Federations and some 300 international equestrian events, ranging from Olympic Games downwards, taking place under its auspices each year. The veterinary aspects of these were the responsibility of my department – a daunting task indeed for a country boy from Ireland. The number of member federations and events increased dramatically during my tenure to become over 100 federations and some 500 international events when I opted for an early retirement, of my own volition, in 1995.

I did, however, continue the liaison for some years afterwards, acting as secretary to various joint welfare committees with World Horse Welfare (then known as the International League for the Protection of Horses) which, on my instigation, had become the unofficial welfare arm of the FEI. The above ran concurrently with my role as secretary/treasurer of the World Equine Veterinary Association from 1991–1999.

Another door opened and in October 1995, I moved to the United Arab Emirates to become Consultant and Official veterinary officer to the UAE Equestrian and Racing Federation based in Abu Dhabi.

Although there were racing duties involved throughout three of the seven Emirates, including the inaugural and the three subsequent Dubai World Cups, my major role was with the rapidly expanding discipline of endurance, or long distance riding, as it was first known.

This culminated in the largest ever Endurance World Championship in December 1998, when 175 horses from more than 37 nations competed in the ride. This merited an entry in the Guinness Book of Records.

The following month found me commencing a consultancy role with World Horse Welfare to co-ordinate and oversee its international training programmes, which operate in a number of developing countries. It was, indeed, a humbling experience to move from the elite world of thoroughbred horse racing and international equestrian sport to witness the poverty of the owners of working equines and their families in such countries as Ethiopia, El Salvador, Fiji, Kenya, Mexico and elsewhere, who utterly depend on their equines, be they horse, donkey or mule, to put food on the table at the end of the working day.

However, there was tremendous satisfaction to be found in training these humble people in farriery, harness and saddle making and nutrition and to see the improvement in both the working capacity of their animals and the standard of living of their owners and their families. It was good to give something back to the underprivileged equine, having spent much of my life working with their more fortunate cousins.

In addition to the training role, which I relinquished at my own request, having recommended that I be replaced by a permanent director of training, I continued to assist with further developing the excellent working relationship between the FEI and World Horse Welfare for some years.

I am pleased to acknowledge that I still maintain excellent relations with the various organisations for which I have been privileged to work during the past 50 years.

I believe that this is the time to introduce my wife and family, based on the fact that they are all involved with horses to a greater or lesser degree. My wife, Sherley, trained as a nurse in the Adelaide Hospital in Dublin and we married in 1960. Our eldest child, Sandra, was born in the following year. She was followed by Martin in 1963 and Philip in 1966.

Following our move to Castlefield, a house with some 15 acres in the foothills of the Dublin Mountains (mere hills to the Swiss), in the early 1970s, Sandy was really able to develop her interest in ponies and other animals, which included dogs, horses and three pet sheep.

At that stage, we acquired a pony called Minnie which, over time, was passed on to Martin and Philip. It was Sandy who basically assisted her siblings in their interest in all things equine and more ponies and horses were gradually acquired.

Through the kindness of Brigadier B.J. Fowler and his family, Rahinstown, Co Meath, Sandy was allowed to ride their daughter Jessie Harrington's international eventer, Amoy now retired, at Pony Club events. Jessie subsequently became, and still is, a highly successful racehorse trainer.

There was general upheaval in the family when I accepted a position with the FEI in 1982. Prior to this, Sandy had just left school and was scheduled to move to a finishing school in Somerset to study domestic science and equestrianism.

Just weeks before her departure, the school informed us that it had closed. This was just before the Dublin Horse Show and while we were unaware at the time, she obtained a job looking after show-jumpers in Italy. After a spell with the Moyersen family, at their base near Milan, she moved on to work for Kevin Bacon, Australian show jumper and a great character. This involved caring, schooling and driving some three or four horses to international events around Europe.

From there, Sandy joined the top-level enterprise run by George Morris at Hunterdon in New Jersey, USA. At the time, George was still competing at top international level. However, by 2005, he had made the decision to sell Hunterdon and accept the role of chef d'equipe of the US show jumping team. Under his leadership, they won the 2005 Samsung Super League series, team silver at the 2006 World Equestrian Games and team gold at the 2008 Olympic Games. At the 2011 Pan American Games, the US team won team gold and individual gold and silver. In addition, a long time student of George's, Rich Fellers, won the 2012 Rolex FEI World Cup Final.

While at Hunterdon, Sandy met Texan farrier, Joe Johnson. At the time, Joe was assistant to Seamus Brady. Seamus had been farrier to the Irish Army Equitation School; based at McKee Barracks in Dublin prior to moving to the USA.

Joe and Sandy married in 1986 when they branched out on their own from their base in Virginia. Sandy quickly adapted to the new profession and as a pair, they acted as official farriers to the US jumping team at a number of top-level international events, including the 1991 Pan Am Games (Cuba), 1998 World Equestrian Games (Rome), 1999 Pan Am Games (Winnipeg) and all World Cup Finals from 1994–1999.

Joe has not enjoyed the best of health in recent times and has now semi-retired, leaving Sandy to carry on much on her own, but now specialising more in dressage horses. Her current monthly itinerary (2017) involves working for two weeks in Florida, one week in Lexington, Kentucky and one week in Ohio. For the past few years, Sandy has also acted as Official Farrier at the Washington International Horse Show in the autumn of each year. In addition, she is an Equine Insurance Consultant working from her home base now in Florida.

When in Rome for the World Equestrian Games in 1998, Sandy photographed an equestrian statue of Marcus Aurelius. It is made of bronze and stands 4.24 m tall. The original is on display in the Capitoline Museum with the one now standing in the open air of the Piazza del Campidoglio being a replica made in 1981, when the original was taken down for restoration. The statue was first erected ca. AD 175. Interestingly, this photo shows a heart bar shoe on the horse's hoof. According to the late Burney Chapman, highly respected farrier from Texas, heart bar shoes were dug up from the old shoeing textbooks and reintroduced to the horse world in the early 1980s, some 1,800 years after they were known to be in use in Rome.

Left to right: Philip, Martin and Sandy on three of Claire Koch's dressage horses in Switzerland.

Martin quickly got the equestrian bug and with his mare, Katy O'Hara, competed at junior eventing level. The climax to this career was to be included in the Irish squad for the Junior European Championship at Achselswang, in Germany, in 1980.

The following year, he injured his back in a fall at an Irish event and this effectively terminated his riding career. He undertook a stud management course at the Irish National Stud under managing director Michael Osborne, in his last year prior to his departure to Dubai to succeed Lord John Fitzgerald as director of the Emirates Racing Association (ERA). This was prior to Martin taking a gap year in Australia working on several stud farms, including that of ex-Olympian eventer, Neal Lavis.

Following a serious car accident, he returned to Europe and initially spent time working for Swiss international dressage rider, Claire Koch, prior to obtaining a position as a lay assistant in an equine veterinary practice in Germany.

He next worked for a horse road transporter also based in Germany, prior to joining international equine shipping agent, Peden International Transport Ltd (now Peden Bloodstock) where he first acted as road manager for the Royal Canadian Mounted Police's 12-week tour of Europe, prior to full employment with the Peden Company under Managing Director, Michael Bullen.

Over several Olympic Games, commencing in Rome in 1960, Michael (three-day-eventing) and two of his siblings, Jenny Loriston Clarke (dressage) and Jane Holderness-Roddam (eventing – Team Gold in Mexico, 1968) were members of UK teams.

Martin succeeded Michael as Managing Director in 1994. Since then, Martin has managed some of the largest and most complicated shipments ever to have taken place, including the last seven Olympic Games and all World Equestrian Games since their inception in 1990.

Martin's speciality is putting together large logistical movements of competition horses and is acknowledged as a foremost expert in the industry. In 2014, Martin was additionally appointed as interim managing director (subsequently operations director) of Janah Management Company Ltd. Janah is the world's largest international shipper of thoroughbred horses. In a typical year, it will transport in excess of 9,000 horses and deliver them to destinations in Europe, the Americas, the Middle East, Africa, Asia and Australasia.

The majority of these horses belong to the Dubai Ruling Family and are transported for breeding or competitive events (racing, endurance riding etc.).

Martin has formerly held the Chair of the International Animal Transport Association's (IATA) Worldwide Equine Committee and in 1998, he was awarded the Robert Campbell Award for Outstanding Service to Equine Shipping.

More recently, in 2011, he was awarded the Bronze Equestrian Cross in recognition of outstanding achievements to German riding and driving sports by the German Equestrian Federation. The Peden Company now comprises Martin, Henry Bullen (Mike's son), Fiona McCormack, Veterinary Advisor, Bella Atock, who manages the German office, Heike Schmitz and two others.

Martin married Inez van Tienhoven in 1992, who had three children from a previous marriage; one of whom, Bella, is now Senior Shipping Consultant, based in the Peden office in Mulheim, Germany. Martin and Inez's daughter, Georgina, is a passionate rider and is now competing in amateur jumping in Germany, under the Irish flag, with some success.

Philip shared the same appetite as his siblings for all things equine as a child. He particularly excelled in school doing anything that did not involve going to lessons: preferring building stages and preparing art exhibitions as well as acting as secretary of various extracurricular clubs and societies.

On leaving school, he was awarded the Wardens Special Prize for Services to the college. Following some casual work in England, Philip spent a few years on the show jumping circuit in the USA, firstly with George Morris (Sandy's boss) and then with one or two other riders/trainers.

Sadly, shortly after returning to the UK from one stint in America, he became critically ill with viral encephalitis. Following some months in hospital, he was well enough to return to work, but the long-term effects of this illness continue to manifest themselves to this day.

Philip spent most of 1992 in Geelong, Victoria, Australia studying Equine Business Management at Marcus Oldham College. On his return, he attained his IATA certificate as a Flying Groom and then worked in this capacity for a number of shipping agents including, Peden Bloodstock.

Prior to the Sydney Olympic Games in 2000, he was working at the Peden Olympic quarantine facility in Aachen, Germany and, due to late qualification, the departure of Jordan's H.R.H. Princess Haya's horse was delayed for two weeks.

During this period, Philip had sole charge of the quarantine facility with just Princess Haya's horse in residence. A couple of weeks later, he received a lovely 'thank you' card from the Princess who was, by then, in Sydney. The Princess was elected President of the FEI in 2006 and served two full terms, the maximum permitted at the time.

Ill health continued to plague Philip and he developed a severe deep vein thrombosis in 2006. This DVT led directly to further health complications and left him permanently physically disabled, unable to work and depending on crutches for mobility. Philip married Gilly Hemesley in 1999 and they have two children, Alexandra and Charlie. They live in the Forest of Dean near Monmouth, Wales.

Sherley had three younger sisters but, like me, her family had no equestrian background other than through her Uncle Blayney (Hamilton) whose horse, Hamstar, won the Irish Grand National in 1948.

Of her sisters, the eldest, Juliet Perrin, made her mark producing show ponies, which were ridden successfully in competition by several of her children, one of whom, – Andrew, is currently Joint Master of the well-known Kildare Fox Hounds.

Mary and her husband, David McCann, have concentrated on breeding performance horses for the world equestrian market of Show Jumping and Eventing at their farm, Hartwell Stud, Co Kildare in Ireland. Sea Crest, followed by his son, the world-renowned Cruising, have been their dominant stallions. Their children, Jonathan, Jenny and Gina are closely involved with the running of the stud.

Diana Gilna Keogh, the youngest, made her name as Diana Gilna, producing and riding show hunters including four Supreme Championships, seven Reserve Supreme Championships and many Hunter Classes at the annual Royal Dublin Society Horse Show over the years. Diana married the well liked Jim Keogh as her second husband.

Diana's daughter, Claire, was still a teenager when she joined her mother in the main arena and together they achieved the highest accolade of Supreme and Reserve Supreme Hunter Champions of that particular show. Sadly Diana died suddenly in 2007.

I fully realise that this introduction exceeds the norm in length, but it covers a long life with horses as the focus.

From Dublin to Dubai, Bern to Brisbane and Lausanne to Lexington, it will be a pleasure for me to share with you some of my experiences and adventures along the way and I hope you enjoy the ride.

Chapter 1

THE EARLY YEARS

Ponies and Horses – School – Student Days – Race-Riding – the
Bicester Horses – Graduation

The International Equestrian Federation (FEI) General Assembly was in session in Amsterdam in December 1983. It had spent considerable time discussing the apparently insolvable problem of how horses, which would compete in the Olympic Games in Seoul, Korea in 1988, could ever return to their home countries after the games. Never before had a major international equestrian event taken place on mainland Asia and nobody knew the equine health risks involved.

The President of the FEI leaned over to the man sitting beside him and, unaware that the microphone was still switched on, said, "You had better send Atock."

Many in the room heard the remark. H.R.H. The Prince Philip, Duke of Edinburgh, president of the FEI, had just instructed Fritz O. Widmer, secretary general, to send me to Korea.

Within weeks, I boarded a flight from Zurich to Seoul, as the sole representative of the FEI, with the single purpose of solving the problem of how to get horses back to their home countries following the games.

****

How did all this come about and how did I find myself in this situation? Let's go back to the beginning. We lived in the north Dublin suburb of Glasnevin. I do not recall what started my interest in the equine species but in 1937, at the age of five, I commenced having riding lessons. Major, later to become Lt Colonel Joe Hume Dudgeon, a British Army officer and one time captain of the British Army Jumping Team, had opened a riding school at Merville, on the Stillorgan Road, in the previous year. Unbeknown to me at the time, he had been a great help in assisting the new Irish Army Equitation School when it was first formed in 1926.

Major Dudgeon initially only accepted adult pupils. He contemplated building an indoor riding school and I believe he sought the advice of my house-building maternal grandfather, Alex Strain, or Grandpa to me. During their discussions, Grandpa persuaded him to give me riding lessons. The major relented and agreed to take me on and I became his first ever child pupil, a fact of which he reminded me on many occasions subsequently. In addition to the major's wife and children, Ian and Kay, the head teacher was Sergeant Major Frazer McMaster, a dour Scot, who did not suffer fools or nervous children, gladly. In fact, his bark was considerably worse than his bite, but he taught in a highly disciplined and military fashion. He certainly frightened the living daylights out of me in the early stages of my tuition, although the female teachers were considerably more sympathetic to a small child.

One of my earliest recollections of this period was of getting a 'leg-up' in the cinder ménage onto Gadlys, a small brown pony. It was not a success – I went into orbit over the pony's withers and landed on my two bare hands on the cinders on the other side. Regardless of this, I persevered and have happy memories of learning to ride Gadlys, Trixie and others during my lessons. These continued on a weekly basis, certainly during school holidays. Thus, my love of ponies and horses began, which was to stay with me for the rest of my days.

The welfare of all animals was always of major interest and concern to me. I hated to see an unhappy dog clearly miserable either through hunger or ill treatment from its owner. The same, of course, applied to ponies or horses. On one occasion I witnessed a workhorse slipping and falling on the street in the city. I watched in horror as the driver whipped it to try to make it get up while it was still attached to its cart. The unfortunate horse tried hard but could not respond on the slippery cobble stones and its frantic efforts were to no avail, certainly not helped by its callous driver. Fortunately, others came to its rescue, released the horse from its harness, packed sacking around its feet to give grip and helped the horse to rise.

Although I was often taken to the Dublin Zoo as a child and later brought my own children, I always had difficulty seeing big cats – lions and tigers – cooped up in cages and the crocodile surviving in a tank barely larger than itself, where it lay, day in day out, without even the possibility to turn around. Even a budgerigar in a cage was certainly not for me.

Contrary to this, I was always impressed by the care the riding school horses and ponies received in Dudgeons. They tended to be out in a field, as nature intended, until wanted for lessons. The grooms, such as Mickey Parr, Jack Reilly and others, were sympathetic in their handling of the animals, and although I never saw any sign of abuse, this would certainly not have been tolerated. The competition horses were, of course, kept in stables, from where they were exercised and trained according to their requirements.

Among those taking riding lessons at the time was Richard Teevan. He and I became great friends and eventually colleagues and remained so until he died in 2001 following a long illness, which was diagnosed within weeks of his retirement from his position of senior stewards secretary to the Irish Turf Club.

Riding lessons concentrated very much on the suppleness of both pony and rider, and one of the exercises taught to demonstrate this was to ride down over a cavaletti (a series of poles on or close to the ground) while removing one's jacket.

Adrian Henry (school friend and later leading orthopaedic surgeon in London) leading AA over a cavaletti while removing jackets.

Presumably yielding to persistent pressure, my parents decided to buy me a pony. Naturally, Major Dudgeon and Mr McMaster became their advisors in the search for a suitable animal. The first pony to be tried behaved well, trotting down over a cavaletti, with me as the passenger.

However, having negotiated the final element, it reckoned that it deserved its reward and put its head down for a mouthful of grass. This resulted in me tumbling down its neck headfirst – out through its ears – landing in a heap on the ground and narrowly escaping becoming the next mouthful. Not suitable.

The next pony to be tried was too strong. Having walked, trotted and gently cantered around a large field, it suddenly eyed the gate at the far side. With increasing tempo, it made for the gate and home. Persistent 'whoas' from me and even more persistent 'whoas' from interested family members went unheeded. Unfortunately, there was a laneway running at right angles outside the gate necessitating a 90-degree turn to the left. Clearly, such a manoeuvre was totally out of the question at the speed at which we were travelling. The alternative escape route was straight ahead over several strands of wire into the next field. Inevitably, we attempted the wire, hit the top and landed in a heap on the far side. Not suitable.

It was third time lucky, however. Judy, a little overweight bay pony, with absolutely no vices, was found in Dunderry, Co. Meath, and she happily came home with us and remained in ours' and Dudgeons' care until the day she died, well into her thirties.

Judy proved to be a great success. She shared her time between Dudgeons' and our home in Glasnevin on the north side of the city. We had no stabling so she lived out in the field adjoining the cricket pitch. It was amazing the number of new friends I, or rather Judy, acquired. There were no problems with traffic in those days. In fact, since the Second World War was declared in 1939 and petrol severely rationed, there were few cars around. I was able to ride Judy on the roads, followed by an army of her young friends. Judy also spent time at Major Dudgeon's establishment, where I continued to go regularly for lessons.

A two-wheeled trap was purchased, to which Judy quickly adapted. Shopping and visits were subsequently undertaken by pony and trap. I became quite a proficient driver. In fact, on one occasion, after we had moved to Ballsbridge, to the south of the city, I was sent on an errand to the nearby village. Whatever I was supposed to purchase was not available. But I knew where I could get it – Grandpa Strain. So, Judy and I set off across the city on the five-mile journey to Glasnevin, where Grandpa lived.

Despite her duties in the trap, Judy was dual purpose. Our greatest claim to fame was at the Royal Dublin Society (RDS) Spring Show where we finished second in the musical chairs – in reality, it was musical buckets. When the canned music commenced, about 20 of us started off cantering bareback in a circle around evenly spaced up-turned buckets. There was one bucket less than the number of competitors. When the music stopped, we had to dismount, find a free bucket and sit on it. The child who could not find a bucket was eliminated. Eventually, there was only one bucket left but two pony and child combinations. Excitement was intense. The music stopped and we both rushed for the sole bucket. The other child beat me to it but Judy and I received a blue rosette for being second, and this was a very proud moment for us both. I did return to compete at the RDS on future occasions but more on this later.

On one occasion, Grandpa decided to take me to spend a short holiday at Hunter's Hotel, Rathnew, Co. Wicklow. This was about 30 miles from Dublin, and we set off with Judy in the trap. We broke our journey on the way at Greystones, where Judy stayed in a field, while we slept in bed-and-breakfast accommodation.

The following morning, we resumed the journey. Some days after arriving at Hunter's Hotel, Judy showed signs of lameness, and although her condition improved, she was still not fully sound when it was time to return home. Grandpa did not wish to put his weight in the trap and so he hired or borrowed a bicycle and while I drove the pony, he cycled beside me all the way home. We did, of course, break the journey again at halfway as on the way down. Whether this proved too much for grandpa or not I do not know, but he died suddenly six weeks later. It certainly proved that he had the welfare of the pony very much at heart.

At the time of his funeral, and presumably to get me out of the way, I travelled by train with Sylvia Dodd, who was several years older than me, and whom I knew through Pony Club, and who subsequently married Gordon Craigie, a member of a well-known North Dublin business and farming family, to a horse show in Duleek near Drogheda.

We went with the horses from Amiens Street Station (now Connolly Station). In our carriage, there were three horses plus Sylvia, Seamus Hayes, who was just starting his career, which was to eventually lead to him becoming Ireland's top international show-jumping rider, and me.

Some years later, Seamus rode the first ever winner of the Hickstead Derby, in 1962 and he was a member of the first Irish civilian team to win the Dublin Nations Cup Aga Khan Trophy on his great horse, Goodbye. We unloaded the horses at Duleek station and rode the final few miles to the show. This was repeated in reverse on the way home after the event.

Although during much of this time we lived in Ballsbridge, a few miles to the south of Dublin, I joined the Meath Pony Club. I believe that this was related to the fact that, at the time, following the war years, Colonel Dudgeon, as he is now, was master of the North Kildare Harriers, whose territory bordered on Co. Meath. He was very involved with its Pony Club.

During every school holiday, there were two or three rallies hosted by various kindly property owners in Co. Meath. These normally involved talks, riding lessons and fun riding. Most of the members were farmers or landowner's children, the majority of whom had their own ponies or horses.

As we did not have transport for Judy, I was unable to bring a pony to these rallies but somebody would always produce an animal for me to ride. On one occasion at a rally, I rode Heartbreak Hill, a retired steeplechaser which, in 1932 (the year of my birth), had started favourite in the Aintree Grand National and despite being badly baulked at Valentine's Brook, had finished sixth in the race.

Fortunately, she was now quite happy to go at my pace and had no longer any ambitions to be first past the post. Having been confined to ponies until then, it was a real thrill to be sitting on a large live steeplechaser. Maybe this experience was the start of my interest in racing?

During the summer holidays, we camped under canvas for a week at the seashore in Mosney, near Drogheda, north of Dublin and close to Butlin's Holiday Village. Many mothers, including mine, helped at camp providing for us children and long into adulthood, friendships made there endured.

This was always great fun although I was never really happy when deprived of modern conveniences. To this day, I still prefer to wash in hot water which comes from a tap in a bathroom, which is preferably warm and en suite, rather than live in a tent in the middle of nowhere.

Among the friends made at the camp were the families: Baggallay, Boylan, Corbally-Stourton, Kelly, Mullins and others.

Kitty Baggallay was a frightening lady and very much from the old school. Her son Denis was a racehorse trainer of some 25 horses, mainly jumpers (steeplechasers or hurdlers), who subsequently gave up training to take up the position of keeper of the Match Book, equivalent to chief executive of the Irish Turf Club.

He succeeded Brigadier E.T. Boylan. The Boylans lived at Hilltown, Drogheda and of their two sons, Eddie, became a successful international event rider and won the three-day-event at Badminton on Duras Eile in 1965 and was a member of the winning team of the first World Eventing Championship at Burghley, UK, in 1966, and the European Championship in Punchestown, in 1967. Clearly, being associated with this great horse ensured that Eddie Boylan's name was firmly written into equestrian history and together they went on to win a number of other major events.

I returned to Pony Club camp one year after I was overage to assist. This was a year in which there was a violent storm one night which threatened to flood the camp. All had to be evacuated. I had my mother's Morris Minor car and the only way to get to Butlin's Holiday Camp, which was the nearest suitable accommodation available, was along the sand on the seashore. Many journeys had to be made to get everyone safe and it was quite scary to drive on the beach in the pitch dark with driving rain in a car overloaded with frightened children, while avoiding high incoming waves from the sea. However, all was achieved satisfactorily, the fallen tents were re-erected, and life returned to normal on the following day.

I continued to spend all my spare time, particularly, during school holidays, riding at Merville both on Judy and, as I improved, also on others. Apart from the RDS Spring Show in May, which was mostly agricultural and the Horse Show in August, which was and still is, a major event in the international calendar, there were only limited opportunities to compete at this time.

One of these was Marlay Gymkhana in Rathfarnham, which was always held about two weeks prior to the Horse Show. I had the good fortune to be offered the ride by the Corbally-Stourtons on Tinkerbelle, a 13.2 hh grey pony mare in a showing class at Marlay, which we won.

Two weeks later, we also won the novice class at the RDS and were 3rd in the open class. I subsequently rode several other ponies in jumping classes at the RDS but with no great success. With the exception of Flyto, who was trained at Merville, I never laid eyes on any other such as Bingo, Dinkey and others until the day of the competition. So, I had no chance to get to know them.

At that time, half way through the round and having jumped the first few fences, competitors had to weave in and out through three posts to show that the pony was under suitable control; if not deemed to be under control the round was penalised. This was certainly the case with Dinkey and me. Although jumping a clear round, we went through the three posts so fast that we were penalised and therefore, did not qualify for any prize.

At this time, there was a very good 13.2 hh pony called Pixie competing. For many years after she retired, her successes were immortalised by the award of the Pixie Cup. Pixie was trained at Kellett's, which was the other major riding school in addition to Dudgeon's in Dublin. Iris Kellett was a top international jumping rider for many years. Amongst her most prominent wins were the Dublin Grand Prix in 1948 and the following year, she was the first ever winner of the Queen's Cup at the White City in London. The then Princess Elizabeth, now Queen Elizabeth, presented Iris with the trophy.

Pixie's rider at the time was about to become overage for that size of pony, hence a new rider had to be found. It was, therefore, with great excitement that Kevin O'Dwyer from Kellett's and I from Dudgeon's were invited to try out Pixie. Pixie had a very low head carriage, which meant that as you approached a jump there was virtually nothing in front of you. Also, she went right into the bottom of the fence before she took off, which made for a difficult ride.

A course of some six fences was built at Kellett's and Kevin went first. He had difficulties and was eventually jumped off. I was next and was unshipped at the first fence. Another round was ordered. Kevin jumped clear and it was again my turn. I was also clear until the last fence where Pixie stopped. I cleared the fence but Pixie didn't, so Kevin got the ride for the following season.

In addition, during each Christmas holidays I was given the present of a hunt. These were always on hirelings and although I was very nervous, I enjoyed the thrill of galloping and jumping, preferably at speed. Natural hunting people enjoy seeing the hounds work, but I admit that riding and jumping were more of a thrill for me. Wouldn't it be fun to ride in a race?

I very much enjoyed my time riding ponies and although Judy was the only pony I ever owned, I was immensely grateful to the owners of other ponies who gave me the opportunity and responsibility to ride their ponies in competition.

Undoubtedly, this experience focused my mind on horses and all they had to offer for the future. It was not only the thought of winning, although this was important in its own right, but just taking part was equally important. Sadly, there can be some people, parents included, who adopt the 'win at all costs' attitude. As with any occupation or sport, winning is always good but it should be the participation that counts and not just who won what. Of the partnership between man and horse, it is the horse that should earn our praise. Without it, we would get nowhere. It is worth recalling here the philosophy of the equine charity, World Horse Welfare, which states, "Use him but do not abuse him." As you will learn in due course, I was privileged to work for this charity many years later.

I next moved on to spending time 'riding out' for John 'Blather' Farrell. Mr Farrell was a large, loud spoken cattle farmer and dealer who trained some 20 point-to-pointers near Clonee just outside Dublin. I obtained my amateur jockey's licence when with him but was never actually given a ride in a race.

Joe Ahern, who was a successful amateur at the time, rode for the stable so I had little chance. Joe's brother, William, was an assistant trainer and he and I became good friends and often represented Mr Farrell at a point-to-point when there were two meetings on the same day and he had runners at both.

On one memorable occasion, William and I saddled three winners while the boss only had one at the other meeting. About this time, I also had the excitement of travelling with Joe to Aintree, (home of the Grand National) Liverpool, where he rode North Littleton in the Topham Trophy over the Grand National fences, although without success.

My allegiance then moved a few miles up the road to Captain Denis Baggallay, whose mother was so involved with the Pony Club, who trained jumpers (steeplechasers and hurdlers) at Loughlinstown, which was close to Fairyhouse, home of the Irish Grand National. Captain Baggallay had been a successful amateur rider in his day and was now a moderately successful trainer of some 15 or so winners per year.

I really enjoyed riding better horses in gallops and also schooling over hurdles and fences. However, I was soon to realise that schooling with two or three horses' upsides was quite different to riding in a hurdle race at speed amongst 15 or 20 other horses. This experience was gained at the now long defunct Baldoyle racecourse at Sutton in Co. Dublin.

Baldoyle was known as a 'tight' track just one mile around so almost continuously on the turn. I had my first ride there in a hurdle race on a horse called Flight Control, owned by Denis Domville and trained by Captain Baggallay. There were 20 runners in the race, which was a novice (inexperienced horses) hurdle race over two miles. Not in my wildest dreams could I have dreamt of the speed at which racing horses could travel and jump. I was apprehensive being in the middle of so many horses travelling so fast.

We jumped the first few hurdles in the middle of the pack, but by the time we approached the starting point on the second circuit, the field had strung out and we were nowhere near the front. As we approached the next hurdle, a horse just in front of us hit the hurdle hard and knocked it flat. Flight Control, showing a lot more intelligence than his inexperienced rider, seized the opportunity and dived for the gap left by the fallen hurdle. Needless to say, I proceeded in a straight line and suffered the indignity of being recorded as 'UR' (unseated rider), which was not a good basis on which to start my race-riding career. I was, however, consoled on return to the weighing room by none other than Pat Taaffe, a young professional jockey at the time. But subsequently, he was highly successful while riding as the first jockey to the great trainer, Tom Dreaper, who numbered amongst his clientele, Lord Bicester, Mr J.V. Rank and the Duchess of Westminster and by P. J. Doyle, a senior professional jockey. Both kindly told me that their first rides in a race had ended in similar circumstances, so I had no need to worry. Regardless of the outcome, it was certainly a great thrill to ride a horse at speed in a race across hurdles and only wetted my appetite for more rides in the future.

This first episode was followed by a ride in a steeplechase around Fairyhouse on a horse trained by Denis Baggallay and called Young Ireland. The race was aptly named the Peter Simple Hunter Chase and was for horses without a memorable track record, ridden by riders with even less. Young Ireland was a front-runner and it was a great thrill to pass the stands in the lead on the first circuit but sadly, not on the second. He jumped brilliantly and fully restored my confidence although we finished unplaced.

I also had a number of rides in point-to-points, which included at least one particularly interesting experience. Whenever possible, even if I did not have a booked ride, I attended these events in the hope of picking up a spare ride. On this particular day, I arrived at the Westmeath Hunt point-to-point, which I had never attended before and guess what, I was offered a ride in the first race. My immediate reaction was to panic as I had no idea of the course and there was no time to walk it. I then thought to myself, *Don't worry, just follow the others*. Not so.

Prior to mounting and having seen the horse for the first time while waiting in the paddock, the owner informed me that this horse pulled hard and liked to be in front. Panic returned. I followed others to the start from where the first fence was just visible. We led into the first and as soon as we were airborne, I frantically scanned the horizon, looking for the second and so on throughout the race. We eventually finished fourth.

P.J Kehoe leading Bill Taaffe – brother of professional jockeys Pat and Toss – and AA on Almaska's Pride – Winner – over the first fence at South Co Dublin Harriers Point-To-Point, 1954.

One day, a good friend, Tony Schorman, who had a lot more race-riding experience than me, asked if I would like to ride a horse at the Bray point-to-point, on the following Saturday.

The owner, Dudley Ireland, had two horses in the race. Tony would ride one and I could ride the other. On Saturday, I saw and mounted Almaska's Pride for the first time. He gave me a lovely ride throughout and as we approached the last fence, Tony and I were upsides sharing the lead. With minimum assistance from me, Almaska's Pride held on to win by a head – my first win.

Immediately after the race, Mr Ireland asked me if I would ride him again on the following Wednesday at the South County Dublin Harriers point-to-point. Again, he gave me a great ride and about three fences from home, I could see that we had a chance as there were only two horses in front of us and they were clearly not going too well. Approaching the last fence, we passed Mr J. R. 'Bunny' Cox, one of the best amateur riders of the day who ranked with the top professionals at that time and we won by an easy five lengths. I was extremely flattered when in Dublin, a few days later, Pat Taaffe, referred to above, crossed the road to congratulate me on my wins and this after he had just returned from success riding at the Cheltenham Festival.

Regardless of my personal lack of success in the saddle, racing was always a major interest. In addition to racing in Ireland, various visits were made to other racecourses further afield and even more exciting visits to the Cheltenham Festival in March, Aintree to see the Grand National the following month, Newmarket for

31

the Cambridgeshire and on the same weekend in October, to Paris for the Prix de L'Arc de Triomphe. These were normally in the company of good friends, Ronny Guilford and David Pim, and were always great fun even if financially debilitating. When I come to think about it, I have no idea where the money came from to fund these trips.

In 1951, while still spending time with Denis Baggallay, often visiting two to three days a week or staying in the house with his family, I received a message one day that Tom Dreaper, the highly successful trainer of steeplechasers, already referred to wished to meet me. What on earth could he want from me? We arranged to meet at the Gresham Hotel in O'Connell Street, Dublin. Mr Dreaper explained to me that Lord Bicester, one of his principal owners for whom he purchased, trained and raced young horses in Ireland prior to furthering their careers in the UK, wanted someone competent to get his horses relatively fit when they came in from their summer holidays on grass and prior to returning to their trainer, George Beeby, in Compton, Berkshire for the winter racing season. Naturally, I was thrilled and honoured and readily accepted. This was the nearest thing to manna from heaven for an impecunious student.

In early July, just before starting my veterinary studies, I packed my case, including my dinner jacket on my mother's insistence that "they may dress for dinner," and set out on the long journey by sea and train to Bicester in Oxfordshire. Tusmore Park, Lord Bicester's estate, was some five miles from the station and I was met by Mr Brookes, the chauffeur, with a large luxurious Rover car. When we arrived at Tusmore Park, Mr Brookes dropped me at one of the cottages on the estate.

This was the home of Mr Anderson, the shepherd, his wife and their Jack Russell terrier. The sheepdogs slept elsewhere. Both were extremely hospitable and friendly. The arrangement was that I would have bed and breakfast with the Andersons and other meals with the staff in the 'big' house. Needless to say, the staff did not dress for dinner in the servant's quarters and hence my dinner jacket quickly became redundant.

Lord Bicester spent several days a week in London, where he was Director of Morgan Grenfell & Co, Merchant Bankers and other companies. Between 1934 and 1956, he had also held the honorary position of Lord Lieutenant of Oxfordshire. I met him briefly on the first morning and next went to the stables and was introduced to Mr Bill, the elderly headman and his two equally elderly assistants.

I met most of the horses which I would ride over the next six weeks, and who were literally a 'who's who' of equine steeplechasing talent in the UK. They numbered amongst them Finnure, Roimond, Silver Fame, Mariners Log, Senlac Hill, Freddy Fox and the now retired Parthenon.

Dick Francis, who all but won the Grand National on the Queen Mother's Devon Loch in 1956, when it infamously collapsed when in sight of the winning post, and who was later to become a well-known crime writer, was retained to ride Lord Bicester's horses when the top Irish jockey, Martin Molony, was not available.

At that time, Martin rode in the UK during the week but returned to Ireland for Saturday racing. In fact, in one season during this period, Tim Molony, Martin's older brother, who rode exclusively in England, was champion jockey. Martin finished second to Tim in England while, in the same season, he was also champion jockey in Ireland – quite an achievement when the Mail Boat from Holyhead to Dun Laoghaire was often the only means of transport between the two countries.

Dick Francis, in his book *The Sport of Queens* devotes a chapter to *Black Gold Sleeves Red Cap,* which were Lord Bicester's racing colours. Amongst the eighteen photographs in the book are three of the Bicester horses: Roimond jumping Beecher's Brook in the 1950 Grand National, in which he finished second to Russian Hero; Silver Fame jumping the last fence on the way to winning the 1952 Cheltenham Gold Cup; and Finnure jumping The Chair at Aintree on his way to winning the 1950 two mile Champion Chase.

For the record, Finnure had also won the prestigious King George VI Chase over three miles at Kempton Park the previous year and prior to that, had won an Irish Cesarawitch at The Curragh.

AA on Roimond.

Harry Bonner, who was a neighbour, showman (he often judged at the RDS Dublin Horse Show and elsewhere) and bloodstock advisor to Lord Bicester had originally proposed Francis for the job as jockey. It was to the Bonner house, Chesterton Fields Farm at Middleton Stoney, that Mr Brookes took me after I had viewed the horses the first morning.

I was given a leg up on a large, slightly overweight chestnut gelding, while Mr Bonner mounted another horse. We set off on the quiet roads, the purpose of which, I believe, was for Mr Bonner to assess whether I would be capable of taking responsibility for such a delicate consignment as these top class chasers. By way of conversation, I asked Mr Bonner if the horse I was riding was one of his hunters. "No son, you are riding Finnure," came the reply. My assessment of Finnure may not have impressed this expert at the time but I must have passed muster, regardless, as the following day I was back riding the other horses.

On one special occasion, Mr Bonner kindly included me in an invitation to dinner with Tim Molony and his wife, Stella, in the local hostelry in Middleton Stoney – a very proud moment for me to dine with the champion jockey and it did my street credibility no harm when I returned to college and related my experience to fellow students with racing interests.

The routine for the first week or two was confined to walking around the park and on the nearby roads and laneways. This progressed to trotting for extended periods. The routing then became; to proceed down the front avenue to the main Oxford to Brackley road, turn right along a grass verge for several hundred yards, right again and through various villages, including Cottisford, Hardwicke, Hethe and back through the rear gate into the park. Many years later, this area and some of these villages were to become immortalised in the successful TV drama *Larkrise to Candleford*, which was based in this part of Oxfordshire. I returned to Tusmore Park on two subsequent years after I had commenced my veterinary training to repeat these procedures.

Obituary Lord Bicester

Lord Bicester's Obituary in the *1957 Horseman's Year (W.E. Lyon)* read:

> *Steeplechasing suffered a grievous loss in February by the death of Lord Bicester, a man of wealth whose outlook on steeplechasing was in direct contrast to that of many other wealthy owners on the flat. A true lover of steeplechasing, he put into the game more than he ever expected to get out of it and for years spent large sums of money in the quest of a Grand National winner.*
>
> *Many were the magnificent horses he had, and Silver Flame, one of the very best of them, won him the Cheltenham Gold Cup amongst his twenty-three victories, but the nearest that Lord Bicester got to win a Grand National was Roimond's second to Russian Hero in 1949. Lord Bicester had a great eye for a horse and those who bought for him in Ireland knew the type he liked. Big weight-carrying horses with plenty of bone and quality, such as Roimond, Finnure, Silver Flame, Marquis II, Royal Approach, Bluff King and Forth Bridge. These were ornaments to National Hunt Racing in more senses than one.*
>
> *Lord Bicester's kindness and integrity will be greatly missed – he was loved*

My swansong at Tusmore Park was in 1953, my final year, when I paraded Roimond at the local Bicester Horse Show. Basil Ancil, Harry Bonner's son-in-law and a successful amateur jockey at the time, rode Silver Fame. A few days later, I travelled with the horses to George Beeby's yard in Compton, Berkshire to return them to their trainer for the coming winter season.

At this time, Bruce Hobbs was assistant trainer to Mr Beeby. In 1938, aged 17, Bruce had ridden the polo pony sized Battleship to win the Grand National, beating Royal Danieli, ridden by Irish jockey, Dan Moore, by a head in a thrilling finish. Dan went on to become a noted trainer from his base across the road from Fairyhouse racecourse and not far from Captain Baggallay's yard. Among his most notable winners in 1980 had been Tied Cottage, the Cheltenham Gold Cup winner, ridden by his future son-in-law, Tommy Carberry. Very sadly, Tied Cottage was later disqualified as a result of theobromine, a caffeine derivative and a prohibited substance, being found in his urine.

Around this time, in one year, there were some 40 samples collected on the UK and Irish racecourses, which revealed the presence of theobromine, which was a constituent of a well-known horse tonic, but regardless, they all had to be disqualified under the rules of racing.

In 1951, the first of what I call 'The Bicester Years,' my mother, probably in frustration because I could not decide what my future might be, spoke to her good friend, Professor John Fleming who knew an Irish veterinarian, Dr Johnny Burkhardt, who was then Director of the Equine Research Station at Newmarket in Suffolk and agreed to advise me on my future. This research station subsequently became the Animal Heath Trust and many years later, I was to become a regular visitor there when, as Head of the Veterinary Department of the International Equestrian Federation (FEI), I met with directors of the day including Dr Brian Singleton and subsequently Dr Andrew Higgins.

An appointment was made with Dr Burkhardt and my mother and I travelled to Newmarket by boat and car. Dr Burkhardt was extremely understanding. He considered that becoming involved in racing as a jockey or a trainer was a great idea but queried if I should not first obtain a profession as a back-up "just in case the racing job failed". He proposed that I become a veterinary surgeon.

I accepted this sound advice and applied to University College Dublin (UCD) to commence my pre-medical studies and duly passed and entered college. Having passed the pre-med exam, which was undertaken alongside agricultural and medical students, I moved on with others to the Veterinary College of Ireland on Shelbourne Road, Ballsbridge to enter the second and subsequent three years of study.

The college was a mere ten-minute bicycle ride from home. The first year was devoted to anatomy and physiology. Anatomy revolved around the dissection of a dead horse or pony. These were usually elderly and were euthanized for the purpose when very often it was the kindest thing to do.

This was an initial shock to me and to some of my colleagues, several of whom had never seen a dead animal before. The purpose of this was for us students to trace every single muscle, tendon, ligament, nerve, artery, vein, joint and all the internal organs that made up the whole animal. It was extremely important to know all we could about the dead animal, before we were allowed to touch a live one. All the time, we had to compare what we found in the horse with that of the ox, sheep, pig, dog and cat.

Over the ensuing years, we studied physiology and biochemistry, animal husbandry and production, pathology, microbiology and parasitology, large and small animal clinical studies and surgery in all animals. This is just a summary. Is it any wonder that we envied our medical colleagues who only had one two-legged species to study?

In our final year, we actually practiced on live animals, under strict supervision of course. These belonged to those not in a position to afford a professional veterinary fee. Being able to see and touch the living and to treat its symptoms was a major step forward, particularly as you saw it (hopefully) recover from whatever ailment with which it had been afflicted. This was an achievement to which we all aspired.

Finally, the great day arrived and in 1958, I received my degree and thought that I knew the lot. I was now a veterinary surgeon and a member of the illustrious Royal College of Veterinary Surgeons (MRCVS). The world was my oyster, or so I thought, although a professor at the Veterinary College often told us, "We all make mistakes—that is why there is rubber on lead pencils and bumpers on motor cars."

I was later to be brought further down to earth with a bang when Col. Dudgeon advised me, "Always remember, the older you get, the more you will realise how little you know;" true sayings that I have never forgotten.

Chapter 2

VETERINARY PRACTICE AND RACING

*Veterinary Assistant in Ireland and England – Own Practice in Dublin –
Veterinary Officer Irish Turf Club – Presentation to International
Conference of Racing Analysts and Veterinarians (ICRAV)*

I was now free to practice my trade. I spent virtually my entire time as a student 'seeing practice' (spending time with a qualified veterinary surgeon learning the intricacies of practice in the field) with Lewis Doyle, a well-respected equine and farm veterinarian based in Navan, Co. Meath.

Prior to graduating, I had agreed to carry on working for him for my first year as a qualified veterinary surgeon. This was mainly to carry out TB testing, which had fallen way behind, having been filed by Lewis in the 'too difficult' tray. It was not that it was too difficult; it was just that it was too boring, and he had much more interesting work to do.

Generally, farm practice was enjoyable. It took place outdoors, often in lovely countryside and in a peaceful environment – unless, of course, you had a disagreement with the farmer. It was still economical to carry out treatment on individual animals and to be responsible for a safe birth was always a rather magical moment even if this was at 5 am in the morning, which tended to be the preferred time for the majority of dairy cows. What was not so enjoyable was stripping to the waist on an early winter morning and putting on a cold rubber overall to assist with the procedure.

Amongst Lewis's clients were many farmers, large and small, the Meath and Tara hunt kennels and stables, a few stud farms and racehorse trainers. Amongst the latter were the Hon. Ginger Wellesley, who had trained The Bug owned by Norman Watchman, to win the Diadem Stakes at Royal Ascot a few years earlier and Jimmie Brogan, who trained close to the Dublin to Slane road.

Jimmie had been a successful jump jockey in his day, and his son Barry followed in his footsteps for a spell before moving to Australia. Jimmie's big winner at the time of my involvement was Gold Legend who won an Irish Grand National in 1958 when ridden by stable jockey, Johnny Lehane.

In addition to training, Jimmie also managed the nearby Waterside Stud for Mr Dick McIllhaga. Subsequently, these premises were acquired by international show jumping rider, Paul Darragh, and his business partner, Alain Storme. It was to this establishment that, in 1995, the young H.R.H. Princess Haya Bint Al Hussein of Jordan came to hone her jumping skills, which culminated in her representing Jordan at the 2000 Olympic Games in Sydney, Australia.

Some years later, in 2006, the Princess was elected President of the FEI – the International Equestrian Federation – and duly completed her highly successful maximum eight-year term in 2014.

Another client of interest at the time was Lord Fingall, Killeen Castle near Dunshaughlin in Co. Meath where he managed some mares for Sir Victor Sassoon. Lord Fingall had ridden the winner of a hunter chase at Cheltenham in the mid-1920s and more recently owned Roddy Owen, which won the Cheltenham Gold Cup in 1959 ridden by Bobby Beasley.

Many Dublin graduates considered it advisable to get experience abroad. So, in March 1960, I moved to Ross-on-Wye in Herefordshire to become second assistant in the practice of Morgan, Daniel and Brown. This appointment was dependent on me being allowed time off for Sherley's and my forthcoming wedding and honeymoon in June.

The experience gained in the Ross-on-Wye practice was immense. Our patients included horses, cattle, (both beef and dairy) sheep, pigs, a few goats, dogs, cats and other miscellaneous small pets. During our time in England, I became ill with a fluctuating temperature of unknown origin. I was hospitalised for some seven days, but the cause was never diagnosed at the time, although these symptoms were to reoccur a few years later.

Early in 1962, we decided that it was time to look at options back in our home country. I bought the nucleus of a large animal practice, from veterinarian Walter Emerson, which he operated from Rathgar, a south Dublin suburb, and who wished to retire. On return to Ireland, we initially set up home in an apartment on the top floor of my mother's three-storey house in Ailesbury Road, Ballsbridge[1]. I inherited the majority of Mr Emerson's practice, which included a number of farms from smallholdings, with one or two cows to estates with up to 600 cattle and also a number of religious institutions. In addition and not long afterwards, I also purchased the Dundrum practice of Willie McDougald, who retired to expand his hobby and to manage a large mink farm based in the midlands. One of Willie's daughters, Jane, went on to marry Paul Darragh, who was mentioned above.

A highly significant event, in which I was involved shortly after starting my practice, was a horrific road accident involving a pony. I was called by the Garda Síochána (Irish police) to an incident in nearby Nutley Lane. The unfortunate pony, which had been hit by a car, was lying on its side in the road, deeply shocked but fully conscious. One hind leg had been totally amputated through the hip joint and the leg was lying on the pavement some two to three metres away from the distressed animal. It was the most ghastly scene I had ever witnessed. I quickly euthanized the pony to put it out of its misery. It was a deeply traumatic situation, not only for me,

---

[1] 1. My mother's house was Olney, 44 Ailesbury Road, Ballsbridge, Dublin. Shortly after we were married in 1960, she sold it to the Belgium Embassy, (46, next door) that knocked the two houses together. Many years earlier, John Boyd Dunlop, (1840–1921) inventor, who developed the pneumatic rubber tyre, lived in 46 Ailesbury Road. Born in Scotland in 1867, he settled in Belfast as a veterinary surgeon where he practised. In 1887, he constructed there a pneumatic tyre for his son's tricycle. Patented the following year, the tyre went into commercial production in 1890, with Dunlop holding 1,500 shares of the Belfast manufacturing company that developed into the Dunlop Company.

but also for the garda, the connections of the pony and others so much so that shortly after returning home, I received a visit from the friendly garda to ascertain that I was OK.

The upstairs apartment in a house in a favoured residential area in Ballsbridge was not really conducive to running a veterinary practice. Not long afterwards, we purchased alternative accommodation in a two-storey house only 200 yards from the main street in the south Dublin superb of Dundrum, which became the base for our practice.

We lived upstairs and converted the basement into the surgery. Following a British Small Animal Veterinary Association Conference (BSAVA) in Dublin, a few years later, the surgery was approved as a training centre for Registered Animal Nursing Auxiliaries (RANAs), only the second practice in Dublin at the time to be so approved. We normally had two nurses in training at any one time.

While all this was going on, I had a re-occurrence of the fluctuating undiagnosed temperature I suffered while working in Ross-on-Wye and which necessitated hospitalisation. Following a range of tests in Dublin, brucellosis (primarily a cattle disease) was finally diagnosed and over several years, a wide variety of treatments were instigated, but none of them alleviated the symptoms of night sweats, exhaustion and depression.

I was advised to stay well away from cattle, which harbour the illness. This resulted in me selling the large animal side of the practice to concentrate on less stressful companion animals. It is worth mentioning at this stage that, as students, we were never taught the rudiments of self-protection against diseases with which we might be in contact. When testing cattle for brucellosis, we had to take blood samples to send to the laboratory for diagnosis. When drawing blood, it was normal procedure to take a sample from one cow in the byre, then place the needle between the teeth (the vet's and not the cow's), before moving on to the next cow…and so on.

Further, when removing the retained placenta from a cow, which might well have aborted, we never used protective sleeves on our arm. We stood immediately behind the cow with our arm fully inside the uterus and our nose and mouth within centimetres of the animals' external genital organs. There is no better way of becoming infected. This was lunacy and a sure way to become infected, but we never realised the dangerous implications of such a practice, nor had we ever been warned, as students, of the risks we would be taking.

One of our early cases in the new premises was a Pekinese puppy who had clearly swallowed a large object, which was stuck in its abdomen. As so often with animal emergencies, it was a Saturday afternoon. I could not yet afford an x-ray machine but I did know a friendly human radiologist who, despite it being a weekend, kindly responded to my request to x-ray my patient.

This revealed a large bone jammed in the stomach and stretching half the length of the unfortunate dog. Following surgery to remove the bone, it made an uneventful recovery and the following morning, it attempted to pick up one of our own dogs' bones to demonstrate its well-being.

Pekinese, ruler and bone, post-surgery.

On another occasion, I received a call from the Gardaí to say that a dog had been seen on the railway track alongside Whitworth Road and opposite Drumcondra Hospital in the north of the city. This was at a point where the track is some 10–12 metres below road level for one or two kilometres. The only access was down any one of a number of metal ladders attached to the retaining wall.

I met several Gardaí in Whitworth Road from where we could see a German shepherd lying on the track some distance below us. It had a fracture of a front leg and was making no effort to move. The Gardaí ascertained that we had only a matter of minutes to get down to the track, diagnose the injury, render immediate first aid and get back up to the road again using the ladder, before the next train from the city to the West of Ireland was due. We managed to extricate the unfortunate animal just in time and transferred it into the care of the Dublin Society for the Prevention of Cruelty to Animals (DSPCA) hospital facility.

By this time, in the late 1960s, our three children were becoming pony mad and when an old country house, Castlefield, with a few acres of land became available in Templeogue, some three miles from Dundrum, we purchased it. This enabled the children to be raised in a semi-rural environment and to fulfil their growing interest in all things equine.

In addition, we established a boarding facility for dogs and cats whose owners were on holiday or needed respite from their pets for whatever reason. I must have been horribly naïve because, after only a few years, I convinced myself that we could manage our affairs just from the income from the boarding kennels. I sold the veterinary practice to Malcolm Argyle and John Bainbridge, colleagues and friends who, at that time, were assistants to N.H. (Ham) Lambert, a highly respected small animal practitioner in Dublin. Ham had, in fact, been a great help to me in establishing the small animal side of my practice and I had always held him in high regard. Was this all a big mistake or did it open the doors to a whole new veterinary world?

One evening shortly before I sold the practice, my good friend from the Dudgeon riding school days, Richard Teevan, called me. At that time, Richard ran a large animal and horse practice in Kilcock, some 20 miles west of Dublin, but was also working part time as stewards secretary (veterinary) to the Irish Turf (Jockey) Club. He told me that Ted Kelly, his then superior, needed to undergo a hip operation and the Turf Club would be looking for a replacement during the three months that Ted would be out of action. My mind went into overdrive. Could this be my ticket to a new career?

At this time, the Keeper of the Matchbook, as the chief executive of the Turf Club was known, was Captain Denis Baggallay, the trainer with whom I spent time as a student and who gave me my first ride in a race. Amazingly, two days after Richard had told me of a pending vacancy, Captain Baggallay contacted me to know if I might be interested. Of course I was interested and a few months later I commenced understudying Ted Kelly prior to his surgery. As it happened, by the time Ted was ready to return to work, a vacancy had occurred as steward's secretary (disciplinary) which Ted readily accepted. This resulted in me remaining in post, but now in a permanent role from January 1972. Not long afterwards Capt. Baggallay retired and was replaced by Cahir O'Sullivan. I enjoyed an excellent working and personal relationship with both he and his wife, Greta, for many years to come.

At this time, in the 1970s, there were 28 racecourses throughout Ireland catering for up to 300 race meetings in any one year. This included Laytown, south of Drogheda on the east coast of Ireland, where we raced on the beach in high summer when the tide was out. Dope sampling (saliva swabs only at this track) was conducted from the boot of my car.

The Turf Club also served the two North of Ireland racecourses, Down Royal and Downpatrick. The original Long Kesh Detention Centre was close to Down Royal racecourse, which was often referred to as The Maze. It was where those from both sides of the political divide were incarcerated during the time of 'The Troubles' in Ireland, in the 1970s. Jockeys often joked that if they went too wide turning into the finishing straight they would end up in The Maze (prison).

Clearly, racehorses were, on the whole, exceptionally well-cared for; otherwise they could not possibly perform to the best of their ability. However, as with any athlete, it is only natural that they did suffer accidents and illnesses, which required veterinary care and the administration of medication. It was the trainer's responsibility to ensure that the horse did not return to full training and racing until it had fully recovered and any drugs administered had been eliminated from its system.

The duty of the VO was almost totally related to overseeing the collection of urine samples or, if unable to collect urine, saliva samples for forensic analyses to ascertain that the horse was drug free at the time of racing. Other duties included confirming horse's identities against their passports particularly on their first appearance on the racecourse and also examining a horse following a poor performance to confirm, or otherwise, the trainer's excuses.

Samples to Laboratory

Samples collected needed to be kept cold, preferably refrigerated, from the time they were collected until they reached the laboratory. That was all very well for one day meetings, when I took the samples home for the night and delivered them to the forensic laboratory in Trinity College, Dublin, the next morning, prior to travelling to that day's racing. But, what about the 2–5 day holiday meetings? Samples collected would remain overnight (or longer) in the boot of my locked car where there was no refrigerator. This was far from ideal.

After a short while, having discussed the issue with Cahir O'Sullivan, I purchased 12 metal toolboxes, each being large enough to accommodate samples from up to eight horses. These full boxes were padlocked to ensure security. I arranged with the Totalisator Board, whose offices were within a few hundred yards of the laboratory and whose vehicle travelled back to Dublin with the day's takings each day after racing, to also take our toolbox back to their offices. First thing the following morning, the laboratory would collect the samples and return the empty toolbox, which would find its way back to me at the next day's race meeting. Problem solved.

A popular horse tonic at the time contained caffeine and one of its metabolites, theobromine, was commonly found in urine samples. In one season alone, in the 1970s, there were over 40 cases in the UK and Ireland. Tied Cottage, a Cheltenham Gold Cup winner, was the highest profile horse to be disqualified. Phenylbutazone (PBZ), often referred to as 'bute', is a nonsteroidal anti-inflammatory drug (NSAID) used for the short-term treatment of pain and fever in animals. It is not a cure for lameness, as popular myth often suggests, but it will help to mask the pain and unsoundness in some more minor cases. PBZ and its metabolite, oxyphenbutazone, were other common substances to be found in urine from time to time.

Any accidents or injuries on race days were treated by the racecourse veterinarian who was normally a local equine practitioner employed by the racecourse. We always had a good and close working relationship with these different colleagues around the country.

Gradually over the years, I became involved with meetings with other racing authorities to consider harmonisation of veterinary rules, regulations and procedures. These included issues such as the updating of mandatory equine influenza vaccination regulations, disease control and the international movement of horses, identification of horses and completion of passports, forensic analyses, and various other procedures. The subjects of these international meetings were normally discussed initially by representatives of the British, French and Irish Jockey Clubs.

Although I was very much the junior member of this group, Major Douglas Witherington, the British Jockey Club veterinary officer and Dr Paul Benazet, the French equivalent, guided me through what I was expected to do, rather like kindly schoolmasters. The other members of our Irish negotiating team included Cahir O'Sullivan, my boss and Keeper of the Match Book, Dr Michael Lambert, Director of the Equine Forensic Laboratory in Trinity College, Dublin and Dr Peter Timoney, highly respected veterinarian and well-known internationally on issues relating to equine diseases and their control.

Dr Peter Timoney

Peter graduated in 1964 from University College Dublin. After filling various posts in Ireland and the USA, he returned to Ireland in 1981, when appointed scientific director of the newly formed Irish Equine Centre. He returned to the US in 1983 to join the University of Kentucky's Department of Equine Veterinary Science. From 1989 to 2006, he served as director of the Maxwell H. Gluck Equine Research Centre. Peter is a World Organisation for Animal Health (OIE) designated expert on equine viral arteritis, and a past President of the World Equine Veterinary Association, of which I was one time secretary/treasurer.

When the British, French and Irish authorities had agreed on what they wanted to achieve, the meetings then moved on to include the German, Italian, and Spanish equivalents. The results of these meetings normally formed recommendations, which were referred for ratification to the International Conference of Racing Authorities (now re-branded the International Federation of Racing Authorities) at its annual meeting in Paris in October. This conference takes place each year immediately following the prestigious race meeting at Longchamp, featuring the richest race in the world at the time, the Prix de l'Arc de Triumph.

In addition to these, there were the bi-annual meetings of the International Conference of Racing Analysts and Veterinarians (ICRAV). Although I was unaware at the time, a small group had met in Newmarket in 1976. However, the first official meeting is credited as taking place in Ireland two years later. This was basically organised by Michael Lambert and his forensic colleagues with a little help from me and our veterinary friends abroad who provided their professional input. The delegates stayed in Dublin and were bussed each day to The Curragh, a major racecourse and training centre, where all the Irish classic races are run and where the actual meetings took place.

Michael Moss, who was among the many delegates who attended, was the first director of Racecourse Security Services Laboratory (RSS), Newmarket, UK and subsequently rebranded the Horseracing Forensic Laboratory (HFL). Michael had been instrumental in setting up the laboratory as an independent entity and for convincing The Jockey Club of the need for a significant research budget and the staff to deliver the research output, which contributed to the UK's pre-eminence in the area of steroid analysis in horseracing. Under Michael's leadership, the HFL expanded to become the largest equine drug-testing laboratory in the world by the mid-1980s. He was also responsible for instigating the first-ever international meeting of racing analysts and veterinarians, which became the forerunner of the International Conference of Racing Analysts and Veterinarians now held biannually as mentioned above.

After leaving HFL in 1989, Michael continued to work in racing as a consultant to various Jockey Clubs, including Macao and Brazil before settling in the Philippines with his second wife Daisy. He was succeeded as Director of HFL by Dr Neville Dunnett and I had the pleasure of working with both of these eminent scientists during my time with the Turf Club and later.

Michael Lambert and I were both invited to Michael Moss's retirement party, which was held in the Animal Health Trust close to Newmarket. During the evening, I was with the two Michaels as they chatted. At one stage, Moss said: "Do you know, I had absolutely no idea that this party was being planned for me," to which Lambert retorted:

"If you had no idea what was going on in your own laboratory, it is high time you retired."

Two interesting side issues of the Irish conference were: firstly, I had occasion to drive M. Jean Romanet, his son, Louis and his wife back from The Curragh, where the meetings took place, to their hotel in Dublin following the first day of the conference. M. Romanet was the Director of the Société d'encouragement du cheval, the equivalent of the French Jockey Club and he proved to be a huge influence on me later in my career.

Secondly, there was an official dinner one night, organised by Michael Lambert in Trinity College in Dublin. In addition, Cahir O'Sullivan agreed to our suggestion that Sherley and I should host an informal party on the last evening of the conference in our home. Some 50 guests attended a casual buffet supper with lots of drink and fun and from which the last foreign guest (I will not mention from which country) departed at 4 am.

Further such conferences, which I had the pleasure of attending for the Irish Turf Club, included Lexington, Kentucky in 1979 and Melbourne, Australia in 1981.

After I left the Turf Club, I continued attending these conferences when representing other organisations: Toronto, Canada in 1983, Hong Kong in 1985 and Louisville, Kentucky in 1988 when working for the FEI and the meetings in the Gold Coast near Brisbane, Australia in 1996 and lastly that in Dubai in 2004 when representing the United Arab Emirates Equestrian and Racing Federation.

I would now like to recall the Melbourne ICRAV Conference in 1981. This was hosted by the Victoria Jockey Club of which my good friend and colleague, John Bourke, was senior veterinary officer. I was charged with making a presentation on the *Welfare of the Horse*. I relied on an overhead projector and transparencies to illustrate my points as PowerPoint had not yet been invented, or if it had, I had certainly never heard of it.

Looking back on this presentation now, many years later, I was pleased when a number of delegates kindly congratulated me, I think genuinely, for drawing attention to a number of welfare issues of concern, which are summarised below. I would now like to share this presentation with you:

One would imagine that the successful thoroughbred racehorse is akin to a superbly tuned and beautifully maintained racing car. This is rarely the case. The car comes off the production line after many years of detailed planning, and is then systematically assembled by highly skilled and trained mechanics to become a smooth operating machine.

The background of the racehorse can be very different. Certainly, on most occasions, much thought goes into the preparation of its ancestry. But after it has been born and reared, it is sent at the ridiculously young age of 18 months, while still totally immature, to a training stable to be assembled into a racing machine.

This should be a highly skilled performance, like the assembly of the racing car, and on many occasions, it is but, unfortunately, all too often it is left in the hands of the un-skilled and the ignorant. This can lead to the production of a wayward machine with a bad mouth and little love for racing.

The potentially good racehorse can be totally ruined by incorrect handling at this stage of its development. Perhaps, this is a gross exaggeration so let us look in a little more detail at the lot of this particular animal.

Undoubtedly, systems vary throughout the many countries of the world so I will confine my remarks to how I see the situation in my own country – Ireland. As already stated, much thought and planning generally goes into the production of the thoroughbred – everybody wants to breed a champion – but it does not necessarily follow that the stallion with the best blood lines mated to the mare with the best blood lines produces the most successful progeny. In fact, often this is not the case and we all know that the high-priced yearlings at sales do not necessarily have the best racing record.

Assuming that a live foal is produced – and the chances of this are little more than 50% – it will run in the open with its dam until weaned. This foaling record is hardly a figure for which the veterinary profession can be proud and it is a figure that has changed little over the years despite miraculous scientific advances. Dr (now Professor) Leo Jeffcott of the Equine Research Station (now rebranded as Animal Health Trust), Newmarket, UK recently conducted a survey of thoroughbred wastage. In 1975, there were 28,500 mares listed in the general Stud Book. Of these, 17,100 were covered – mated – 9,675 foals were born but only 5,573 were named. Of the remaining, 3,089 went into training and 2,758 actually raced in their first season. This figure represents 9.68% of runners from the 28,500 mares originally listed. Perhaps, there is food for thought in these figures.

I understood from the subsequent discussion that the Australian figures at the time were much the same as those for the UK.

One wonders if mares might be better off if humans would stop interfering with them. Such 'interference' includes sending unsound or defective stallions and mares to stud in the first place. Following weaning, however, the foal will then join companions of its own age and run loose in large paddocks during the daytime while being housed and fed at night, over its first winter.

During this period, a pattern usually develops – a leader appears and plays a dominant role. Some will say that the others will not pass the leader either in the paddocks or subsequently on the racecourse, while a different view maintains that if they are watched closely, sooner or later one will emerge from the herd to challenge the leader and this is your future racehorse.

Having reached the age of 12–15 months and having been handled in and out of the paddocks, the yearling is broken on the stud to lunge and long rein and eventually goes to the trainer in the autumn, often via a yearling sale. When the youngster reaches the trainer's yard its troubles can really start. There are a large number of very good trainers but there are also a number of mediocre ones. In Ireland, we have some 700 trainers and permit holders in total training some 4,000 horses.

The methods used to break horses vary enormously. This is a most important exercise, which will play a major role in determining how the animal eventually performs. Many are ruined at this stage. This may well be due to circumstances as the old, traditional breed of horseman has virtually disappeared and many of those now working with horses have not been brought up with them. In some cases, when contemplating a job, they have 'tossed up' between the local factory, with regular hours and weekends, free and the local trainer who offers neither. This is not a sound basis on which to start working with horses. In addition, many of these youngsters have their sights set on becoming jockeys. Few of them make the grade and they are then liable to take out their frustrations on the unfortunate horses under their care.

One wonders how important training really is and how much actually depends on the horse's inherent ability. It would be fair to say that few horses are out of their stables for much more than one hour per day. Surely, this is amazing – to have a fit, tense, excitable, natural herd animal cooped up in an often-small stable for 23 out of every 24 hours. This is akin to the management of battery hens and must be a recipe for psychological problems to place a thoroughbred in such an environment. One could hardly imagine a human athlete allowing his fit muscles only one hour's exercise per day. Even greyhounds are likely to be allowed freedom to romp in a compound during their non-training hours. It would be interesting to learn the opinion of a sports physiotherapist on this subject.

However, to return to training methods, let me give you a few examples personally known to me. One of our most successful national hunt trainers takes his horses out of their stables for only half an hour per day. They cross the road, are ridden up a laneway into a large field, where they gallop one, two or three laps before proceeding back down the laneway and into their stables again. Day in, day out, this is the routine.

Another of our trainers goes to the sales in Newmarket each year, buys well-bred fillies, which have disappointed on the racecourse, takes their rugs off, brings them home, turns them loose in fields with others and beds them in a deep litter stable or barn overnight. They grow long, dirty coats and are occasionally groomed with a curry comb. They are ridden out for 1½–2 hours each day, walking, trotting and cantering over a 250-acre farm and jumping whatever might come in their way, such as ditches and hedges. For the remainder of the day they run free, admittedly with a shelter, to socialise, roll, gallop and do what they like. These fillies come to the races, often looking like hairy goats and run and win their fair share of races.

Presumably, their success is very much related to the relaxed atmosphere of a small stable and a more natural and interesting existence, as against the confines and strict routine of a more fashionable stable in a large training centre. The sequence to this is that with a winning record and happy in themselves, they are put in foal and are sold on at a handsome profit.

Without doubt, the best steeplechase mare we have had in Ireland in many years, which includes winning the Cheltenham Gold Cup, is trained on the side of the Dublin Mountains (hills to those from Switzerland or other countries, which are privileged to have real mountains) where there is not a flat field in which she could gallop for five miles. She does a lot of roadwork over the hills and gets an occasional gallop on the sands by the sea.

So, is it the training system or is it the horse?

We have 28 racecourses in Ireland and apart from The Curragh, no centralised training or racing, so that horses must normally travel on race days to the course to arrive shortly before their race. The more affluent trainers travel their horses by luxury lorry but a number of the smaller stables use car and trailer. Anybody who has travelled in a trailer will realise that it is not a pleasant experience. The horse must survive the effects of several hours in a draftee, swaying trailer while breathing in sickening exhaust fumes. Soon after arrival, the horse is expected to pull out at the top of its form, run in, and possibly win a race – a big ask. A recent survey measured the effect, admittedly on ponies of a five-hour journey by trailer. The results showed varying degrees of mental arousal and altered heart and blood pictures, which in several cases took up to 36 hours to return to normal – and we expect horses to run at the top of their form virtually straight off the back of a trailer. Interestingly, the more seasoned travellers were more upset by the experience than those on their first trip.

It is often said that 'good horses make good jockeys' and there is no doubt that it is a joy to watch a good rider, perfectly balanced and in tune with his horse during the race, gather it together for its final effort. He, or she, will ride it out with hands and heals in rhythm with the horse's stride while maintaining the necessary balance. A few very successful jockeys ride with extremely short stirrup leathers. It will have taken time to perfect this style.

Regrettably, some young aspiring riders seem to have the impression that their senior's success is directly proportional to the length of their stirrup leathers. The end result is that their only hope of remaining in the saddle is with the help of God and the horse's mouth. Towards the finish, they tend to use the whip excessively, as they are totally unable to use hand and heal from this unnatural position. Regardless of this rather negative comment, there are many exceptionally good junior and senior jockeys riding both on the flat and over fences.[2]

Under the Rules of Racing, horses must always run up to their maximum ability. This presents a very real quandary for the jockey. If he does not ride the horse out to obtain its best possible placing in the race, he leaves himself open to the wrath of the stewards for not trying hard enough. If, however, he uses his whip excessively to assist in obtaining the best placing, he is liable to be subject to a penalty of a fine and/or suspension by the same stewards for 'abusing' the horse.

In the more valuable races with high prize money and hence a larger percentage payment for the jockey, the temptation can often be to win regardless and accept the consequences afterwards. Winning regardless tends to imply excessive use of the whip. It is not a pleasant site to watch a horse receiving a very real beating towards the end of a race. While this is bad enough in a relatively short flat race, to witness the same at the end of a three mile, or longer, steeplechase in heavy ground with horses clearly exhausted is not for the faint-hearted. Swinging the whip to encourage the horse to run on is one thing but truly beating it is unacceptable. This is a dilemma

---

[2] See similar sentiments expressed by Stan Mellor, champion National Hunt jockey 1960–1962, in Henrietta Knight's most readable book, *Not Enough Time*, which is about her life with another three times champion jockey, Terry Biddlecombe, champion 1965, 1966 and 1969. *Not Enough Time*, 2015, Head of Zeus Ltd., Page 227.

for both jockey and steward although, to their credit, the stewards recognise the issue and are now taking steps to find a solution (as of 1981).

Exercise-induced pulmonary haemorrhage (EIPH) refers to the presence of blood in the airways of the lung in association with exercise. EIPH is common in horses undertaking intense exercise. Horses that experience EIPH may also be referred to as 'bleeders' or as having 'broken a blood vessel'. In the majority of cases, EIPH is not apparent unless an endoscopic examination of the airways is performed following exercise. However, a small proportion of horses may show bleeding at the nostrils after exercise, which is known as epistaxis. According to Dr Jim Pascoe of the United States, some years ago, 40% of race horses endoscopically examined by him showed evidence of lung haemorrhage post-race. Does this mean that racehorses are being pushed beyond the level of their natural ability or is lung haemorrhage normal in the racehorse?

The best known treatment available for this malady is probably the diuretic, frusemide, commonly known by its trade name, Lasix. It is in common use in North America, where many horses are treated with Lasix prior to racing and where it is legal in most states to do so. In the UK and the majority of other racing jurisdictions, however, medication rules are stricter and do not permit horses to race with frusemide present in their system. Some clinicians treat horses perceived to have EIPH problems with frusemide during training, but there is no hard evidence that this reduces the risk of haemorrhage during races. Many other treatments have been used for EIPH but none is consistently effective.

When the race is over, it is normal practice to wash/hose the horse down. Probably, the correct method is to sponge the horse with lukewarm or tepid water, scrape it dry, put on a cooler and walk the horse quietly around until it has dried off.

The alternative method, sadly often witnessed in racecourse stables post-race, is reserved for the attendant in a hurry. A few buckets of cold water are thrown over the horse, a rug is put on, the horse returned to its stable and the attendant goes about his business, often to attend to another runner in the next race. Five minutes later the unfortunate horse is invisible in the mist of steam emanating from his stable.

The next alternative, also often sadly witnessed, is the lazy version and often employed in winter under miserable weather conditions. A couple of buckets of icy-cold water are thrown over the horse (as before) and the attendant stands, chatting to a companion as he removes the plaits and the horse shivers. The sequel to all this is when the trainer explains to the worried owner a few days later that the horse picked up a 'virus' at the races. It is quite amazing the number of trainers who are totally unaware that this sort of treatment is meted out to their charges.

There is no doubt that the trainer's lot is not an easy one. Good owners are thin on the ground. These individuals are people who breed horses and know them. They realise that horses are not machines and that if a horse is ill or injured, the trainer can readily discuss the problem and expect reasonable understanding. Most such cases will require veterinary attention and periods of rest, which can be agreed to without too much difficulty.

The other breed of owner is the prosperous businessman, who considers that the owning of a racehorse, or two or more, is a status symbol, which will enhance his standing in business and socially in the community. He must be difficult to deal with as, without any inherent knowledge of horses in general, he cannot understand that *it is not possible to remove the injured part and replace it with a spare as he does in his factory. As for giving time for an illness or injury to be overcome – that is just not considered. He is liable to demand that his horse gets back onto the racecourse too quickly and while still unfit, which of course gives rise to further problems for the unfortunate animal.*

There is one area in which the racehorse is more fortunate than its show-jumping cousin. The racehorse is normally asked to perform on relatively fewer occasions during the year. For horses involved in the international jumping circuit it can be a different matter. The successful ones must compete, almost without rest, for months on end, travelling to one event after another, spending their time either in transit or in strange temporary stables, which are often much too small for the larger horses.

*Naturally, many find that their legs have difficulty standing the strain of constant jumping, twisting and turning at speed on joints that were never designed to make such movements. Luckily, or unluckily depending on your viewpoint, the ensuing discomfort can be masked by the use of the anti-inflammatory drug, phenylbutazone, which is currently legal in sport horses (*you will read more about this in another chapter*). Luckily in the sense that this will minimise the pain to some degree and unluckily because the pain-alleviating drug permits the horse to continue to compete, when nature and all that is good in veterinary medicine is crying out for it to be rested to prevent further injury to damaged tissues.*

When the horse's racing career is concluded, what happens next? The successful entire may well retire to stud to perpetuate the cycle, often in luxurious surroundings. The not so successful may become so-called 'country stallions.' It is not unknown for the less fortunate of these to remain cooped up in dingy, dark stables on a deep litter bed, only to be produced when there is a mare to be covered. The mares, admittedly, often not in the top bracket, are often kept on a low level of nutrition during the winter and then fail to conceive. Considering the conditions under which many of these animals are kept, it is no wonder that fertility rates are so low. Ignorance and lack of education and knowledge can be responsible for a great deal of hardship for some of these less fortunate horses.

The non-breeding animals may be retrained and thrive in second careers, as leisure horses, hunters, family pets, riding school or competition horses in various different disciplines. The less fortunate may find themselves in lower grade racing or in a meat factory. The latter may not always be the worst option if it prevents the horse from slipping further down the ladder into uncaring hands.

One further item which bothered me and which I did not mention in my presentation was the situation at one south of Ireland racecourse where there was a large central water-trough in the stable yard from which horses could drink directly and stable lads could fill buckets to give to individual horses and also to wash their horses after racing. Potentially, drinking from this common water source could enable the spread of disease to other horses. While I had no evidence to prove that this had actually happened, I did draw the attention of the chairman of the Trainers' Association to the matter, but he was not unduly concerned.

However, I have diverted, so let's go back to racing in the real world. One day I set off for Wexford races in the southeast corner of Ireland. On arrival, there was no sign of activity on the track and I suddenly realised that racing was not at Wexford that day but at Tramore, one and a half hours' driving time away. I arrived at Tramore a half hour after the first race! The stewards were not best pleased and quite rightly gave me a severe reprimand. Perhaps, it was time that I started to consider a new career path?

Chapter 3

INTRODUCTION TO FEI

Doping Control Dublin Horse Show – Acting as Foreign Official –
Olympic Games Moscow – World Cup Final Birmingham – Appointment
to FEI

According to the Royal Dublin Society (RDS) website, in 1941, Frank O'Reilly first joined the RDS, the historic show grounds in Ballsbridge, a south Dublin suburb, where the prestigious Dublin Horse Show is staged in August each year.

In the 1980s, first as chairman of the Executive Committee (1981-87) and then as president (1986-89), he steered the RDS through a difficult patch, which threatened its very survival. Frank was instrumental in bringing the tenth FEI World Jumping Championship to Dublin in 1982, the first to include a compulsory horse inspection before the start of the event. It was also thanks to him that anti-doping controls were established at the Dublin Horse Show.

Knowing of my role in the Turf Club, Frank called me one day in the mid-1970s to say that the Federation Equestre Internationale (FEI) which was the world-wide governing body of dressage, (show) jumping, (three-day) eventing and (carriage) driving, wished to introduce anti-doping controls into international equestrian sport and could I help to set this up for the Horse Show?

As a student, I used to cycle from our home to the Veterinary College in Ballsbridge, and passed the RDS en-route. In essence, this was all highly convenient for me, assuming that my boss, Cahir O'Sullivan, would agree.

Following my approach to him, Cahir kindly spoke to the senior steward of the Turf Club, who gave his permission. I also had to seek the support of our racing team to ensure that they would be available to cover racing in my absence. As soon as everyone was in agreement, I commenced organising the infrastructure at the RDS to enable suitable stabling with an adjoining small 'office' to be erected adjacent to the 'pocket', which was the area in which the horses gathered prior to competing and to which they returned immediately afterwards. In fact, this was not ideal as it was under the Anglesea Stand and hence quite noisy, but it worked well enough through several shows prior to and including the World Jumping Championship in 1982.

It was during these initial events that I met, for the first time, Professor Leo Jeffcott, who had been appointed by the FEI as Foreign Veterinary Delegate and whose role was to ensure that the FEI's veterinary regulations and general regulations were applied equitably to all competitors. The other members of the Veterinary Commission were Dr Murty Hynes as President, Adair Linton, a local practitioner with a special interest and expertise in equine matters and myself as Associate Member. At the time, Murty had recently retired from his position as

Director of Veterinary Services of the Irish Department of Agriculture. Leo was considerably younger than me and had attained international acclaim in a wide number of veterinary fields over many years. He was very efficient, easy to work with and is still an esteemed friend and colleague.

The other notable presence whom I met on this occasion was Fritz O. Widmer. Mr Widmer had recently been appointed as the FEI's secretary general and this was his first visit to the Dublin Horse Show. Frank introduced me to him. He was highly impressed with the event in general and of particular interest to me, with how the doping control was organised and executed. Not long after the show, Frank called to thank and ask me if I would be willing to have my name placed on the FEI's List of Event Veterinarians. This had been at Fritz Widmer's request. It was explained to me that for major international events either the FEI or the organisers, depending on the status of the event, must only select veterinarians included in this list to officiate at their event. Naturally, I was delighted to accept, subject to Cahir O'Sullivan's approval. As always, the long suffering Cahir did not stand in my way.

Resulting from this, over the ensuing few years I was appointed as Foreign Veterinary Delegate at a number of international events: 1978 – European Pony Championship at Lincoln UK and the Junior European Three-Day-Event Championship, Burghley (both in the UK); 1979 – Junior European Jumping Championship, Gijon, Spain; 1980 – Olympic Games, Moscow, USSR; 1981 – FEI World Cup Final, Birmingham, UK. In addition I was appointed President of the Veterinary Commission in 1980 – European Junior Jumping Championship, Millstreet, Ireland and in 1981 – European Pony Championship, also at Millstreet.

Joan Mullins, who was well-known to me through the Pony Club and also as a client when I was working for Lewis Doyle, was the Official International Jumping Judge at Lincoln, and we flew over together. At the time of the Lincoln event the height of ponies was measured in 'hands', although this has now been decimalised; 4" make a "hand", so pony competitions were designated as being (no higher than) 12.2", 13.2" or 14.2".

Different countries treated pony measurements with different levels of distain. The Lincoln event was for 14.2" ponies, so I was amazed to find one European country's pony's passport describe the animal as 14.5", which is equivalent to 15.1". As this pony was 3" above the required height and hence at a distinct advantage when jumping a fence, clearly it was not permitted to compete. The height of ponies had always been and continues to be a contentious issue.

Burghley was my first introduction to top-level three-day-eventing, although admittedly this particular event was for juniors. This magnificent estate near Stamford in Lincolnshire, was owned by the late Lord Burghley, where he annually hosted a major ***** three-day event, five stars being the highest category. Lord Burghley himself was a noted athlete. He had won the Gold Medal for the 400 metres hurdle race at the 1928 summer Olympic Games and the Silver Medal four years later in addition to many other titles.

At Burghley, Colonel John Hickman, a highly respected Cambridge University veterinarian, who held many important positions within the veterinary political system, including President of the British Equine Veterinary Association and Deputy Chairman of the FEI's Veterinary Committee, was President of the Veterinary Commission and Michael Gibson, a well-known local equine practitioner was the

Associate Member. They both proved to be admirable teachers with vast exp[...] in this discipline. They guided me through my duties as Foreign Veterinary Dele[...] with great sensitivity and instantly made me feel like an accepted member of th[...] team. Mike's mother was the judge when I rode Tinker Belle to win a 13.2" pony class at the Dublin Spring Show as a child. Other officials I met at this event included Major General Jack Reynolds, then secretary general of the British Equestrian Federation but later to become president and Colonel Gustav Nyblaeus, Swedish Official International Dressage judge of considerable note, both of whom I was to come across many times in the future.

The most exciting and dramatic assignment for me came out of the blue in 1980 when I was invited to officiate at the Olympic Games in Moscow. This was to prove to be an amazing experience. As I had to fulfil my Turf Club commitments as best I could Sherley and I only flew to Moscow on the day of the opening ceremony so we actually missed this special occasion. As the British Airways plane taxied towards its parking bay at Moscow Airport, I was requested over the Tannoy to identify myself. We were invited to leave the aircraft first and were immediately met by a welcoming party headed by Professor Igor Bobylev. We were escorted to the VIP lounge and our passports were taken from us to be checked elsewhere. I had known Prof Bobylev's name for some time. He was expected at the ICRAV conference in Ireland the previous year but was unable to make it and a deputy replaced him. He was President of the Veterinary Commission at these games so I realised that we would be working closely together for the next two weeks.

Having become fully acquainted with those who welcomed us, which included our interpreter for the duration of the games, our passports were returned to us. We were ushered out and into one of a fleet of limousines, now fully loaded with our luggage. We were whisked away on specially delegated traffic lanes reserved for the Olympic Family to the enormous and luxurious *****Moskva Hotel.

This hotel was solely for the use of the President of the International Olympic Committee (IOC), presidents and secretary generals of all competing international federations, technical delegates (TDs) and other VIPS. As the veterinary TD, I qualified to be in this illustrious company.

We had been invited to join Fritz Widmer, FEI secretary general for dinner. We arrived at the appointed hour and were reintroduced to Col. Nyblaeus, whom we had already met at Burghley two years previously, and one or two others. Col. Nyblaeus, as FEI Vice President was attending the games while representing H.R.H. The Prince Philip, Duke of Edinburgh and President of the FEI, who was unable to attend. Before we commenced our meal, I caught sight of the President of the IOC, Lord Killanin entering the dining room with his wife. I knew Lord Killanin well from his connections with racing in Ireland.

n was Chairman of Galway Racecourse and a good friend of
After each day's racing at Galway, he always invited us to his
drink. In addition to the five-day Festival meeting in July, there
ier one or two-day meetings at Galway during the year and Lord
)itality qualified him to be a 'friend' of officials. In addition,
and I shared a common affliction. We both suffered from
brucellosis and tended to compare notes whenever we met.

On the occasion of our first meeting at the Moscow Olympics, I was very touched when Lord and Lady Killanin approached our table and I had the privilege of introducing them to the representative of the President and to the secretary general of the FEI. After some small talk, he kindly invited Sherley and me to his room for a nightcap after dinner. As I already knew, Lord Killanin liked his whisky – with ice. At this stage, he and his wife had been staying in the hotel for several days but he explained to us that he had had great difficulty obtaining ice for his drink. He then demonstrated that by standing under the chandelier in the middle of the bedroom, looking up and speaking clearly, "Please, may I have some ice for my drink?" the result was almost instantaneous. He advised us to remember to be careful as to what else we might say in the bedroom.

I was highly conscious of the fact that we were already late for the games and although the first equestrian event was still several days away, there were various duties which I needed to perform. These included checking the stable accommodation, the feedstuffs, ensuring that all horses had received a basic clinical examination on their arrival, to ensure freedom from disease, check their identity against their passports and various other stipulated duties, not least of which was the organisation and practical aspects of the doping control.

However, regardless of all the above Prof. Bobylev was more interested in showing us the sites of Moscow. Finally, he relented. He assured me that all was well with the accommodation and fodder and the horses' health did not give rise for concern. Eventually, we did manage a cursory inspection and found the 450 available stables impressive with large comfortable and airy, loose boxes. Following more pressure, Prof. Bobylev produced the passports for the 98 horses due to compete.

It took several hours in the office to check the mandatory details before gathering them up, at which point the professor asked, "Where are you going?"

"To see the horses," I responded.

"Why do you want to see the horses?" came the reply.

"To check their identity against their passports."

This was an Olympic Games and yet, confirmation of the identity of the participating horses was of little interest to him.

Regardless, we managed to go through the exercise and confirmed as best we could that the horses present were in fact the ones that had been officially entered. It is worth bearing in mind that at this time the standard of completion of passports varied widely from country to country and often left much to be desired.

The horses were, of course, re-identified against their passports at time of inspection on the day before their first competition and again at any future reinspections and also when selected for sampling at doping control. This inspection was based on a modified format of that already used in the three-day-event discipline.

All appeared to be in place for the doping control to be carried out successfully. The FEI Veterinary Rules, 3rd edition 1977, were applicable at the time of the Moscow Games. In this rulebook, forbidden substances were described as stimulants, depressants, tranquillisers, local anaesthetics and masking agents (later editions of the rules/regulations, which were revised on a four-year cycle, became more specific). There will be more on this subject in a later chapter.

In fact, all was not quite so with the arrangements for the doping control. In attempting to collect samples, it is important that the attendant designated to collect the urine remains calm and quiet to encourage the horses to relax in the stable. The Moscow collectors wore white coats (startling to a horse) and when the horse straddled to urinate, they came charging into the stable brandishing the urine pot, frightening the horse and, as a result, very little urine was collected. I had absolutely no knowledge of what forensic laboratory was analysing the samples, other than an 'official' laboratory or of the results of the analyses.

This, of course, was understandable as the results should have been reported directly to the secretary general of the FEI, and to nobody else. I was totally unaware of the situation regarding the human athletes. In retrospect, as this was an Olympic Games, I had naively assumed that this was all being overseen by some higher authority.

The programme of competitions followed the normal pattern: First the three-day-event, next dressage and finally jumping. The host nation won the team medal in all three disciplines. ITA were 2nd and MEX 3rd in the three-day-event, BUL were second and ROM were third in dressage; and POL were 2nd and MEX 3rd in jumping.

Of the individual medals, three-day-event: ITA 1st (Federico Roman riding Rossinan) URS 2nd and 3rd; dressage: AUT 1st (Elizabeth Theurer riding Mon Cherie), URS were 2nd and 3rd; jumping: POL 1st (Jan Kowalczyk riding Artemor), URS 2nd and MEX 3rd.

The entire event course was surrounded by soldiers standing shoulder to shoulder. At the end of the day, the route from the course to the nearby subway station was similarly also entirely enclosed by soldiers standing shoulder to shoulder, who guided us in a diminishing funnel to the train, which would take us back to the city.

Igor Bobylev was an excellent host and between competitions, managed to show us much of the sites of Moscow, which included visits to the Bolshoi Ballet and the National Circus. While being driven to the circus, which Igor was unable to attend, our interpreter told us that our driver would not be available to collect us after the end of the performance and that we should take a taxi back to the hotel. We thought little more of this until we all emerged out onto the street following a magnificent performance, to find that we were not alone in wanting a taxi.

Initially, they came in convoys, then rapidly diminished and finally ceased. The multitude had deserted us; next the streetlights began to dim and one by one were switched off. This was not a comfortable position to be in and we were at least 15 minutes driving time from our hotel and had no idea in which direction. We started hailing private cars and finally one stopped. The driver and a male passenger sat in the front. Without a word and without getting out of the car, the passenger leaned back and opened the rear door. We had little option but to get in – clearly we were gullible tourists. I managed to get out the word 'Hotel Moskva', the driver nodded and we drove off. The two men chatted to each other in the front. To them, we did not exist. Finally, the hotel loomed up in front of us. The car stopped. I offered some notes (cash) in thanks. A wave of the hand dismissed this gesture. The door opened, we got out; I tried to express our thanks before our kind friends disappeared into the night without a word or a smile.

During the Closing Ceremony on 3rd August 1980, Sherley photographed Lord Killanin addressing the huge crowd of over 80,000 people. This was to be his last games as President – he was succeeded by Juan Antonio Samaranch.

Immediately following this, we attended a magnificent reception hosted by the organising committee of the games in the Palace of Congresses in the Kremlin. There must have been several thousand people present including Leonid Brezhnev, first secretary and chairman of the Communist Party, along with many other senior party members, athletes and officials from all the different sports that comprised the games, a number of whom we recognised. Food and drink flowed from numerous outlets strategically placed around the enormous hall. It was a wonderful evening.

After we returned to Ireland, Lord Killanin very kindly autographed the photo Sherley had taken during the Closing Ceremony; it now hangs in our drawing room.

Lord Killanin, President IOC, addressing the 80,000 spectators in the Lenin Stadium, Moscow.

At the time, I felt honoured to have officiated such a major event. It was only some time later that I discovered that many of the officials were not necessarily first choices. Due to the politics of the times these games were boycotted by many of the major nations and it became necessary to appoint officials from 'neutral' countries. Coming from the Irish Republic I qualified for the role.

During the next two years, as you will have noted, I acted as President of the Veterinary Commission at both the European Junior Jumping and Pony Jumping Championships respectively, both of which took place at Noel C. Duggan's Greenglens Equestrian Centre in Millstreet, Co Cork in Southern Ireland.

Ass G's Peculiar Behaviour

There was a rather bizarre incident at the first of these events. One day, I was alerted to the fact that Ass G, a horse on the German team, was behaving in a peculiar manner. I went to the stables with Dan Hutch, an equine practitioner, and who was Associate Member of the Veterinary Commission.

Ass G was perfectly normal in the stable, but once outside, he repeatedly kicked out with both hind legs. Clearly, there was something bothering him. Dan examined him, including an internal rectal examination but could find nothing abnormal. This was a mystery. The same behaviour was repeated each time he was led outside his stable. During the day, Dan continued to monitor the horse and administered various soothing medications. Early next morning, I met a journalist known to me, who commented that it was great that Ass G had recovered and was ready to compete. I contacted Dan who knew nothing of this. Eventually, the story emerged.

The German Chef d'Equipe, not satisfied that enough was being done to treat Ass G contacted a well-known veterinarian in Germany, Dr Peter Cronau. I did not know Peter at the time, but he told me his side of what happened some years later. He received the call from the Chef d'Equipe, requesting help. He took a flight from Dusseldorf to Cork later that night and then travelled by taxi to Millstreet, where he arrived around mid-night. He met the Chef d'Equipe, went to Ass G's stable, conducted an internal examination and discovered a large bolus (not unlike a large ball of knitting wool) of ascarid worms passing into the rectum and straight into his hand. He removed the bolus, administered a mild laxative and departed the scene.

As there were no further flights back to Dusseldorf in the early hours of the morning, the taxi driver took Peter back to his home. His wife made the spare bed available in which he had a short but good night's sleep. A fine-cooked breakfast awaited him in the morning, whereupon the taxi driver drove him back to the airport for the first flight of the day back to Dusseldorf. The fee requested was the return fare from the airport to Millstreet and back. Bed and breakfast were free gratis as the taxi driver's contribution to an Irish welcome.

Peter and I had a good laugh over the story when we met some years later and have since become good friends.

At Millstreet, we were all dumbfounded. Clearly, this bolus of worms was causing Ass G some discomfort as it passed through his gut and Peter had arrived just at the psychological moment when the bolus entered the rectum and straight into his hand. Ass G made an uneventful recovery and went on to compete during the event.

In 1981, the same year as the Pony Championship at Millstreet, I was appointed to act as Foreign Veterinary Delegate at the Jumping World Cup Final held at the Exhibition Centre in Birmingham, UK in April of that year. On this occasion, the event was sponsored jointly by Volvo AG, Sweden and the Dutch Ministry of Agriculture – the flowers provided to decorate the arena and the fences were quite magnificent – although in subsequent years, Volvo AG were the sole sponsors. Fritz

Widmer, the FEI's secretary general, was present at Birmingham for this event. We had of course met previously in Moscow and in Dublin but now had the opportunity to talk. I have indicated earlier that I felt that it was time to move on from the racing job and see what other opportunities there might be in the equestrian world. I conveyed this to Fritz and asked his opinion. Completely out of the blue, he said that there just might be an opening for me in the FEI if I would be interested.

Within the next few weeks, Fritz Widmer discussed the possibility of my joining the FEI team with the President, H.R.H. The Prince Philip, Duke of Edinburgh, who apparently agreed in principle. Following some correspondence, Sherley and I were invited in August to make a three-day inspection visit to the headquarters of the FEI in Bern, the beautiful Swiss capital. This was clearly a 'getting-to-know' visit. The Veterinary and Legal Department had been established in 1979. We met some of the staff, including Madame Monique Wettstein-Deyme, who had been appointed its first head and whom I might eventually succeed. I was surprised at how small the secretariat was, occupying just one upstairs floor of an attractive building, with a limited staff. M. Robert Michels, Head of the Sports Department, who I had met when officiating at one of the Millstreet championships and some others. Monique, a non-veterinarian, had previously worked in the Legal Department of the Societe d'encouragement et des steeple-chases de France (French Jockey Club). She lived in Zurich and worked in the FEI on a part time basis. Her major function appeared to be handling dope cases, issuing passports to National Federations and Report Forms to Veterinarians and Appeal Committees officiating at international events.

On the last evening of our visit, Sherley and I were dining alone in the Schwizerhof Hotel in Bern, where we had been staying, when I was called to the telephone. It was Mr Widmer, who advised me that Prince Philip, who was currently competing in the World Driving Championship at Zug, would like to meet us. Zug was not far from Zurich Airport and he proposed that he would collect us, on the following morning, rather earlier than arranged to enable us to detour to Zug to meet Prince Philip prior to travelling to the airport for our flight home.

We met in the unlikely venue of the men's changing rooms in Zug Football Stadium, which was near to where the championship was taking place. This turned out to be more of a chat than an interview but it must have gone down well because Sherley was invited back in October to select accommodation for us. A few weeks later, I was invited to attend the FEI Annual General Assembly, which was scheduled for the second week in December in Vienna.

This seemed logical as the assembly took place once a year in December, so it would be a good opportunity to meet the key players in equestrian sport, rather than delay it for a year, and prior to commencing work in January. Imagine my surprise when I was introduced to the Bureau to discover that not only Mr Knud Larsen, who was a member of the Ground Jury at Gijon and at one of the Millstreet championships, but also two Irishmen who I knew well, Frank O'Reilly from the RDS in Dublin who initiated my setting up the medication control for the Horse Show some years earlier and John Wiley, who was the National Hunt handicapper for the Turf Club, and for whom I rode a horse in several point-to points, regrettably without distinction.

This was all very exciting for us and I had kept Cahir O'Sullivan fully informed with developments. He kindly said that he would be sorry to see me leave but wished us both well. The day after I returned from Vienna saw the Atock family set off on a two-week Christmas holiday to Gran Canaria, the last such holiday we would all take together as a family, before beginning a new career based in Switzerland in January 1982.

Family photo: Christmas in Gran Canaria. seated left to right: AA, Sandy and Philip – standing Sherley and Martin.

Chapter 4

HISTORY OF EQUESTRIAN SPORT

*Changing Function of the Horse – Move to Bern – FEI Secretariat – Vet.
Committee and Regulations*

Before proceeding further, it is worth taking a look at the development of equestrian sport over the years. Here I am indebted to Max E. Ammann's authoritative research on this subject[3].

> *The origin of the partnership between man and horse goes back to prehistory. There is evidence of this partnership in the art and literature of ancient China, Egypt, Persia and Greece. Xenophone wrote 'The Art of Riding' 2000 years ago. The horse played its part in peace and in war. It was used for practical purposes in agriculture, hunting and transport and it was also used for recreation and sport. Most of the sports were purely local and depended on the culture and traditions of each particular community. Some of these sports were based on military skills, others were derived from hunting, but it is probable that wherever horses were used, some form of racing will have taken place.*
>
> *Equestrian sports as we know them today, particularly the Olympic disciplines of jumping, dressage and eventing were born in the middle of the 19th century. The Societe Hippique Francaise was founded in 1865 and a year later, it organised its first Concours Hippique (Horse Show). This led to the first organised national 'circuit' of such Concours.*
>
> *In July 1868, the Royal Dublin Society (RDS) included in the program of its annual 'Horse Show', for the first time, two jumping competitions: the 'high leap' and the 'wide leap' – both derived from the Irish passion for foxhunting. The Irish Times, obviously referring to the high leap, reported on 31st July 1868 that the fence was raised to six feet, which was jumped in magnificent style by Richard Flynn's Shaun Rhue, to whom first prize of ten pounds was awarded.*
>
> *A few years later, in 1872, a show took place at Bratislava in the Austro-Hungarian Empire, which included a demonstration of what could be achieved with well-ridden horses. The same year, a 'Society for the Award of Prizes for Well Trained Riding Horses' was founded in Vienna. The Society presented its first prizes for riding horses in Bratislava on 25th April 1873. In 1883, the society changed its name to 'Campagnnerereiter Gesellschaft' and is still active today.*

---

[3] Ammann, Max E. *History of International Equestrian Sport*, Bern, Switzerland, Federation Equestre Internationale printed in Switzerland 12/1989

The Cercle Equestre Royal of Belgium, founded in 1877, organised its first Concour Hippique in the Bois de la Cambre, in 1881. In 1884, a Concour Hippique took place in Turin as part of a national exhibition. Taking part was a team from the Italian Army Cavalry School, which was soon to become the most influential riding centre in the world.

Holland saw its first Concours Hippique in 1886. Upperville, Virginia and Springfield, Massachusetts, both lay claim to being the oldest horseshow in America. However, there is no evidence that jumping competitions were included in the program of the first Upperville show in 1853. Thirty years later, jumping competitions were a feature of the first National Horse Show in New York, which was held in the old railway depot on Madison Square.

Towards the end of the 19th century, this new type of horse show with its equestrian competitions was beginning to be recognised for its value as a performance test for national breeding stocks, and for horses needed for military purposes. These shows also became highly popular entertainment for a population which was still, to a large extent, dependent on the horse. In the last years of the 1890's, driving joined jumping and show riding.

Major events in the early years of the 20th century were the first ever International Concours Hippique in Paris in 1900, prompted by the Paris World Fair. The Society Hippique Francaise decided to add three days of international competitions to its Concours Hippique Central and it thus became the first CHI (International Horse Show). However, this had little to do with the international sports programme organised in conjunction with the World Fair and which subsequently became known as the Second Olympic Games.

Apart from the best French professional and gentlemen riders, the only foreigners competing in Paris in 1900 were some Belgian riders and the Italian Count Trissino, who rode Oreste and Meloppo, both trained by the brilliant Italian riding instructor, Federico Caprilli.

The Championnat du Cheval d'Armes, also in France in 1902, was the first ever Three-Day-Event. The International Army Horse Show in Turin, also in 1902 and the International Three-Day-Event in Brussels in 1905 followed. There were many other 'firsts' in those years: a Concours Hippique in Switzerland (Yverdon) in 1900, Barcelona (1902), Madrid (1903), a Three-Day-Event in Portugal (1904) and the indoor show in London (1907). Of special significance was the big international event at the Italian Army riding centre at Tor di Quinto in 1908. The first Nations Cup Competitions, for national teams of three or four riders, were organised in 1909 in San Sebastian and London and in the same year, such familiar international events as Lucerne, Lisbon and New York came into being.

The idea of including equestrian sports was already raised when the first Olympic Games were being planned for 1896 in Athens, but due to organisational problems and the lack of Greek interest in equestrian sports, nothing came of it. The first serious attempt to include riding as an Olympic discipline was made by a group of Swedish officers led by Count Clarence von Rosen. He appealed to Baron de Coubertin at the IOC meeting in 1906.

As a result, he was asked by the Baron to draft an Olympic equestrian programme. This was presented to the Olympic Congress at The Hague in 1907 and was accepted for the 1908 Games, to be held in London. However, when the

Organising Committee received the entries from 88 riders from 8 nations, it took fright and backed down. Fortunately, the next Games of 1912 were awarded to Stockholm and there was no difficulty in accepting the programme proposed by Count von Rosen in 1907.

In the autumn of 1911, the invitations were sent out to the military departments and to the National Olympic Committees. The three-day-event was limited to officer entries but the jumping and dressage competitions were open to civilians. 62 competitors from ten nations with 70 horses eventually took part in the competitions, but they were all officers.

The growth of modern equestrian sports had been very rapid, but at that time only a relatively few competitors were involved in international competitions. They all knew each other and they probably also knew all the judges and they were quite prepared to accept any local variations to the fairly simple rules which existed at the time. With the advent of the Olympic Games, it became obvious that some internationally recognised rules for the three Olympic disciplines were becoming essential. Eventually, in May 1921, delegations from ten national equestrian organisations met in Lausanne to discuss the formation of an international federation.

On 28th May 1921, the meeting chaired by the President of the International Olympic Committee, Baron de Coubertin, took place with representatives of 10 nations present. The following day, representatives of the United States, France, Japan and Sweden decided on the constitution of an International Equestrian Federation. The delegates of the six other countries present in Lausanne – Belgium, Netherlands, Italy, Norway, Poland, and Switzerland – accepted in principle the new Federation.

On 24th November in the same year, the first Congress of the new International Equestrian Federation was held in Paris with Belgium, Denmark, United States, France, Italy, Japan, Norway and Sweden being present. The new Federation thus started with eight-member nations. Since the Statutes stated that the President has to come from the country of the next Olympic Games, a Frenchman, Baron du Teil, was elected the FEI's first President. Cdt. Georges Hector, also a Frenchman, became the first secretary and subsequently a secretariat was established in Nice. For the first time, in 1924, this third running of Olympic Equestrian events took place under the jurisdiction of the Federation Equestre Internationale (FEI).

1930 saw the first FEI Dressage Championship, outside of the Olympic Games, organised in Lausanne, Switzerland, in the form of a Grand Prix de Dressage. There were no FEI Championships in the other disciplines until after World War II.

Having concentrated its main efforts during the first years of its existence on establishing rules and regulations for the equestrian events at the Olympic Games, the FEI in 1931 published its first comprehensive Rule Book. Among its features were rules for the Nations Cup for teams of jumping riders, as well as for record-breaking attempts, in both the high and long jump. At the same time, the FEI published its first Bulletin and by 1931 it had a membership of 24 nations.

1939 saw the outbreak of World War II and by this time, the FEI had a membership of 31 nations. From 1941, there were only three official international events during the war years: 1940 in Rome and New York and 1941 in New York. International activity resumed in 1946 with jumping events held in Switzerland,

Dublin, New York and Toronto. On 22nd October, the FEI Congress (Annual General Assembly) was held for the first time since 1939. General Baron de Trannoy, who had competed in the first two equestrian Olympic Games in 1912 and 1920, was elected as President of the FEI.

Cdt. Georges Hector, who had been the secretary general of the FEI from its founding until the previous year, died in 1952. The first FEI Championship in Jumping for juniors was held in Ostende, Belgium. In 1953, the FEI organised the first Jumping World Championship (with exchange of horses) in Paris and its first European Three-Day-Event Championship in Badminton, UK and in 1957, for the first time, an FEI Championship for women riders was held. The Ladies Jumping Championships were abolished in 1974.

H.R.H. The Prince Philip, Duke of Edinburgh, who was elected as President of the FEI in 1964, succeeded Prince Bernhard of the Netherlands. In the following year, the FEI introduced the President's Cup honouring the most successful Nations Cup team of the year. Great Britain was the first winner. The FEI also decided on the still valid rotation of Championships with the World Championships, in which the four finalists must ride each other's horses, being held in the even non-Olympic years while Continental Championships can be organised in the odd years.

In 1970, the FEI took driving as a fourth discipline under its wing. The first International Driving event under the new FEI rules was held that year in Lucerne, Switzerland. The following year, the first European Driving Championship was held in Budapest and the first World Championship followed in 1972 in Munster, Germany.

1978 saw the World Cup for jumping riders introduced. It consisted of preliminary leagues in different parts of the World culminating in a World Cup Final. Volvo was the sole sponsor of the World Cup in its first season. The FEI also organised the first European Pony Championship at Lincoln, UK (at which I officiated as Foreign Veterinary Delegate). *In the following year, the first World Cup Final was held in Goteborg, Sweden.*

Fritz O. Widmer was appointed secretary general in 1976. He had been an industrialist until 1978. He was Commander of a Cavalry Squadron and was subsequently appointed lieutenant colonel and a member of the Swiss army staff. He rode until 1960 nationally in all three Olympic equestrian disciplines and internationally in dressage and jumping. He was an FEI Judge in jumping and judged dressage nationally up to Grand Prix level. Before he was elected secretary general of the FEI, he served as central secretary of the Swiss equestrian federation, as its vice-president.

In 1981, the FEI created a new category of Young Riders (16–21 years old) as a bridge between the Juniors (14–18) and the Seniors (over 18 years old). In 1982, the FEI introduced the first International Dressage competition.

The General Assembly in 1986 elected H.R.H. The Princess Anne, as its new President, succeeding her father who retired after 22 years in the role. The FEI introduced a new annual competition, called the Prince Philip Trophy, honouring the most successful nation of the year, based on placings at Championships and Games of the respective year. By 1991, the FEI had 91 member nations.

Mr Widmer had commuted to Brussels prior to moving the secretariat to Bern, Switzerland in 1979. The secretariat in Brussels had been cited in the same building as the Belgian Equestrian Federation. M. Robert Michels, who assisted the SGs of the day, lived in an apartment in the building. and the story goes that in the morning he served the Belgian Federation, came home to lunch with his wife and in the afternoon performed FEI duties.

In 1979, M. Michels also moved to Bern where he became Head of the Sports Department, which covered all disciplines, until various heads of discipline were recruited in succeeding years. He remained with the FEI in Bern until his retirement in the mid-1980s, following which he and his wife returned to Brussels, where sadly he died not long afterwards.

Early January 1982 saw me enter the FEI headquarters in Schlosshaldenstrasse, Bern, Switzerland, as the first veterinarian to be appointed head of its Veterinary Department. My wife, Sherley, followed a month later. My department consisted of just one office for me to share with my part-time secretary. There was no job description so I spent the first few weeks and months working through files to try to get an idea of what I was supposed to do. This became a case of both learning by my mistakes and trying to understand the complexities of the organisation of which, up to now, I knew little.

From my perspective, apart from Robert Michels, the only other personality in the office at the time, who I had previously met, was Max E. Ammann. Max had a huge influence on equestrian sport as the jumping World Cup (WC) series was his brainchild and he was the director of this highly successful worldwide event.

Max E. Ammann

Max had previously served as President of the Swiss Press Association and as Foreign Correspondent in New York for Swiss, German and Austrian newspapers during which time his attention switched to equestrian sports coverage. Max was the co-founder and first President of the International Alliance of Equestrian Journalists when formed in 1974 and it was Max who thought up the concept of a World Cup series for jumping, as was already successful for tennis and golf. He discussed the idea with Prince Philip, President of the FEI, who liked the idea and who asked him to set up the competition for the FEI. Max was then appointed World Cup Director, with an office in the secretariat. He was also author of a number of equestrian books in addition to some on art, which was very much his hobby.

The first World Cup Final took place in Goteborg, Sweden in 1979, the second in Baltimore, USA in 1980 and the third, which was sponsored jointly by the Dutch Ministry of Agriculture and Volvo and at which I was privileged to officiate, took place in Birmingham, UK in 1981. Volvo thereafter became the sole sponsor.

Max E. Ammann and AA in (serious) discussion at an event in St. Gallen, Switzerland.

I had met Max in Birmingham at the World Cup final in 1981 and subsequently in Dublin at a World Cup qualifier; and was delighted to find that his office in the FEI secretariat was just across the corridor from mine. We became good friends and often had lunch together. Others on the staff at the time were the SG's personal assistant, Barbara Bream and Vera Bernasconi, who was Head of Administration. M. Marbot, who had retired from the Swiss watchmaking industry attended to the mail and Mrs Weder provided a cup of coffee in the morning and tea in the afternoon, although second cups were not encouraged. There were two or three additional secretarial staff and that was the full complement of the world equestrian sport's governing body headquarters in 1982.

Over the next few years we were joined, in 1987, by Captain John P. Roche, initially Head of the Jumping Department but now Director of Jumping and one time Irish international jumping rider, Catrin Norinder of Swedish nationality, who was appointed Head of Eventing and responsible for the equestrian component of Olympic Games, but now as with John, director of these disciplines and Irmgard Nienstedt from Germany, who became Head of Dressage and who retired a few years after me. I enjoyed a good and friendly relationship with all three department heads.

Managers of the various departments of the FEI Secretariat in 1989. Left to right AA (Veterinary), John Roche (Jumping and Driving), Irmgard Nienstedt (Dressage and Special Disciplines), Etienne Allard (Secretary General), Catrin Norinder (Three Day Event, Olympic Games and Calendar), Rene Ziegler (Director) and Peter Witschi (Administration, Finance and Personnel).

The 'Irish Connection' after a meeting at the FEI Secretariat. Left to right: John Roche, Patrick Carew, Conor Crowley, Robbie Lowry and AA.

Apart from John and me, who were both Irish, the connection extended, in the early 1990s, to include Lord Carew, Chairman of the Jumping Committee, Conor Crowley, Chairman of the Finance Committee and Lord Lowry, Chairman of the Judicial Committee.

Although long after my time, I believe that it is also worth mentioning here that Sabrina Ibàñez first joined the FEI in 1991, working initially in the Eventing Department under Catrin Norinder. She left the organisation briefly in 1995 to work in her family's business in the USA, returning to the FEI in 1998. She was appointed FEI secretary general in 2014, following a proposal to the FEI Bureau from newly elected President, Ingmar De Vos, who had vacated the role on his appointment and which had received unanimous support.

Not insignificantly, I was to learn that French was the official language of the FEI. My limited knowledge of this language ended with my school days so this presented a mountain to climb. Mercifully, English was widely spoken in the office but there was always the danger that a conversation would break into French and I would be left ignorant of the discussion. Worse were to be the occasions when I was supposed to take the minutes of a meeting, which commenced in English and then suddenly switched into French, at which point I had little or no knowledge of the subject under discussion. This required subsequent discreet enquiries from the main orators.

Additionally, I discovered that all meetings, although largely discussed through the medium of English, had then to be translated into French and that this then became the authoritative version. This was a rather ludicrous situation, which did change some time later when English superseded French as the official language.

Initially, there were no regular office meetings but, depending on the subject matter, various members of staff would suddenly be summoned to an immediate meeting with the SG, without any prior knowledge of the matter to be discussed. Hence, there was no possibility to prepare in advance. Eventually we, the staff, did manage to obtain a 10 am meeting every Tuesday with a prior agenda and minutes taken. This was a big step forward.

The atmosphere in the secretariat was not always as congenial as we might have liked and the staff seemed to come, go and be replaced with monotonous regularity. I have no doubt that the secretary general had the very best intentions for the FEI as an organisation, but he was a hard taskmaster and difficult to please. In fact, the tension in the office, on many occasions, was palpable. This was unsettling for the staff, including myself and naturally this effected Sherley as well.

Within two years of commencing work in the FEI and in discussion with the secretary general, we made a decision for Sherley to return to live in the UK and for me to remain based in Switzerland and to commute to home as and when feasible. On one or two occasions, I did consider moving on and was, in fact, interviewed for Douglas Witherington's position as chief veterinary officer to the British Jockey Club on his retirement and although not accepted for this role, which was given to Brian Abraham, Douglas's second in command, I was offered a supporting role, which I declined. Eventually, I decided that my FEI job was exciting, worth fighting for and became ever more determined to make a success of my position.

At this time, and through the World Animal Health Organisation (Office Internationale des Epizooties – OIE) I had met Professor Ulrich Kihm. Ueli, who was Swiss, chaired a very important OIE committee, which was responsible for monitoring the more serious worldwide animal diseases, including those affecting the equine. At the time, he was Director of the high security Viral Institute in Basle in Switzerland, which specialised in research and diagnostic services for such diseases. We met from time to time and he was always extremely helpful to me with any concerns I had with equine disease and issues in relation to international equestrian sport. Ueli knew of the difficulties we had living in Switzerland but had never fully understood them. Some years later, by which time I was well settled in the job, he was promoted to chief veterinary officer of the Swiss government veterinary service, which entailed a move for him and his family to Bern. Shortly after the move, I invited him to lunch. "Now, I understand your problems," he said when we met, "I have only moved from Basel to Bern and I find myself being treated as a foreigner, so you, as a genuine foreigner, had no chance!"

I was delighted that finally he appreciated how we had felt during our early years in the country.

Sometime later, when we were struggling with the threat of African horse sickness prior to the Barcelona Olympic Games in 1992, Ueli came, at my invitation, to the first World Equestrian Games in Stockholm, Sweden, in 1990 to speak to a gathering of all the top equestrians involved in the sport who were seriously concerned about bringing their horses to Barcelona two years later. He was able to convince them that the situation was under control, contingency plans were in place and that their horses would be perfectly safe to travel and compete in Spain.

However, let's go back to the FEI secretariat. I learned that the Veterinary Committee was formed at the behest of the FEI President in 1966.

History of Veterinary Committee

In 1966, there were two nominees to be the first chairman – Professor Igor Bobylev (Soviet Republic) and Dr Joseph C. O'Dea (USA). Professor Bobylev was elected. Subsequent chairmen were Dr Peter Cronau (GER) from 1990–1998, Professor Leo B. Jeffcott (GBR) 1998–2006 and Dr John McEwen (GBR) 2006–2014. The latter two were, of course, after my time although I knew both of them well. The members of this committee from its inception, were as follows: Professor J. Jany (USA) 1966–1972, Professor R. Bordet (FRA), 1966–1974, Professor P. Mullaney (IRL) 1966–1974 (Prof Mullaney taught me pathology as a vet student in Dublin), Dr F. Santisteban Garcia (ESP) 1966–1974, Dr Paul Benazet (FRA) 1974–1978 (Dr Benazet was my old French racing colleague). Dr R. Archer (GBR) 1974–1979, Dr J. O'Dea (USA) 1974–1978, Dr A. Wasowski (POL) 1976–1980, Professor R. Zeller (GER) 1976–1980, Professor J. Hickman (GBR) 1978–1982 (who helped me so much at Burghley), Professor H. Gerber (SUI) 1978–1982 (with whom I had close contact as he was based in Bern and was a good friend to the SG), Dr H. Fernandez (ARG) 1980–1984, Professor H. Breukink (NED) 1980–1984, Mr C. Frank (GBR) 1982–1988 (without a PhD veterinarians in the UK and Ireland are not normally referred to as 'Dr'), Dr R. Armendariz (MEX) 1982–1983, Dr D. Frappier (CAN) 1983–1986, Dr P. Cronau (GER) 1984–1988, Maj. Gen. S. Srivastava (IND) 1984–1988, Professor J. F. Chary (FRA) 1986–1991, Dr J. O'Dea (USA) for the second time 1986 – 1991, Professor R. Shimizu (JPN) 1989–1993, Dr J. P. da Costa Periera (POR) 1989–1993, Dr P. Cronau (GER) for the second time but now Chairman, 1990–1998, Professor L. Jeffcott (GBR) 1991–1995 (prior to becoming chairman in 1998), Dr M. Simensen (USA) 1991–1995, Dr F. Barrelet (SUI) 1993–1997 and Dr W. Niederer (NZL) 1993–1997, by which time I had departed the FEI.

The first Veterinary Committee meeting I attended took place in Cambridge, UK, in May 1982. The committee at this time was, of course, chaired by Professor Igor Bobylev with Col. John Hickman, both known to me from previous events, as his Vice Chairman. Prince Philip, President of the FEI, flew in by helicopter for the first day of the two-day meeting.

The subject matter included assessing the impact of the revised Veterinary Regulations (VRs), which had become effective from 1st May 1981 (all rules and regulations are revised on a four-year cycle). This edition had increased in size from the 1977 version of 45 pages to 75 pages in the newer version, which went into much greater detail. The significant modifications included a new chapter dealing with veterinary control at international events (responsibilities of Veterinary Commissions, inspections and identification of horses, special arrangements for three-day-event and driving).

There was an extended chapter dealing with drugs and medications and a new chapter on the Standard Sampling Procedure for Prohibited Substances. In addition, there were four appendices: Horse Passports, Instructions for Collecting Samples, a List of Prohibited Substances and a Standard Method of Examination for Nerve Sensation.

The main concern of this latter appendix, was to ensure that horses did not compete if one or more limbs have been desensitised, either by a nerve block (as for a tooth extraction in the human) or by surgery to cut the nerve and permanently 'freeze' the lower limb. While acceptable in a leisure horse gently walking or trotting on the road, this is a dangerous procedure in a competing horse travelling at speed over fences. The problem was that there was no scientific method of establishing if a horse's limb, or part of, had been desensitised. Hence, the relevant appendix in the VRs, which was headed 'Standard Method of Examination for Nerve Sensation' read as follows:

"As there is no satisfactory method at the moment to detect desensitisation in the horse, it was decided at the General Assembly 1980 that no ruling could be made. This appendix will be published when an adequate method of detection is available and approved by the General Assembly."

The general gist of this appendix was still included in the Veterinary Regulations of 1998 and in all intervening editions, 18 years after the 1980 ruling was made and three years after I retired.

Clearly, I had nothing to do with the production of the 1981 Veterinary Regulations (VRs) as I only joined the FEI a year later in 1982. However, if we now look forward some 12 years, to the 1994 VRs, in which clearly I did have input and which by now also included an index, the regulation had grown to over 200 pages. Much of this increase was due to further clarification of various regulations but also to the inclusion of relevant extracts from other disciple rulebooks. This assisted the Veterinary Delegates and Commissions if they need to consult members of the Ground Jury on any issues relevant to their specific discipline.

At the 1982 Cambridge meeting, Prof Bobylev felt that we must place more emphasis on the specific problems of the African, Asian and South American countries. He was also concerned at the number of horse related accidents and the state of unsoundness of many competition horses. He drew attention to the fact that in the past ten years only one veterinary symposium had been held in a developing member country.

However, a positive outcome from this meeting was the confirmation of a 'fitness to compete' Horse Inspection, first used at the Moscow Olympic Games and to be repeated at the forthcoming World Jumping Championship in Dublin. Horse inspections had already been the norm in the Eventing discipline for some years but the Dublin inspection was to be a serious wake up call for the sport horse industry as a whole and for my introduction into the realms of international equestrian sport.

Following this first meeting in Cambridge and in the interim pending the next revision of the VRs in four years' time, I immediately commenced looking at how these regulations could be further improved for the future. One area that really did require immediate clarification was references to horse examinations and inspections. In fact, looking back, there was no provision in the relevant 1977 VRs for a Ground Jury Horse Inspection at the Olympic Games in Moscow although all were informed in advance, on site, that this would take place. After all, these inspections were standard procedure in the three-day-event and driving disciplines, so why not in dressage and jumping?

Subsequent to the Cambridge meeting and following wide discussion within the Veterinary Committee and with knowledgeable competition veterinarians in the field, the following wording was adopted by the General Assembly at its meeting in Amsterdam in 1983. This was widely circulated to be effective immediately and was, of course subsequently published in the 1985 VRs.

Examination – *The term 'Examination' is used to denote a clinical examination by a veterinarian to establish the general state of health of a horse. A horse cannot be eliminated from an event or competition as a result of an examination. After an examination, any horse that is not considered to be fit to take part in the event or competition, for which it is entered, must be presented for inspection by the Ground Jury and Veterinary Commission.*

Inspection – *The term 'Inspection' is used to denote an inspection by the Ground Jury together with the Veterinary Commission to establish the fitness of a horse to take part in the event or competition for which it is entered. This inspection must conform to the requirements of the relevant discipline.*

In practice, all horses were required to undergo an examination on, or immediately following arrival at the site of an event. This must be conducted by a veterinarian and was clearly intended to ensure that no horse arriving at the event was unfit and/or carrying any infectious or contagious disease. If the examining veterinarian considered that there were grounds for concern that horse would be immediately placed in isolation, pending further investigation.

On the other hand, the inspection was conducted, normally on the day before the first competition, before the lay Ground Jury, with representatives of the Veterinary Commission in attendance to provide an expert opinion if invited to do so. This inspection was often erroneously referred to as the 'Vet Check'. It was not a Vet Check – it was a 'fitness to compete' horse inspection. In case of disagreement between the Ground Jury and the Veterinary Commission it is the President of the Ground Jury who makes the final decision. So, do not blame the vets in future if you think that an incorrect decision has been taken!

So, let us now move on to the World Jumping Championship in Dublin, which took place in the following month, June 1982, and see what happened there – you may be surprised.

Chapter 5

CONTROVERSY AT CHAMPIONSHIP

Horse Inspections – Repercussions – Aftermath

As already indicated, I had informed Fritz Widmer, secretary general (SG) of the FEI, when accepting the role of Head of the Veterinary Department that I should have time off to honour my commitment to organise the doping control at the World Jumping Championship in Dublin in 1982. The veterinary commission at this championship was composed of president: Mortimer (Murty) Hynes (IRL), foreign veterinary delegate: Dr Heinz Gerber (SUI), associate members: Adair Linton (IRL) and me.

Murty Hynes was the recently retired Director of Veterinary Services of the Irish Department of Agriculture. Although horses were not necessarily his prime area of expertise, he was well-known and respected as a man of integrity in his own country. Heinz Gerber was an extremely knowledgeable and highly respected international veterinarian. Whenever a 'nasty' equine disease popped up anywhere in the world, it was invariably Heinz and Jack Bryant (USA) who were the first professionals to call. Adair was a top equine practitioner, and I was there because of my expertise in the field of sample collection for forensic analyses.

The first compulsory Horse Inspections in all disciplines had been held at the Moscow Olympic Games in 1980, and this was only the second time that a horse inspection would be officially carried out at a major international jumping event.

The schedule for these examinations and inspections in Dublin was clearly relayed to all participants well in advance of the event so there was absolutely no excuse for them not being aware of the procedures as outlined, as some were later to make out. The condition of many of the horses presented at the Horse Inspection left much to be desired.

I wrote the following article immediately after the event, and it was published in FEI Bulletin No. 6/1982. It caused quite a degree of controversy. I make no apology for the article itself and although it was sanctioned by the SG, I accept full responsibility for what was written, although in retrospect, I do accept that the use of the words 'dramatic improvement' in the first paragraph was probably not justified:

The Horse Inspection at the World Jumping Championship in Dublin in June can only be considered disappointing. 98 horses representing 16 countries were presented, inspected and trotted up on the day preceding the first competition, following a pre-arranged time schedule. Of these, fully 10% were definitely lame and a large percentage of the remainder showed varying degrees of unsoundness.

73

The lame horses were re-inspected several hours later, during which time most of them showed a dramatic improvement in their original condition. The Ground Jury decided that, in addition to the random selection, these horses should be permitted to compete but should be specifically selected for medication control during the course of the championship.

It must be considered worrying that so many horses, supposedly representing the best in the world, should be seen in such a condition.

The inspection was conducted rapidly and averaged approximately one and a half minutes per horse. The horses were presented by their grooms with only a few Chefs d'Equipe and riders attending. The fact that so many showed irregular paces was probably due to the fact that they were taken directly from their stables to the inspection area without being given an opportunity to walk around and 'loosen up'.

Chefs d'Equipe are strongly advised to take this inspection more seriously in future as a repetition of the standard experienced in Dublin brings little credit to the sport.

To say that this article caused a furore is an under-statement. The first to tackle me following publication was the secretary general. He was furious, so much so that I feared for my job. Despite the fact that he must have approved the text to be published in the first instance, he obviously had no idea of the potential consequences. I understand that he had received a number of phone calls castigating him for permitting this to happen. In fairness, in subsequent correspondence, he did support the need to publicise the issues. The June Bulletin is not circulated until July but, when received sometime in mid-August, the newspapers took up the story, which was much embellished in many cases. The following headlines set the tone:

12th August: *Dublin Evening Press*: *Dope Given to Horses at Dublin Show; The Standard (UK)*: *– Show jumping cruelty public does not see; The Times (UK)*: *Horses die for honour, glory, but mostly money.*

13th August: *Irish Independent* – *Dope and Cruelty at RDS Charges* – *denial by riders; Irish Times*: *Claim that 10 Horses drugged at RDS denied; The Daily Mail (UK)*: *Cruel show riders killing the horses; The Daily Mirror (UK)*: *The horse dope a vet wants banned.*

14th August: *Irish Independent*: *DRUGGING ROW – NO HELP TO INDUSTRY; Irish Press*: *A CRUEL ROUND* (Editorial)

15th August: *The Daily Mirror (UK)*: *A price too high* (Comment)

20th August: *Dublin Evening Herald*: *Horse Doping: Britain lashes FEI report* (British Equestrian Federation); *Dublin Evening Press*: *Show jumper rejects dope allegations* (Aidan Hennigan quoting David Broome); *Horse and Hound*: *BEF President defends show jumping: WHY, THIS FALSE ACCUSATION MUST BE ANSWERED* (General Sir Cecil Blacker, President British Equestrian Federation) and *Unfair attacks on show jumping – but no room for complacency* (Town and Country)

21st August: *Daily Mail (UK)*: *Riders hit back in drugs row* (David Broome)

27th August: *Horse and Hound*: *Inaccurate and irresponsible – that's my verdict on the FEI report* (David Broome), and *Let's get 'bute' into perspective* (Loriner)

However, amongst all the above, a quote from Harvey Smith is particularly worth recording: "The reason I don't go to European or World Championships is because I do think that they are too much. A lot of horses are asked to jump what they can't jump. But that is not the riders' fault or their greed, it's the governing body's fault, the FEI. They build fences too wide, with rails too heavy and courses too long. This causes stress on horses and also makes a bad spectacle..."

Correspondence to and from the FEI, and those involved (and not necessarily involved) multiplied. These included letters from General Sir Cecil Blacker to the FEI and to The Times and David Broome, President of the International Jumping Riders Club to the FEI and Horse and Hound in addition to many more.

However, after the dust had settled, Heinz Gerber wrote a long letter to Horse & Hound in an attempt to put all the published comments into perspective. Extracts from this were published in Horse & Hound in its issue dated 10th September 1982 under the heading, "Don't make vets scapegoats for what is wrong in show jumping," and are summarised below:

Following the considerable publicity given to show-jumping, as a result of the report of the publication of the FEI Veterinary Commission at the Dublin World Championship, Observer in Horse and Hound (August 20) so rightly refers to the 'torrent of nonsense', which had appeared in the national press.

But, Observer went on to point out that there was 'no room for complacency,' and it seems to me that something approaching complacency is still present in the attitude of some well-known riders and officials as indicated by their comments in the same issue. What they say is only partially correct, while the attacks on Mr Mortimer Hynes were in substance unjustified and in some cases quite vicious.

I feel that veterinary surgeons are being made scapegoats for much of what is wrong in modern show jumping. This is not acceptable and I would like to underline a few facts.

The official Veterinary Commission was asked to conduct an inspection of all horses on the day before the competition started. The aim of such an inspection is to ensure that no truly unsound horses compete. However, the rules do not permit any medication testing on the day of this inspection. A horse may therefore be presented under any kind of medication. This renders the inspection of little preventative value.

Secondly, the veterinary surgeons do not have the final say on whether or not a horse is allowed to compete. This is the Ground Jury's job. Any implication that the Veterinary Commission in Dublin first raised a fuss, and then let the horses compete, is therefore unfounded. Personally, I feel that decisions should be taken by veterinarians on the sole ground of soundness.

However, if soundness had been the criterion in Dublin, not even half the horses would have been allowed to compete. Definite lameness was present in ten out of fewer than 100 horses at the first inspection.

It was decided to look again at these animals on the same day and after a few hours. Eight of them were improved, but not all that 'dramatically'. It is, of course, anybody's guess what had happened in the meantime. Without the possibility of medication testing, allegations of medication or certain physical measures will always crop up.

Only two horses had to be shown again the next morning: both were still lame on hard ground, but worked more or less acceptably on soft ground.

If these findings are not cause for concern, then the people responsible for show jumping should publicly state that they are in show business and not in a sport, of sorts. There really is no room for complacency.

And, even though the 'lay press' has published a 'torrent of nonsense' and 'arrant rubbish', this may turn out to be a good thing. It may force people in this sport to take a hard look at the true cause for concern.

A horse may show temporary unsoundness due to some commonplace condition. In the best possible world, treatment would be in order. But, because medication is abused, and is also mainly used to mask crippling conditions, and not to treat a commonplace injury, there is no other solution other than a ban on all 'foreign substances'.

General Sir Cecil Blacker's defence of show jumping in Horse and Hound (Why This False Accusation Must Be Answered. August 20th) is on the whole correct, but certain items need mentioning. The FEI was not only right to publish the relevant statement; it simply could not do otherwise. Silence would have been equivalent to closing eyes to the truly unsatisfactory state of soundness in Dublin.

It is incorrect to say that, "Most teams were inspected immediately after the horses descended from their horse boxes, stiff after very long journeys." Most horses arrived one or two days before the inspection in Dublin. Moreover, Chefs d'Equipe knew at what time their horses would be inspected. They were free to walk and exercise them for as many hours as they wanted to. They were certainly not forced to show their horses stiff after a journey. To imply that is a cheap and disappointing excuse. The third test did not concern four but two horses.

Most horses that were lame at the first inspection were dope-tested throughout the week, but it is not true that the four, which were lamest, were tested on the same day. So, Gen. Blacker's conclusion regarding 'bute' is not precise. I agree with Gen. Blacker that the allegation that international show jumpers are enabled to perform, because they are dosed with 'bute' is indeed false.

And, it is improbable that English and Irish laboratories would not detect other drugs, although some are very difficult to detect. As long as unsound horses are used so frequently, such allegations will not disappear. The suspicion will remain that medication, surgical operations or simple disregard for the horse make the wheels go round.

In the same Horse and Hound a number of riders were quoted:

David Broome says that 'bute' is 'preventative medication'. Incorrect. Prevention in this case is before the fact. It used to be quite a common and bad practice in eventing. 'Bute' is not reasonably used as a prophylactic agent, but as a drug to meet chronic, incurable conditions. It does not even heal: its anti-inflammatory properties are analgesic.

It is to some extent refreshing to read Harvey Smith's statement, although the apparent separatist tendencies would certainly not be good for British show jumping.

Pam Dunning mentions prize money. I agree that is not the incentive. Nobody in his/her right senses would ever claim it to be. But, sponsorship and commercial horse dealing are indeed forces to be considered.

Ted Edgar says that the veterinary surgeon in Ireland should be sued. He should go ahead and do so; he would lose his case quickly and, I hope, expensively. Mr Hynes's statements were, in substance, correct and I would support them unequivocally. I might have chosen a few other words, but who knows what the press has added or distorted.

Paul Darragh may deplore the fact that Mr Hynes revealed the contents of my report to the FEI. However, he did not do so in a misleading manner, he just voiced his opinion a bit strongly. If Mr Darragh thinks that the future of show jumping hangs on a thread, he may be right. But, it does so not because of Mr Hynes, but the sorry state of affairs that Mr Hynes has underlined.

Lionel Dunning can be happy to have good doctors and surgeons, because 'bute' would certainly not have cured him. It was probably used as a supportive aid to treatment and carefully so because of its well-known toxicity.

Ronnie Massarella is not right in different respects: ten horses were re-inspected a second time and two a third time. Those two were not sound on re-inspection. He (not me or Murty Hynes) mentions horses' names; he forgets the worst of all. What Mr Massarella says about the causes of unsoundness in the three horses he names is not correct and much too weak. I cannot give diagnosis here, but I could easily prove that this is playing down conditions, which would normally prevent the use of these horses as simple hacks. Mr Massarella does make a very good point, though: the paddock, maybe, or gentle work under controlled medication.

It is notable that the four worst horses at Dublin could not make it through the week; they went to pieces although one came close. The four finalists were sound horses, although one showed lameness for a few steps during the individual final.

In addition to all this, Murty Hynes was hounded by the media, quoted and misquoted, when in essence all he did or said was to support what Heinz Gerber had written in his published letter to Horse and Hound. Sadly, he felt that he was left with no option other than to resign as the Irish Equestrian Federation's Contact Veterinarian to the FEI.

So there it is. I have no wish to labour the point any further, but I venture to suggest that this 'torrent of nonsense' and 'arrant rubbish' may have started a watershed, which, over time, stimulated the many improvements that have subsequently been instigated into FEI disciplines over the years.

An interesting postscript to all this was a few months later while attending another international event, the president of a major national equestrian federation castigated me for the article I had written for the FEI Bulletin. He told me at some length that my article had, "set the jumping discipline back some 20 years..." but, after a pause, added, "...but you did the right thing." My actions had finally been vindicated.

But now let us take a look at drugs in equestrian sport.

Chapter 6

DRUGS IN HORSE SPORT

*Conflicting Opinions – The Phenylbutazone Issue – Potential
Consequences – NSAID Conference*

The FEI for the sport horse sector and the majority of racing authorities maintain that horses taking part in competition must be healthy and compete on their inherent merits. The use of a 'prohibited substance', as defined by the respective authority, might influence a horse's performance or mask an underlying health problem and could falsely affect the outcome of the competition. This can have repercussions on the confidence of the public both in the betting market in racing, the overall performance of competition horses and subsequently, in the breeding shed in all disciplines. It can interfere with the genetic potential of the horse and of its lineage and be detrimental to the horse's welfare. The old adage that the mare could not be kept sound on the track or in competition so, we sent her off to stud is just not acceptable.

It can be a major problem to keep horses healthy and sound. The dividing line between the treatment of injury and disease on one hand and the preparation of horses for competition on the other is narrow and not easily defined. It is obviously correct to use medication to cure injury and disease but patently wrong to use drugs to influence performance or to enable an unfit or unhealthy horse to return to competition before it has fully recovered.

It is accepted that the commercial aspect of the sport places great demands on those responsible to compete with their horses to the best of their ability, often more frequently than they should. This places the competitor and his or her veterinarian in an unenviable position. A solution must be found to balance the ever-increasing sophisticated analytical methodology, which now has the ability to detect minute amounts of prohibited substances and the practical day-to-day requirements of the equine athletes.

The days when horses raced on hay, oats and water long before dressage, jumping and the FEI ever existed, probably terminated in biblical times. This was when Adam and Eve ate the forbidden fruit. They did so, not because they were hungry, but because the serpent deceived them into believing that the fruit would render them God-like.

Folklore and fairy tales are full of the belief that magic substances exist, capable of imparting supernatural powers. Think of Popeye, the sailor, who obtained enormous strength and ability from eating spinach. Think of the early Romans who fed their chariot horses a mixture of honey and water and suffered crucifixion when caught and think of poor Daniel Dawson who was reportedly hanged on Newmarket Heath in 1812 for overdosing and poisoning horses with arsenic.

I am indebted to my good friend and colleague from student days, Professor Tom Tobin, another Irish veterinary graduate, based in the Gluck Equine Research Centre in Lexington, Kentucky and author of *Drugs and the Performance Horse* for this useful information. Tom actually graduated in Dublin in 1964, six years after I did, although remarkably he can still quote the roll call in my year.

Those competing at international events are responsible for ensuring that no drug or medication is administered to a horse in the period before a competition so that the substance or its metabolites (minute break down products of a drug) or derivatives, might be present and detectable in the horse's body fluids or excreta at any time during the event.

The philosophy of the vast majority is, therefore, that the horse must compete in a drug free state. Similarly, the first paragraph of *Article 6 of the International Agreement on Breeding and Racing* states that *no horse shall, at the time of racing, show the presence in its tissues, body fluids or excreta of any substance, which is a prohibited substance.* Some 45 racing administrations, but not all, are signatories to this agreement.

The more liberal North American view point, in the majority of states, takes the position that, if a horse is a little sore or stiff what is the problem with giving him phenylbutazone (PBZ – bute) to ease his aches and pains prior to competition/racing?

The more correct response is to certainly give it some bute, but do not ask it to return to competition/race, until it is fully sound and the drug has cleared its system.

Let's carry the argument a stage further, and give an extreme example. Would anybody really want to see a superb young horse, which is jumping brilliantly on its inherent merits beaten by one, which was once equally brilliant but can now only manage to compete at this level when propped up by drugs?

In 1995, the Californian Horse Racing Board modified its ruling on authorised medication. With the exception of authorised bleeder medication with Lasix, it states that "no substance shall be administered to a horse within 24 hours of a race."

But negating all of that, it goes on to state that "not more than one of the following non-steroidal anti-inflammatory drugs (NSAIDs) may be used at any one time: phenylbutazone, oxyphenbutazone, naproxine, flunixine or meclofenamic acid."

Threshold levels in blood plasma have been established for each of these. In addition, threshold levels have also been established for acepromazine, mepivacaine, promazine, albuterol, atropine, benzocaine, procaine and salicylates. Is there anything left in the chemist's shop that cannot be used?

The American Association of Equine Practitioners (AAEP) justifies this controlled therapeutic medication for performance horses on the basis that it improves and protects the health and welfare of the equine athlete. There is surely an anomaly between these conflicting viewpoints.

Why do the majority of regulatory authorities take this stand not to permit drugs at the time of competition? Primarily, the policy is designed to protect the fairness of the sport, the welfare of the competing horses and their integrity in the breeding shed. Public perception of equestrian sport can be adversely affected by reports of drug misuse involving abuse to animals and particularly to horses – remember the media furore following the World Jumping Championship in Dublin in 1982 and the numerous reports of drug use in a wide variety of other sports up to the present day? In the racing industry where vast sums of money are often wagered on the outcome of a race, it is essential that the public maintain confidence in the honesty of the participants, both human and equine. Of equal importance is the need to prevent competition success for a horse with potential hereditary problems, which could perpetuate the defect in its progeny. Such issues may include breathing difficulties, which could require surgery, bursting blood vessels resulting in lung haemorrhage (bleeding), soundness issues due to lack of bone or tendon problems and so on.

So, what is the International Equestrian Federation's stand on this complex issue? It's 1975 Veterinary Manual stated that "no horse shall be eligible for competition if it is found to have received a 'forbidden substance'" (later rebranded as a prohibited substance). A forbidden substance was defined as, "a stimulant, depressant, tranquilliser, local anaesthetic of masking agent."

In 1977, an international conference of racing administrators, analysts and veterinarians meeting in Rome, Italy formalised a list of prohibited substances. This list referred to substances acting on the various body systems e.g., *Substances acting on the respiratory system, Substances acting on the locomotor system* etc., Although this was primarily a racing conference, which I attended as Veterinary Officer to the Irish Turf Club, the FEI was also represented.

While the FEI General Assembly subsequently adopted the list in principle, it recognised the need, at the time, for the continued use of some form of non-steroidal anti-inflammatory drug (NSAID). The Veterinary Committee, in consultation with research workers and other experts in its member countries proposed that all NSAIDs be included in the prohibited list with the exception of phenylbutazone (PBZ – bute) and oxyphenbutazone (OPB), its metabolite, at a certain permitted level. Member NFs at the time were asked to put forward their proposal. I well remember, while still working for the Turf Club, being asked by the Irish Equestrian Federation to join with Professor Martin Byrne, Irish team veterinarian and Dr Stan Cosgrave, a highly respected equine practitioner, whose practice specialised in thoroughbred racehorses, as a 'so-called' expert group, to give our opinion on the FEI proposal. We recommended the total abolition of any drug, including phenylbutazone, at time of competition.

The General Assembly in 1980 adopted a maximum permissible level for PBZ of 4 micrograms per millilitre of blood plasma (4 ug/ml), adding that if OPB was found in the same sample, it would be considered to be a metabolite of PBZ. This worked well for a time. However, it soon became apparent that the high levels of OPB being found were inconsistent with it being a metabolite of PBZ. The supposition was that both NSAIDs, PBZ and OPB, were being administered at the same time (a cocktail?) and the horse was therefore receiving considerably more anti-inflammatory medication than was intended by the regulatory authority.

In 1982, which was my first year with the FEI, sampling was carried out on 323 horses at 44 international events. This revealed 34 positives to PBZ, seven of which were above the permitted level. Of these, three were disqualified and the riders each received a six months ban. Due to procedural problems, such as incorrect or inadequate recording of the horse's details, incorrect labelling and/or numbering and/or sealing of the samples, the laboratory taking excessive time to report the results or sending the results to the host national federation instead of solely to the FEI and more, no action could be taken against the other four. In addition, there was one positive for caffeine, possibly arising from food contamination.

In recognition of the abuse of the regulation regarding PBZ/OPB levels the 1984 FEI General Assembly agreed to modify the maximum permissible levels of PBZ and OPB to an aggregate concentration of five ug/ml. This permitted the use of PBZ up to a limit of four ug/ml with, in addition, one ug/ml as the expected amount of OPB, if it was present as a metabolite. Effectively, therefore, the permissible level of NSAID was raised from four ug/ml to five ug/ml.

Representatives of NFs of several member countries drew the attention of the 1987 General Assembly to the fact that PBZ and in fact, all other drugs were banned under national law in their countries for use in horses at time of competition. The question arose as to how the FEI could continue to condone its continued use under these circumstances. These countries indicated that they reserved the right to sample horses at international events in their countries and to take appropriate action against offenders under their national law.

Shortly afterwards, a number of NFs, sponsors and welfare lobbies started to exert pressure on the FEI to prohibit the use of PBZ at any level – the so-called 'zero option' was demanded. The FEI's major sponsors went so far as to state that they would withdraw their support, if the FEI did not act. This was during the period leading up to the first World Equestrian Games (WEG) in Stockholm, Sweden, in 1990.

FEI World Championships

Prior to the WEG being conceived, the FEI world championships were all held in different countries. In 1984, for example, of the main disciplines, the Jumping World Championship took place at Aachen in Germany, Dressage in Goodwood, UK, Eventing in Gawler, near Adelaide in South Australia and Driving in Szilvasvarad, Hungary. Eventually, at Stockholm all six FEI disciplines competed for honours and all on the one site:
- Dressage: 68 Participants (22 countries),
- Jumping: 75 Participants (26 Countries),
- Eventing: 84 Participants (22 countries),
- Driving: 52 Participants (18 Countries),
- Endurance: 81 Participants (19 countries)
- Vaulting: 61 Participants (15 countries).

As can be imagined, the WEG was a major exercise for organisers, volunteers and officials.

It is also of considerable note, that the General Assembly in 1989 approved the introduction of the FEI's new Medication Control Programme (MCP), first muted in 1984, which was subsequently to prove so successful in upgrading the standards of control of doping within the sport.

The 'zero option' raised its head in no uncertain terms in the lead up to the WEG in Stockholm. Sweden was one of the countries whose national law prevented the use of any drugs at the time of competition, whereas the FEI, as the ruling body of the games, still permitted the use of some medications up to a maximum level and this included phenylbutazone. The Swedish veterinary authorities insisted that the games must be run under Swedish national law. Naturally, the FEI could not agree. This resulted in stalemate.

FEI Veterinary Committee Vice President, Dr Joe O'Dea was a highly respected American veterinarian, with vast experience of top-level equestrian sport, horseracing, and breeding. He reports the WEG issue in his book *Olympic Vet* where he states: "Finally, Alex set up an informal meeting following a Veterinary Committee meeting in Paris, for us to meet with the veterinary representative of the World Equestrian Games. Our (FEI) stance was that the World Equestrian Games was no different from Olympic Games and the host nation, upon accepting the right to host the Games, also accepted the rules and regulations of the IOC or the FEI, whichever were applicable. We went through the rationale for our rules, and how they protected the horse, the horsemen and the sport. The Swedish veterinarian offered nothing in rebuttal. Helpfully, Alex got his 'Irish' up, and was clear in his insistence that the FEI rules must prevail. The other committee member remained silent. The meeting ended without any acquiescence."

Some years later, Joe very kindly hand wrote in the fly piece of my copy of his book *Olympic Vet* a note thanking me for what I had done.

The WEG turned out to be a highly successful event with no specific doping or other problems. The concept of having all disciplines competing at the same venue has continued every four years to this day, although this has become a heavy burden on those national federations and organisers willing to host such events with in excess of 1,000 horses participating.

The original Medication Sub-Committee (MSC), which was in existence when I arrived at the FEI in 1982, was composed of Professor Heinz Gerber, the well-known and highly respected Swiss veterinarian, Dr Michael Moss, Director of Racecourse Security Services, which was the Newmarket forensic laboratory, but later rebranded as the Horseracing Forensic Laboratory and Professor Manfred Donike, Michael's opposite number in Germany, who also acted as advisor to the International Olympic Committee (IOC).

This sub-committee had served its purpose well over the years while mostly reacting to difficulties as they arose. However, it was felt that its function needed to be revamped and become more proactive with a view to keeping all drug related matters under constant review. As this was such a complex issue, the FEI Veterinary Committee, which advised the Judicial Committee, also needed guidance on whether substances found on analyses were likely to be a deliberate or accidental infringement of the regulations.

A new committee, which was formed in 1992, was made up of the French Racing Authority's (France Galop) veterinary expert, Dr Roland Devolz as Chairman, Dr Andrew Higgins, Director, Animal Health Trust, Newmarket, UK, who had been appointed Honorary Scientific Advisor to the FEI in 1988 and Professor Michael Lambert, Director Equine Forensic Unit, Trinity College, Dublin and forensic analyst to the Irish Turf Club, as members. This group met the challenge head on and kept us all very much on our toes. Andrew's appointment as Honorary

Veterinary/Scientific Advisor was hugely significant and a great help to the FEI in general and to me personally.

Following much background consideration, the PBZ issue was back on the agenda for the FEI General Assembly in Rio de Janeiro, Brazil, in 1993. The Chairman of the Veterinary Committee, Dr Peter Cronau (GER), based its arguments for the total abolition of the substance on the following points, which were circulated to all NFs, well in advance of the meeting:

- Phenylbutazone (PBZ) is already prohibited for horses at time of competition under national laws in Finland, France, Germany, Norway, Sweden and Switzerland;
- 151 out of 474 international events in 1992 (32%) took place in countries where PBZ is already a prohibited substance;
- PBZ has never been permitted in the endurance discipline;
- No other non-steroidal anti-inflammatory drugs (NSAIDs) are permitted, so why allow PBZ?
- The anti-inflammatory effect at site of injury can significantly exceed the detection limits in urine and blood samples, indicating that the drug is still active even if it cannot be found;
- Due to variation in metabolism of individual horses, it is difficult to calculate dosage and still remain within the permitted level;
- Toxic effects have been shown by scientific research;
- FEI sponsors are totally opposed to its use;
- A sport in which horses require medication is not consistent with the FEI's stated policy that horses must compete on their inherent merits.

The South-American countries were totally opposed to the abolition of PBZ so, on the night before the voting took place, in Rio de Janeiro, I inveigled an invitation to sit at dinner with the major players in this region. Peter Cronau took his seat with another group of potential 'dissidents'. We had an enjoyable evening with lots of good-humoured banter interspersed with serious discussion, but at the end I feared that we were set to lose the vote.

Prior to the vote taking place the following day, there was a prolonged debate in session but, eventually, in a secret ballot, the Bureau's proposal to include PBZ in the List of Prohibited Substances was carried by 46 votes for to 31 votes against.

Those speaking for the abolition included, much to my surprise, Argentina (representing much of South-America, including my friend from dinner the previous night), Denmark, Germany, Jordan, Liechtenstein, Norway, Oman, Poland and Switzerland. Among those opposed to the proposal and who wanted PBZ to remain as a permitted substance were Great Britain, Netherlands, Italy, USA and Zambia. In retrospect, it had been a good dinner with our South-American friends.

Left to right: AA, Professor Igor Bobylev, past FEI chairman Veterinary Committee and Dr Peter Cronau, current chairman at FEI General Assembly, Rome, 1995.

In reaching this decision, it was fully realised that the banning of PBZ would require a detailed review of the demands placed on competition horses and maybe even to the format of the various disciplines. Just because the same format has always been used in the past, when pharmaceutical assistance was permissible, did not necessarily mean that it was optimum for the future, in view of the changing circumstances.

There was a general feeling that laboratory methods were becoming too sensitive and hence drugs were being detected in lower and lower concentration. Certainly, this ongoing expertise was welcome and necessary to detect the more modern, highly potent substances, which can be used in minute quantities.

But, is it really necessary to delve deeper and deeper into detecting more and more minute quantities of substances, which realistically can have little influence on a horse's performance?

At the same time of course, the analyst and the relevant authorities must be continually vigilant to watch for new substances becoming available on the market, which could have effects when administered in very small amounts and even as 'cocktails' with other such substances.

To address these problems, consideration was given to the possibility that certain substances only be detected using specified but less sensitive methods. In addition, the FEI persuaded its official laboratory to establish and make available a list of detection limits for some of the more commonly used therapeutic substances. Realising the dilemma facing veterinarians who wish to give the best possible support to their equine patients this list was made available to the International Treating Veterinarians Association (ITVA). Threshold levels, which already existed, were kept constantly under review for naturally occurring substances in the horse or alternatively which may be found in normal and ordinary feeding.

For many years, the Veterinary Committee had invited representatives of the various riders associations to send delegates to its annual meeting to discuss areas of mutual interest or concern. It valued these contacts and while obviously both parties were not always in agreement or saw the problems in the same light, it did give the possibility to appreciate each other's point of view.

Clearly, it particularly welcomed the newly formed International Treating Veterinarians Association and looked forward to constructive dialogue with this association to the ultimate benefit of the health and welfare of the competition horse.

Equestrian sport needs the confidence of the general public. To achieve this requires positive media coverage. It is up to those involved to ensure that the image projected to the public is one of a healthy, clean and enjoyable sport for both horse and rider. As World Horse Welfare, the welfare arm of the FEI at the time, constantly reminds us that we must ensure *the use and not the abuse* of the horse.

The General Assembly in 2006, meeting in Kuala Lumpur, elected H.R.H. Princess Haya Bint Al Hussein of Jordan as the 13th FEI President to succeed H.R.H. The Infanta Dona Pilar de Bourbon from Spain, who had completed her maximum term of eight years in the role.

Among the new President's many excellent initiatives, following her appointment was the concept of a Clean Sport, 'To respect that the innocent party (the horse) in our sporting pursuits is protected and nurtured'

While this concept in itself was highly commendable, it included the introduction of a so-called progressive list of prohibited substances, which, amongst other substances to be permitted, saw the re-introduction of PBZ. Although this move was extremely controversial at the time, the 2009 FEI General Assembly in Copenhagen, accepted the Progressive List by a narrow vote of 53 to 48. This version of the prohibited list, which allowed the use of the NSAIDs, Phenylbutazone, Flunixin (Banamine) and Salicyclic Acid, only one substance at a time, and then only up to defined initial maximal levels, was therefore adopted as the future FEI prohibited substance list and it was scheduled to come into force on 1st January 2010.

Amongst the federations and individuals who opposed this move to re-allow the use of NSAIDs were a number of veterinarians, some of us retired, myself included, who were active in ensuring that PBZ became a prohibited substance in 1993. Having lived through the period building up to its abolition and being highly conscious of all the reasons behind this decision we made our feelings known to the president.

Due to the ongoing controversy, implementation of the Progressive List was postponed to allow for further discussion. This included a congress, which was held in the Olympic Museum in Lausanne in August 2010.

FEI President, H.R.H. Princess Haya, welcomed the FEI initiative to hold a Congress on *Non-Steroidal Anti-Inflammatory Drugs Usage and Medication in the Equine Athlete*, declaring it as long overdue and the first real opportunity to bring together all the new science on NSAIDs, since the FEI's 1993 ban on their use in competition.

"Knowledge and an understanding of all aspects in the debate on NSAIDs is key to an informed decision," the FEI President stated in her opening address.

"What we all most want from this Congress above all else is to give us, the FEI family, the tools and the confidence to have the wisdom to do what we all so clearly have shown we want to do– that is what is right for our partner, the horse," she said, emphasising the universal message of the Congress and the paramount principle of the sport, the welfare of the horse.

Leading research and other experts outlined the current state of knowledge on NSAIDs to over 200 Congress participants representing 29 nationalities. The participants heard that there was now a substantial amount of new scientific evidence on the nature of NSAIDs, including improved ways of detecting them, their effect on the body and their side effects, as well as the effect of low levels of intake and combining different NSAIDs.

I was privileged and honoured, 15 years after retirement, to be invited back to present the *History of NSAIDs in Equestrian Sport*, from the initial introduction of Phenylbutazone and its metabolite, Oxyphenbutazone, as a permissible substance at a level of four micrograms per millilitre of blood plasma, as reflected in the FEI Veterinary Regulations 1981, to the reasons behind their abolition in 1993. Clearly, there were many attending this congress who had not been aware of the background to this rather momentous decision some 17 years earlier. That evening, I had the added pleasure of being invited to join the President, as one of her guests, at her table for dinner.

The whole NSAID congress was an unqualified success and ultimately resulted in the unanimous approval by the FEI General Assembly, meeting in Chinese Taipei in November 2010, to adopt the modified Equine Prohibited Substances List to come into effect on 4th April 2011.

This new list consisted of two groups of substances: banned and controlled medication.

- Banned substances are not permitted for use in horses under any circumstances;
- Controlled medications, which include NSAIDs, are acknowledged as substances with therapeutic veterinary benefits, but are not permitted during FEI events because of the potential for their misuse.

Effectively, this ruling recognised the benefits to horses for the use of NSAIDs under appropriate circumstances, but 'not at time of competition'.

Those of us involved in assisting to bring this decision about breathed a huge sigh of relief.

Chapter 7

MEDICATION CONTROL PROGRAMME

Historical Review – Comparison with Racing – Proposal to FEI –
Introduction of MCP

Shortly after I joined the FEI, I drew the attention of the Veterinary Committee to the unsatisfactory state of its current drug-testing programme.

Coming from a racing background, I already had a reasonable understanding of how it should operate. In my opinion, the FEI programme was not fit for purpose.

There was a Standing Sampling Procedure laid down in the Veterinary Rules/Regulations (VRs) 4th edition, 1981, which was the rule book still in vogue in 1983/84. It was ambiguous on a number of points, and there was confusion as to who was responsible for different segments of the entire sampling procedure and this needed clarification.

The reasons behind this were that a veterinarian, not necessarily the official Veterinary Delegate but, as stated in the VRs, a 'trained assistant employed by the event Organising Committee', supervised by 'a member of the Veterinary Commission' should collect the samples from selected horses at an event. In practise, the Organising Committee rarely if ever employed an assistant for this purpose and the entire procedure tended to be performed by the Veterinary Delegate (VD) who, however well qualified he might be as a veterinarian, was most likely inexperienced in medication control duties. The VD was expected to:

- Collect urine and/or blood samples at an FEI event, in accordance with a laid down procedure;
- Record, pack and seal the samples in a pack supplied by an 'approved' laboratory (although which 'approved' laboratory was not specified, and nor was the sample pack);
- Forward the samples to the 'approved' laboratory for forensic analysis;
- A number of forensic laboratories worldwide, were approved by the Association of Official Racing Chemists (AORC), but these laboratories were not listed in the VRS so, at the time, not all samples were sent to a laboratory with the necessary approval.

Furthermore, this was all organised under the umbrella of the National Federation hosting the event, which was expected to pay the costs. However, regardless of this, the laboratory was expected to report solely to the FEI and not to the federation, which employed and paid them. Because the veterinarian and/or 'trained assistant' were, understandably, unfamiliar with the procedures, the paperwork, and the chain of evidence required when a subsequent positive case was investigated by the Judicial Committee often left a lot to be desired.

Why could this not be run on the same lines as in racing? I drew all this to the attention of Fritz Widmer, the formidable FEI secretary general, in 1983, but nothing much happened until the following year. In 1984, the autumn Bureau meeting took place on a cruise boat on the river Nile, sailing between Luxor and Aswan. This in itself proved to be a challenge. In addition to the members of the Bureau and FEI staff, there were other guests attempting to have a relaxing holiday on the same boat. Our meeting room turned out to be the dining room for all the guests. Its dual function meant that we did not gain access until approximately 10 am, following a leisurely breakfast and we had to vacate again by 12 noon to enable the staff to set up for lunch.

In the afternoon, we tended to visit one or more of the numerous historical sites begging our attention on the shoreline and in the evening, there were usually interesting social functions to attend. We tended to cram in another short meeting between returning from site-seeing and pre-dinner drinks.

One evening, after dinner, I ventured onto the upper viewing deck, where I took in the warmth (and smell) of the Nile. Shortly afterwards, Prince Philip appeared on deck on his own and I seized the opportunity to ask him if I could have a word. I outlined my concerns over the problems associated with the current medication control as organised by the FEI and how I could see them being resolved. He liked my idea and said that we would discuss it in session in the morning.

Next day, he briefed the Bureau on what I had told him. The Bureau accepted these ideas in principle, and instructed me to make a proposal for its consideration. I was happy to oblige and I produced a proposal on the following lines, which was presented to the Bureau at its December meeting in Bern[4].

I opened by saying that doping was an emotional and topical subject and the majority of international sports federations were currently striving hard to be seen to administer a dope-free and healthy sport.

The FEI, I continued, was in a unique position to other international federations in that it controlled two living entities: man and horse, against only one, the human, in other sports. The nearest equivalent to equestrian sport was horse racing whether it be Thoroughbred or Standard Bred. Both wished to be seen to administer a sport, in which the normal performance of a horse during a competition (or race) was not affected, either deliberately or unintentionally by the influence of drugs and medication or any form of veterinary treatment.

It can be a major problem to keep horses healthy and sound. The dividing line between treatment of injury or disease, on the one hand, and the preparation of horses for competition on the other is very narrow and not easily defined. In principle, it is obviously right to use medication to cure injuries and disease, which should be followed by an appropriate rest period, but it is patently wrong to use drugs to influence the performance of a horse during competition.

---

[4] This proposal was subsequently up-dated in the late 1980s prior to its acceptance in 1989.

The major racing authorities commenced the serious introduction of the control of doping towards the end of the 1950s, and the FEI introduced its programme in the mid-1970s. Previous FEI Veterinary Rule books referred to 'forbidden substances' and listed stimulants, depressants, tranquillisers, local anaesthetics and masking agents as being within this category, but it was rather ambiguous as to what procedures were to be followed if any of these substances were found. The 1981 Veterinary Regulations – (not Rules as heretofore) was the first occasion that a list of prohibited substances was published. These were described as, 'Any substances acting on different bodily systems such as: Substances acting on the central or peripheral nervous system; Substances acting on the autonomic nervous system etc. '

The control of the use of drugs in sport was kept constantly under review by racing administrators. Since 1977, meetings of forensic analysts and official racing veterinarians, supported by their administrators, had been held on a regular basis, as follows:

- 1977 – Newmarket, UK;
- 1978 – The Curragh, Ireland;
- 1979 – Lexington, Kentucky;
- 1981 – Melbourne, Australia;
- 1983 – Toronto, Canada;
- 1985 – Hong Kong;
- 1988 – Louisville, Kentucky.

I represented the Turf Club up to 1981 and the FEI or UAE Equestrian and Racing Federation at subsequent meetings:
- 1994 – Stockholm, Sweden;
- 1996 – Gold Coast, Australia;
- 2004 – Dubai, UAE.

Despite all this, it had to be accepted that the doper was normally ahead of the administrator and this was accepted at the Louisville meeting. If the analyst did not know what the doper was using, how can he know what to look for?

This meeting appointed an 'expert' group of two analysts and two veterinarians to look into the matter. The experts were asked to investigate the actions and concentrations of endogenous and normal nutritional substances, the presence of which could be regarded as natural to the horse and not evidence of illegal medication.

I was one of the two veterinarians appointed, but resigned after a short spell as I did not feel that I had sufficient pharmaceutical qualifications for the position. I felt that there were others with a far greater knowledge of pharmacology that would be more suitable for the role. In the event, Professor Heinz Gerber, my Swiss veterinary colleague who officiated at the World Championship in Dublin, was appointed to replace me and join Dr Cliff Irvine, a veterinarian from New Zealand. He also joined internationally renowned forensic analysts, Dr Michael Moss, Director of Racecourse Security Services – later to be re-branded as the Horseracing Forensic Laboratory – Newmarket, UK and Dr David Crone, Director of the Royal Hong Kong Jockey Club's forensic laboratory.

The first international survey of anti-doping control conducted by the racing authorities covered the period 1983-1986. The FEI conducted a similar survey. The results of the former indicated that the racing authorities in Europe analysed 51,340 samples during this period of which 170 or 0.33% revealed the presence of a prohibited substance. During the same period, and in the same geographical zone the FEI collected 1,669 samples of which 37 or 2.22% revealed prohibited substances: 24 of these were from jumping events, seven from three-day events, four from dressage and two from driving.

There were various reasons for this, the most important of which was the incessant competition that many of the FEI horses must undertake compared to their racing cousins. The fact remains that too many drugs were being used, particularly in jumping horses. It was accepted that the commercial aspects of the sport placed greater demands on riders to compete with horses probably more frequently than they should.

When the FEI's Transport Stress Research Project was introduced, and which you will hear about later, the President of the FEI, H.R.H. The Prince Philip, emphasised the necessity not to lose sight of the 'over competing' aspects of the sport, which added to the dangers of injury and increased the amount of travelling involved.

There were, of course, other factors: the ground surface on which horses were required to jump was not always ideal; horses were often required to compete at speed against the clock, which necessitated twisting and turning on joints never designed to make such movements. One heard riders complaining of enormous courses and back breaking fences. (Remember Harvey Smith's comments following the World Championship in Dublin?)

It was not surprising that horses' joints were unable to take the continuous strain and some could only continue to compete with the aid of drugs.

For some time, efforts had been made to resolve many of these factors: by modifying the international calendar with a view to minimising travelling; paying more attention to the ground surfaces, on which the horses must practice and compete and to the courses being built. (Horses normally spend considerably more time in the practice arena than they do during the actual competition). It is a fact of life that courses must be demanding or there will be no viable competition. But there were grounds for limiting the number of events in which a horse may compete in a given period, the number of competitions in which they may compete per event, the severity of fences and the materials with which they are built(e.g., light, rather than heavy poles in shallow, rather than deep cups).

Under Veterinary Regulations (mid 1980s) the President of the Ground Jury and the President of the Veterinary Commission/Veterinary Delegate are responsible for selecting horses to be sampled and for ensuring that the subsequent sampling procedures are correctly performed. The event's Organising Committee is responsible for paying all the costs involved, although the laboratory is required to only report to the secretary general of the FEI – understandably, this was often not respected.

The collection of urine and blood samples (Sample A and Sample B – see Box below) from a horse and the subsequent handling of these samples by a veterinarian, who was, of course, acting on behalf of the event's organising committee, appeared to be simple.

However, the procedures were fraught with difficulties as proven time and time again with FEI samples over the years. On many occasions, samples were handled incorrectly and there were continuous examples of incorrect procedures and incorrect sealing. Why? Because the veterinarians acting at the events had little or no experience of what they were doing, as they undertook the task so rarely and they were attempting to do their work while often being pressurised by unsympathetic owners, riders or grooms. The result – mistakes in procedure, which necessitated abandoning otherwise bona fide dope cases.

Explanation of 'A' and 'B' Samples

As soon as urine and/or blood has been collected, it is divided into two separate containers. One container is labelled 'A' and the second container is labelled 'B'. On receipt of the containers at the forensic laboratory the chemist analyses sample 'A' and places sample 'B' in the refrigerator. If no urine is collected a similar procedure is followed with blood. If sample 'A' reveals the presence of a prohibited substance, the analyst reports the fact to the FEI through the Secretary General, who refers it to the Veterinary Department for action. The Veterinary Department informs the National Federation of the Person Responsible (PR – the rider or driver of the horse) who has the option to accept the result. Or, if he/she wishes, to have the 'B' sample analysed in the presence of an approved witness of their choice, in the same laboratory as first analysed, to confirm or refute the first analyst's findings. Regardless of whether the result is confirmed, or refuted, the file on the case is then passed to the Judicial Committee for their consideration and judgement[1].

Postscript: Dr Andrew Higgins has informed me (2016) that A and B samples are not universal. Brian Sheard, who was Director of the Horse Racing Forensic Laboratory (1996–2001) and who succeeded Neville Dunnett in this role came from the Home Office, and repeatedly said, "If you can convict a murderer on the evidence from a single laboratory, you should be able to report a horse positive."

He felt that A and B samples were an archaic system. Interestingly, greyhound racing has never used A and B samples, but has relied on a single test report from HFL and this has never been challenged.

What was the equivalent in racing? It was the national racing authority and not the racetrack that employed the veterinarian who was therefore trained by and answerable to that authority. The samples were sent to the laboratory contracted to analyse all samples in the authority's jurisdiction. The result – by performing this task on a regular (often daily basis) mistakes were virtually unknown and never interfered (in the author's ten years' experience employed by a national racing authority) with subsequent judicial procedures. In addition, there was an excellent urine collection rate (being the body fluid of choice for the analyst) of 95%, compared to just 50% with FEI samples.

The basic problem was that the FEI had very little direct control over the existing programme. The Ground Jury and the President of the Veterinary Commission/Veterinary Delegate, whoS selected or assisted with the selection of horses to be sampled, were guests of the organising committee. In many cases, the veterinarians were established equine practitioners who often numbered many of the competitors amongst their clients. This in itself was not necessarily a bad thing but when it came to selecting horses to be sampled then, with the best will in the world, there had to be a potential conflict of interest. The laboratory was also employed by the organising committee and paid by them, although it was expected to report solely to the FEI.

Further, it was not difficult for competitors to know in advance which events would be sampled. They could then plan their itinerary to avoid these events and compete freely with a medicated horse with little possibility of being caught. There was the added advantage that with the excessively low urine collection rate even if a horse was selected for sampling, there was still a 50% chance that no urine would be obtained, which enabled the horse's medication to remain undetected. There had even been malicious suggestions that some horses had been trained not to pass urine and there was no doubt that some did appear to be extremely nervous when the urine collector approached it.

It had been known for some time that the current programme was inherently unsound and attention was first drawn to this in 1983. The President informed the Bureau at its meeting in Luxor/Aswan in October 1984 that there were strong grounds for the programme's reorganisation at the earliest opportunity. Many other references were made at veterinary meetings, Bureau meetings, General Assemblies and in public by the past and present Presidents and others to the urgent necessity to move forward on this issue. Dr Peter Cronau, (GER) Chairman of the Veterinary Committee made a proposal in 1986 and a further detailed proposal was received from Dr Joe O'Dea (USA), member and Vice Chairman of the Veterinary Committee towards the end of 1987. However, the Finance Committee had decided that funds were not currently available. It was mentioned that the costs in time to the Veterinary Department to handle the many cases processed, many of which were unnecessary, was quite considerable.

It was planned that initially the new programme would only operate in Western European Groups one and two – (French speaking and English speaking European nations respectively). It was based on the racing authority's principle and a modified version of that operated by the American Horse Shows Association (AHSA) Drugs and Medication Control Programme, which was run under the most able control of its Director, Dr John Lengel. John kindly invited me to spend time with him and his team at its offices in Columbus, Ohio during the planning stage of the FEI programme. The AHSA operates throughout the North American continent, which was considerably larger than our patch of Western Europe. During this trip, Joe O'Dea invited John Lengel, George Maylin, the forensic analyst at Cornell University, New York, and me to visit him at Saratoga during the racing festival as his guest. We had a most productive meeting. It was reassuring for the FEI to have the support and collaboration of the AHSA, the substantial North American federation, very much on side in the planning stage and in an advisory capacity on into the future. John and I continued our professional and personal relationship for all my time with the FEI when my successors took up the mantle.

When accepted, the FEI's re-organised Medication Control Programme (MCP) will come under the direct organisational and financial control of the FEI, which *will appoint an administrator to manage the programme on its behalf.* [5] *The FEI will set up a fund from which it will employ, under contract:*

- One or more veterinarians with equine experience, but not actively involved in international equestrian sport, in each Western European member NF, to collect samples from events in their country (or further afield if requested). They would be fully trained in all the relevant procedures and would be referred to as Testing Veterinarians (TVs);
- Following a selection procedure, the FEI would appoint its own forensic laboratory to carry out analyses of all samples collected on its behalf;
- The FEI would contract a forwarding agent, which would collect samples from the event, on request of a TV, and deliver them directly to the approved FEI laboratory.

Prior to an event:

- The administrator would instruct an appropriate Testing Veterinarian to attend a certain event, and brief him/her on the category of the event. On arrival, he/she would consult with the President of the Ground Jury/ Veterinary Delegate, and agree on the procedure and number of horses to be sampled. The TV would be responsible for ensuring that the samples were correctly collected, recorded and transported by the forwarding agent to the laboratory,
- The laboratory would analyse the samples and transmit the results directly to the FEI and nowhere else,
- If the analyses revealed the presence of a prohibited substance, the administrator would liaise directly with the Chairman of the Medication Sub-committee and/or Judicial Committee and instigate follow up procedures as appropriate.

The advantages of this system were that at all times the FEI would have direct control over every aspect of the sampling procedure. This would reduce potential problems to a minimum. In the event of a positive finding the FEI would be dealing with known, trained personnel who would have no biased interest in a particular horse sampled. If a change of procedure were required at any time, contact with all relevant parties would be straightforward. In addition, it was understood that organising committees would welcome being relieved of their inherent responsibilities in organising these complex procedures at their event.

Allied to all this, it had long been known that some competitors and their trainers used unacceptable practices to make their horses' legs sufficiently tender (hypersensitisation) that will ensure that they make extra effort to cleanly jump a fence rather than inflict more discomfort on itself. These practices varied from rubbing irritants onto the skin or injecting irritants under the skin, inserting pricking devises under bandages and boots and other methods. All these practices were already in the public domain. It was not unusual to find horses being rapped in the stables at night, and early morning 'schooling' at major and minor events was

---

[5] The appointment of Administrator never actually took place. I just absorbed the function into my other existing duties.

common place and often taking place 'off-site', which was totally against the rules. A form of rapping could even take place in the practice arena before competition when under the supervision of a steward. It was not difficult for a rider colleague to place himself and his horse close to a fence thereby shielding the malpractice from the steward.

Discarded syringes had been found at events. There were grounds for suspicion that some riders/grooms were not only 'treating' their own horses but also maliciously 'treating' other rider's horses as well. Veterinarians did not leave used syringes lying around but others did not necessarily have the same scruples.

As laboratory techniques became more sensitive, so too were drugs becoming more sophisticated, thereby requiring more minute doses that were difficult to detect. 'Cocktails' of these minute substances complicated the issue further.

The FEI needed to concern itself with the consequences, if these practices were to become public knowledge. As a senior jumping rider once told me, "Sooner or later, a groom, who is dismissed from his job, will vent his dissatisfaction by selling his story to the newspapers." If this happened then there would be a scandal.

The introduction to the standard sampling procedure for prohibited substances emphasised quite clearly that the first and most important requirement for the control of prohibited substances was the strictest possible stable security. Absolutely correct, but where does it operate? The international stables at the Royal Dublin Society's show grounds in Dublin for one. There is one door in and one door out, both manned 24 hours a day with movements in both directions recorded in a logbook and signed. In far too many cases, stable security has been represented by nothing more than a rope or wicker fence, which becomes a minor inconvenience for those wishing to enter the controlled zone.

What is stable security expected to achieve? It is supposed to keep unauthorised people (i.e., the general public including mothers pushing babies in prams) out of the stable area and away from the horses. Security will not stop a potential doper who is much more likely to be another competitor or groom with authorised access. The regulations state clearly that the person responsible (competitor who rides or drives the horse) is responsible for its security.

There was great similarity between the problems facing the FEI today and those which faced the major racing authorities 25 years ago. Many racing authorities relied heavily then, and some still do, on amateur stewards to regulate the sport. However, with the advent of major investment in bloodstock and significant increases in prize money and betting turnover, it was not possible for these stewards to maintain control on a day to day basis without assistance. Thus came the introduction of Stewards Secretaries or, in some cases, Stipendiary Stewards. These officials attended race meetings, on a daily basis and hence came to know the individuals and horses concerned, their quirks, the types of malpractice in vogue. Most importantly, they were able to advise the stewards on the correct and consistent interpretation of the rules.

While it is not suggested that Ground Juries need assistance with judging competitions, it is suggested that FEI stewards, who only attend a limited amount of events per annum, cannot possibly control the legal (and sometimes illegal) activities of numerous competitors or be aware of the current malpractices in stables, practice arenas and elsewhere in vogue today, without assistance. This could be tackled if *the FEI were to employ a small number of paid Stipendiary Stewards who would attend, certainly, the major events of the year, where they would rapidly come to appreciate the ever-evolving problems. In many cases, ex-mounted policemen would fill the role perfectly. The success of their work could be judged in different ways, as recorded by two racing Stipendiary Stewards when discussing the previous day's racing. One stated that he had an excellent day, "I caught seven offenders". The other, who had officiated a different race meeting, replied that he had had a far better day, "I caught no offenders". Let us hope that someday the FEI can honestly state that it has no offenders.*

Despite the above proposal, it was not until February 1988 that a Working Party, chaired by Professor Vittorio de Sanctis (Italy), second Vice President of the FEI and chair of the Judicial Committee, met in Frankfurt and recommended that, as the FEI financial situation had now improved sufficiently, the modified Medication Control Programme (MCP), as proposed by me, should become effective as soon as possible. Professor de Sanctis briefed the General Assembly at its meeting in Budapest, Hungary in 1989 on the Working Party's recommendation. This was accepted and it was agreed that the programme should commence on 1st January 1990 in FEI Groups one and two (Western Europe) with a view to expanding further afield in the future[6].

However, it was all systems 'go' with the MCP and there was no time to lose! The Medication Sub-Committee produced a bidding document, which was circulated to all Association of Official Racing Chemists (AORC) member laboratories. A selection process was established. There were some eight responses from which the internationally renowned Horseracing Forensic Laboratory (HFL), Newmarket, UK was selected to become the FEI's first official Forensic Laboratory. This appointment was subject to review on a four year cycle.

Some 15 veterinarians[7] from the majority of Western European National Federations were selected for training as Testing Veterinarians (TVs) and a European-based Forwarding Agent was appointed to be responsible for collecting samples from events and delivering them directly to HFL. The manufacturer, based in the UK, who already produced sampling kits with which we were all familiar, undertook to supply the necessary kits to the TVs on request. Naturally, this required many meetings and discussions with all the relevant parties, which finalised with a briefing session for the new TVs, which was held in the autumn of 1989 at the University of Utrecht, Netherlands, by kind invitation of Professor H. J. (Henk) Breukink. Henk had been a past FEI Veterinary Committee member (1980–1984) and now became a TV. In addition, he oversaw a number of his team at the university operating as TVs within a specified radius of the university.

---

[6] Plans are currently (2016) afoot for the MCP to expand beyond Western Europe.
[7] It is estimated that some 100 Testing Veterinarians have been trained and worked for the MCP from its inception in 1990 up to the present time.

FEI Medication Control Testing Veterinarians

The initial complement of MCP Testing Veterinarians, appointed when the MCP was launched in 1990, comprised:

- Fred Barrelet (SUI),
- John Brazier (GBR),
- Henk Breukink (NED),
- Jean-Francois Bruyas (FRA),
- Roberto Busetto (ITA),
- Francisco Camancho (POR),
- Gunter Eisenhardt (GER),
- Dermot Forde (IRL),
- Francoise Hess-Dudan (SUI),
- Roger Johnson (GBR),
- Peter Kallings (SWE),
- Carsten Grondahl Nielsen (DEN),
- Manuela Pigato (ITA),
- Manuel Rodriquez (ESP),
- Adam Wasowski (POL)

Amongst many others to follow in subsequent years, were:

- Liisa Harmo (FIN),
- Jean-Philippe Jamme (FRA),
- Miklos Jarmy (HUN),
- Georgino Porcino (ITA),
- Karina Poepperi (GER),
- Frans J. Ter Beek (NED),
- Anne Trevis (GER),
- David van Dooren (BEL),
- Colin Roberts (GBR),
- Alexandros Rotas (GRE).

Clearly, there were others after my time which, with one or two exceptions, I did not know.

None of this would have been possible without the sterling help of my team in the secretariat. These included Debbie Ripplinger – I gave her away at her wedding, as her parents were unable to make the journey from the USA. Having subsequently left to raise a family, she returned many years later, to work with John Roche in the Jumping Department, Nicole Birbaum, my secretary at the time and Marianne Klay. Marianne, who came from a Swiss equestrian background, fully understood all the ramifications of what we were trying to achieve with the Medication Control Programme. She communicated well with the Testing Veterinarians and it was largely thanks to her that the programme not only got off to a good start, but prospered in its first year. Naturally, others followed in her footsteps as the programme and other work continued to grow including Cynthia Parker, Brenda Viret and many more too numerous to name. I am grateful to them all.

Against a background of emotionally charged criticism, based on media exposure in Germany of abuses to horses at a well-known competition stable, the first World Equestrian Games (WEG), in Stockholm, Sweden in 1990, at which the MCP was launched, was a great success both from the organisational and sporting perspective. 300,000 spectators, 2,500 volunteers, 1,400 journalists, 800 horses and 500 riders representing 40 nations competed over some 14 days at this historic event.

In addition, the President of the FEI, H.R.H. The Princess Anne, who had succeeded her father, H.R.H. The Prince Philip, Duke of Edinburgh in 1986, had announced a number of new initiatives in the 1990 Annual Report. These included, the creation of an Equestrian Ethics Committee, the establishment of the centralised Medication Control Programme, increased severity of sanctions as included in the revised General Regulations, the introduction of a study into Transport Stress in horses, investigation into sensitisation and desensitisation of horses' legs and a more clearly defined and responsible role for competition stewards with the appointment of an overall Senior Steward and a Contact Steward in each member National Federation.

So, not only had effective medication control arrived into international equestrian sport but many additional improvements were instigated to protect the health and welfare of competition horses in the coming years, as you will find out later.

We instigated an annual meeting of the MCP Testing Veterinarians to receive their feedback, review the previous season and make modifications to up-date the programme, where necessary. This ran concurrently with the meetings of the Medication Sub-Committee and the Veterinary Committee. In addition to serious meetings, there was still time for a little fun and relaxation. The last meeting that I attended of this group was at Cambridge, UK in February 1995. As a parting shot, the Testing Veterinarians presented me with an 'MCP' tie. This was covered with lots of little pigs, and created great amusement amongst the donors. It was only then that I realised that MCP stood, not only, for 'Medication Control Programme' but also for 'Male Chauvinist Pig'. The last laugh was on me!

Chapter 8

INTERNATIONAL MOVEMENT OF HORSES

Global Disease Situation – Liaison with Official Authorities – Practices and Problems

For the purpose of considering the international movement of horses, and its inherent problems, its history can be divided into three phases. The first period is prior to the first World War (WWI), the second to the period between the two World Wars and the third dates from the end of WWII to the present time.

During the first period, the horse was indispensable for national survival, both economically and militarily. In those early days, the horses transported us – now we transport them. Contagious diseases were not unknown, but movements 'en masse' over long distances were exceptional, other than in times of war, and outbreaks of disease had every chance of remaining localised. The second period, between the two World Wars, saw the gradual decline in the importance of the horse and a reduction in the number of people who understood them. The final period, covering the last seventy years, has seen the rapid disappearance of the working horse, and of the majority of people who worked with and had knowledge of them.

The people today do not depend on the horse for survival and it may, therefore, be loosely classified as a leisure animal. As such, it has tended to be virtually abandoned by government health authorities and even within these authorities, few have had the opportunity to receive even a basic knowledge or understanding of the horse.

At the same time, due to rapidly developing mechanisation, there has been considerable and significant increase in the international and truly global movement of horses for competition, racing, breeding and trade. It is difficult to assess the vast numbers of horses that travel the globe every year by road, sea and air from country to country and continent to continent. In addition, in 2012, around 54,000 (down from well over 100,000 10–15 years previously) stressed horses were packed into lorries and driven long distances mostly from Eastern European countries to slaughter in Belgium, France and Italy for human consumption. Exhausted, diseased, injured and travelling for days over thousands of miles, these horses were desperate for food, water and rest. Very few horses are slaughtered for human consumption in the UK, and most of this meat is exported to France and Belgium. There is still no legitimate live animal export trade of horses for slaughter from the UK.

Transport Stress Research

You will read later in this book of the collaboration between World Horse Welfare and the FEI. This commenced in the early 1980s when World Horse Welfare generously agreed to fund a research project into the stresses imposed on horses during transport. The funds for this were awarded to the Irish Equine Centre and the University of California. Both centres performed an amazing amount of research over the following years and produced many relevant papers, which were published in the scientific journals.

Equine Transport Workshop and Conference

In 1999, an International Workshop on Equine Transport took place in Middleburgh, Virginia, USA. This was sponsored by the Massachusetts Society for the Prevention of Cruelty to Animals (MSPCA) and USA Equestrian. Based on the results of this workshop the FEI/World Horse Welfare Joint Committee on Equine Welfare decided not only to build on this workshop but also to address the more practical issues through the eyes of those actively involved in shipping and managing horses throughout their travels.

Hence, the Second International Conference on the Transportation of Horses took place in July 2003, at Hartpury College, Gloucestershire, UK. The conference was opened by Captain the Hon. Gerald Maitland-Carew, chairman of World Horse Welfare and it was sponsored, once again, by the MSPCA but also by the FEI, World Horse Welfare, and Peden Bloodstock, which at the time annually shipped some 3,500 horses around the globe, including the majority of major events including Olympic Games, World and other Championships and events.

The Organising Committee was chaired by Dr Andrew Higgins, Chairman of the Joint Committee on Equine Welfare and I was secretary. The Veterinary Research Group met in parallel session, chaired by Dr Frederick Derksen, Michigan State University, USA. 135 delegates from 25 different countries were addressed by a wide variety of experts in the horse transportation business. The subjects covered included:

- Veterinary concerns in moving horses;
- Road transport;
- Roll-on Roll-off ferries;
- Aircraft design; the role of the Team Veterinarian and the professional Flying Groom;
- Current practices and problems in long distance transport;
- Training for equine handlers;
- Certificate of Competence for equine handlers (professional flying grooms);
- The Shipping Agent;
- The insurance perspective;
- European and international rules and regulations;
- Welfare of horses during transport;
- Potential to spread disease;
- Competition and disease;

- And finally, the many issues relating to the long distance transport of horses for slaughter, which was of particular interest to World Horse Welfare which was, of course, one of the sponsors.

Dr Des Leadon, Irish Equine Centre, who led much of the FEI/World Horse Welfare Transport Stress Research Project, addressed the latter conference on *Current Practices and Problems Associated with the Long Distance Transport of Horses*, which really put the complexities of the whole horse transportation business in a nutshell. In his presentation, he said:

The evolution of the jet stall has revolutionised the international transport of horses in the last 10 years or so. These stalls have been designed for a maximum of three horses, side by side, separated by partitions. Access to the horses, for feeding and watering and for their expert travelling grooms is provided at the front of the stalls. Placing three horses in a jet stall can be likened to travelling 'economy' for human air travellers. Horses can, for a higher price, also travel two to a stall (business class) or even enjoy a stall entirely to themselves (first class), if economics allow. A maximum of 29 jet stalls containing 87 horses can be carried by a 747 Jumbo Jet. Most horses tolerate confinement, jet noise and repeated take-offs and landings remarkably well. Although some lose no weight during their journey, it is not unusual for horses to lose about 20 kg, or 4% of their bodyweight, on a 24-hour journey.

Some horses, often unpredictably, will suddenly resent confinement. This occurs in less than half of one per cent of horses that travel. Caring attention and re-assurance and access to modern injectable tranquillisers are generally sufficient to restore calm. Extreme frenzy can be almost impossible to control in such a confined space and has, very rarely, resulted in fatality.

Like their human counterparts, a minority of equine passengers may develop aviation related disease. Although colic and other illness may manifest itself at altitude, as it can anywhere else, the principle problem associated with long distance transport of horses is respiratory disease. Known colloquially as 'Shipping Fever' this disease has been recognised for well over 100 years. The disease had from then until relatively recently, an incidence of about 6%, i.e. 94% of horses transported long distances were unaffected by the combination of pneumonia and pleurisy that is Shipping Fever. The clinical signs include depression, reluctance to drink, increased rectal temperature and increased respiratory rate with other signs of respiratory disease. Research by the late Dr Daria Love and her colleagues in the University of Sydney has shown that holding a horse's head high for protracted periods, even on the ground, can predispose to the development of this disease. Studies funded by World Horse Welfare and the International Equestrian Federation (FEI) and carried out by the Irish Equine Centre have shown that bacterial numbers in the air in the cargo hold can increase dramatically during a journey especially at refuelling stops.

This conference reviewed some five years of research to reduce the risk to horses from transportation. A small 18 page booklet was subsequently produced and the proceedings were published in the scientific literature.[8].

Disease risks

Clearly, the considerable international movement of horses can create problems for these wonderful and often hugely valuable horses that need to be addressed. This constant travel multiplies the risk of spreading infectious diseases between each other and the indigenous equine populations in the countries they visit, not to mention the heightened incidence of transport stress. A horse may make an intercontinental journey, leaving home, travelling and arriving at its destination apparently healthy, but incubating a disease, which it may subsequently spread to the susceptible population following arrival. Clearly, disease is the major issue that interferes with horses travelling, so let us take a look at the general situation in the recent past and at the main diseases of concern.

Examples of the devastation caused by outbreaks of disease include African horse sickness (AHS), in the Near East and South West Asia and later in North Africa at the end of the 1950s and mid-1960s, which killed more than 300,000 horses. During the 1960s, there were serious outbreaks of equine infectious anaemia in the USA, France and Japan. This is not to mention the epidemics of equine influenza in Hong Kong and South Africa or, more recently problems with contagious equine metritis, viral arteritis and African horse sickness, which appeared in Spain in 1965 and 1966. The further outbreak in Spain in 1987 and in the two subsequent years, also in Portugal and Morocco, placed the Olympic Games in Barcelona in 1992 in jeopardy.

---

[8] Leadon, Frank and Atock, Recommendations to Horse Owners and their Representatives on the Transport of Horses, Bern, Switzerland 1990, 17 pages

Symptoms of Some of the Main Equine Diseases

African horse sickness (AHS): AHS is a disease of equines in sub-Saharan Africa, which is spread by biting insects, principally midges. Global warming has extended the region hospitable to midges and hence the threat that AHS and other such diseases could become common in Europe and elsewhere in the future. The disease causes fever, sweating, breathing difficulties, discharge from the nose, and swelling of the eyes and/or head. It can be fatal in horses but is less likely to be fatal in donkeys, mules and zebras;

Contagious equine metritis (CEM): CEM is an extremely contagious venereal disease that is acquired primarily via breeding. While this disease can be carried by either mares or stallions, it is the mare that suffers the ill effects of the infection. Stallions do not show any symptoms of CEM, but mares will often have a thick discharge from the vagina, and will be unable to conceive during the point at which the infection is active.

Equine infectious anaemia (EIA): EIA is spread by the horsefly. It is a virus that causes destruction of the horse's red blood cells, causing anaemia, weakness and death. EIA has become endemic in certain parts of the world, but is rarely found in the United States. There is no cure for the disease but the Coggins Test is a simple routine diagnostic blood test.

Equine influenza (EI): EI is caused by various strains of the influenza virus that affect the upper and lower respiratory tract of horses, donkeys and mules. The virus is similar to the flu virus that affects humans, but it is not identical, so horses cannot be infected by human influenza or vice versa. Protection is afforded by vaccination, which is compulsory for horses competing in FEI events and by the major racing authorities.

Equine piroplasmosis (EP): EP is a tick-borne disease that affects horses, donkeys, mules, and zebras. The disease is transmitted via ticks or through mechanical transmission by improperly sanitised surgical, dental or tattoo instruments or through the reuse of needles and syringes.

Equine viral arteritis (EVA): EVA is a very serious viral disease of horses. EVA occurs in both Thoroughbred and non-Thoroughbred populations. EVA is currently a relatively common disease in Europe, and other parts of the world but is rare in the UK. However, the risk of it increasing in prevalence within the UK, with potentially very serious welfare and economic effects, has increased over recent years. Signs of equine viral arteritis can include: conjunctivitis (bloody tissue around the eye known as 'pink eye'), swelling of testicles or udder and also around eyes and lower legs, abortions (failed pregnancies in mares), fever and runny nose, depression, lethargy and stiff movement.

Venezuelan equine encephalitis (VE): VEE is caused by a mosquito-borne viral pathogen. VEE can affect all equine species, such as horses, donkeys, and zebras. After infection, equines may suddenly die or show progressive central nervous system disorders. Humans can also contract this disease. Healthy adults who become infected by the virus may experience flu-like symptoms, such as high fevers and headaches.

The incursion of Venezuelan equine encephalomyelitis into Texas in 1971, which was quickly localised and diagnosed, was understood to be at considerable financial cost to the American administration. Approximately 50,000 horses died and some 31,000 human cases were recorded of which 310 died in Ecuador alone.

As a result of the above, countries understandably jealously guard the health of their national herd by imposing restrictions on the importation of animals from countries which they consider pose a disease threat. Few guard them more strenuously than the island nations of Australia and New Zealand, which particularly wish to protect their enormous sheep populations.

As you have already learnt, the Tripartite Group of France, the United Kingdom and Ireland some years ago developed a common policy on the movement of horses between their three countries for racing, breeding and competition purposes. The Tripartite Group has now been somewhat superseded by the European Union's requirements, which have established an agreed import policy for horses from third countries i.e. those from outside the member states. Once entry of these horses has been achieved into one member state they can then move relatively freely within the other states.

If we look back to 1956, the Olympic Games took place in Melbourne, Australia. Due to the restrictive import requirements imposed by the Australian Government authorities at the time, while it was feasible for horses to travel to compete in Australia, they could not then return to their home countries. Hence, an alternative equestrian 'Olympic Games' took place in Stockholm, Sweden. Thirty years later, in 1986, the World Three Day Event Championship was awarded to Gawler, near Adelaide, South Australia. In the years prior to Gawler, negotiations took place between the FEI and the Australian veterinary authorities, which resulted in a criteria being established whereby horses from the Northern hemisphere could travel to Gawler to compete and return to their country of origin afterwards. These negotiations surely also assisted in paving the way a few years later for the Dermot Weld, Irish trained gelding, Vintage Crop, to not only travel to Melbourne but to win Australia's prestigious Melbourne Cup in 1993. Vintage Crop returned in the next two years to finish sixth and third. In 2002, Dermot Weld sent Media Puzzle, again from Ireland, to win another Melbourne Cup. Since then many European horses have run with credit in the cup and other prestigious races in Australia.

Adequate control measures to prevent the dissemination of the various equine infectious diseases are dependent on their early diagnosis and the prompt reporting of disease outbreaks. Although diagnostic facilities within a particular country may be limited, the considerable international resources, which are available can be utilised by others, providing requests for assistance are made promptly. Once the condition has been diagnosed, the information can be reported through official channels, such as the World Organisation for Animal Health (OIE) if a notifiable disease (e.g., African horse sickness and others) or through various informal contacts between individuals and organisations working in the field if non-notifiable (e.g., equine influenza and others).

To facilitate the exchange of information at a scientific level, a number of international conferences took place, commencing in 1966, under the auspices of the Grayson Foundation in the USA, the Societe d'Encouragement (French Jockey Club) in France and the OIE.

In 1978, a conference in Madrid, which I attended as part of the Irish Turf Club's delegation, involved equine sporting regulators and national veterinary services concluded that exchange of information at national and international level, with particular reference to non-notifiable diseases, was essential.

Various attempts have since been made to get this initiative off the ground and a Collating Centre was established in 1986 at the Animal Health Trust in Newmarket, UK and this has served the industry well for both thoroughbreds and sport horses. The FEI is incorporated within its communication network. In addition, in 1987, a meeting was held in Paris under the auspices of the OIE and attended by the major equestrian organisations represented by the International Conference of Racing Authorities, the World Trotting Association and the FEI. The meeting agreed to organise a permanent co-operation in conjunction with OIE in establishing diagnostic and epidemiological surveillance of the most important equine infectious diseases incorporating a system of communication between the relevant equestrian authorities in close co-operation with national veterinary services. In summary, notifiable diseases must always be reported to OIE but now other networks have been established to cater for the non-notifiable, but no less important, diseases.

So, how does all this affect the FEI? Every four years, the Olympic Games take place. These include the equestrian disciplines of dressage, jumping, and eventing and involve some 300 horses. Every four years, in the even years between the Olympic Games, the World Championships are scheduled for all the FEI disciplines, currently incorporating jumping, dressage, eventing, driving, reining, vaulting, endurance, and para-dressage with some 1,000 horses competing. In the odd years between the Olympics and World Championships, Continental Championships (European, South American etc.,) are organised and in addition, there are Regional Games such as the Asian Games, Pan American Games, Mediterranean Games and others. Many of these are for senior riders/drivers, Young Riders, Juniors, and Pony Riders.

In an earlier chapter, you will have learned that in 1986, for example, there were four World Championships in the major disciplines:

- Dressage took place in Cedar Valley, near Toronto in Canada—44 competitors from 16 nations took part;
- Jumping was at Aachen in Germany – 72 competitors / 23 nations
- Three Day Event, Gawler, South Australia – 43 competitors / 8 nations,
- Four in hand Carriage Driving, Ascot, UK – 40 drivers / 12 nations.

This was the last time that World Championships were to take place at different venues in different countries. In future, commencing in 1990 in Stockholm, Sweden, they would all take place at one venue and be known as the World Equestrian Games (WEG). WEG has continued to flourish thereafter, taking place in: 1994 in Den Hague, Netherlands; 1998 in Rome Italy; 2002 in Jerez de la Fontera, Spain; 2006 in Aachen, Germany; 2010 in Lexington, Kentucky, USA and in 2014 in Normandy, France. In 2018 they will take place in Tryon, North Carolina, USA.

As one can imagine, transporting 1,000 horses from around the world takes organising, and this tends to be handled by a specialist equine shipping agent. Depending on the venue, some horses can travel by road but a large number will do so by air. The big advantage of the latter means of transport, from the horses' perspective, is that they do not have to queue at check-in, as do we humans. Their paper work is checked prior to boarding the lorry taking them from quarantine to the airport.

On arrival, they merely leave the comfort of their lorry, enter their jet stall, are driven to the aircraft where a hi-low lifts them on board and where their next meal is awaiting them – none of this nonsense of waiting until the aircraft is at 35,000 feet before being offered drinks and food. The horses are met on arrival and whisked away by the agent directly to quarantine or to the event stables depending on their health status.

Many other international events take place each year. This represents considerable movement of competition horses from country to country and continent to continent. This, of course, does not take into account the additional movement of thoroughbred horses for racing or breeding or indeed those destined for slaughter for human consumption – but that is another issue which we will refer to later on.

I had nothing to do with the transport of horses to Moscow for the 1980 Olympic Games as, although an official at the games, I was not yet in the employment of the FEI. However, shortly after I arrived at the FEI and to further my knowledge of all the ramifications of the international movement of horses I met with British Ministry of Agriculture, Fisheries and Food (MAFF but now DEFRA) veterinary officials, at their base at Tolworth, just outside London. Andrew Turnbull, kindly discussed and helped me to understand the difficulties for the international movement of horses for competition purposes due to the wide range of health requirements demanded by different countries. At this time, I also met with Michael Bullen, Managing Director of Peden Bloodstock, a UK based shipping agent specialising in the transport of competition horses to major events. Both contacts were to prove highly valuable in the future.

It was realised, at an early stage, that the equestrian Olympic Games could not take place in Seoul, Korea in 1988 under health controls existing at the time. This was due to the fact that no international equestrian event had ever taken place on the Asian mainland and there was lack of knowledge of the equine disease situation in that part of the world. This was not to suggest that Korea had specific health problems but rather to the fact that that its health status was not internationally recognised. Even if the games did proceed, the majority of countries participating would not allow their horses to return to their country of origin after the event – try telling that to an international competitor and explain that he must abandon his horse after the games, never to see it again.

I was sent to Seoul, on the instructions of H.R.H. The Prince Philip, FEI President, during the General Assembly in Amsterdam, in December 1983. I travelled on my own to Korea, in April 1984, with the express purpose of finding a solution to this problem. I was warmly welcomed on my arrival and during my six days in Seoul, I was accompanied throughout by Korean veterinary officials and an interpreter. During this time, we had intense meetings, interspersed with pleasurable social events. Among those organisations I visited and where I met with senior representatives included the Ministry of Agriculture and Fisheries, the Institute of Veterinary Research, the National Animal Quarantine Station, the National University Veterinary Faculty, the Korean Horse Affairs Association and, of course, the Seoul Olympic Organising Committee (SLOOC). These visits concluded with a final meeting of all authorities at the headquarters of SLOOC.

The following year, the FEI autumn Bureau meeting was held in Seoul. It is normal, prior to a major event, for the FEI to organise such a meeting to enable the Bureau to meet the key members of the Organising Committee and to view and approve the proposed sites for the actual event.

Following a request from the Indian Equestrian Federation, I travelled on from Seoul to New Delhi, where I had organised a Veterinary Course. This was held at the magnificent army barracks at Meerut close by. I had never been to India before and it was a shock to see the abject poverty of so many people virtually on the doorstep of the barracks. Once through the gates, we entered a different world: manicured lawns, a band playing, drinks flowing, with the poor on one side of the gate and the affluent on the other.

The conclusion of the visit to Seoul was that I strongly recommended that the Korean authorities should ensure that the experts of their relevant organisations be fully represented in the Korean delegation to the following month's World Organisation for Animal Health (OIE) conference in Paris. This they did and this was to be the start of many long and protracted meetings and negotiations with national veterinary authorities and the OIE itself. In fact, I found myself chairing a meeting at this first session with the chief veterinary officers of all the major countries, which would normally send their horses to an Olympic Games. The difficulties identified in Seoul and subsequently recognised in Paris were eventually resolved after several years of intense negotiations. This allowed horses to compete in Seoul and to return home after the games.

Interestingly, at least one of these meetings took place with Dr Bom Rae Kim, Director of the Korean Animal Health Division and his colleagues, in the British Ministry of Agriculture (MAFF) offices in Tolworth, UK. It was chaired by Iain Crawford, who had been one of the assistants in the Ross-on-Wye veterinary practice with me back in the early 1960s and who was now Director of Veterinary Field Services in MAFF – a small world.

Veterinary course Meerut: AA seated to the right of Maj Gen RKR Balasubramanian (Retd), President Indian Equestrian Federation.

AA making a point with a Korean colleague.

Sadly, and presumably as equestrian sport was virtually unknown in this part of the world and regardless of the excellent facilities, there was lack of effective promotion and spectator attendance was poor. Only 10,000 attended the final jumping competition. Although the Korean Broadcasting System was good, little was transmitted worldwide, although 32 nations participated in the three disciplines.

The Pan American Games took place in Havana, Cuba in August 1991. In preparation for this and with a view to assisting veterinarians in the region, Dr Joe O'Dea (USA), Vice-President of the FEI Veterinary Committee and I organised a three-day veterinary course to take place in Mexico, in February 1990. Thanks to local contacts in Mexico, this was based at the beautiful Cocoyoc Hotel, which was in the countryside close to Mexico city. 32 veterinarians representing Cuba, El Salvador, USA, Honduras, Venezuela, Columbia and Mexico attended. Immediately following the course Joe, the three Cuban veterinarians, Dr Raul Armendariz (Mexico) and I proceeded to Havana.

We were joined there by Dr Noel Vanososte (Venezuela) who was Vice President of the FEI at the time and advisor to the Cuban authorities. We spent a very productive three days meeting with representatives of the organising committee and others at the equestrian centre at Lenin Park, the National Institute of Veterinary Medicine and other sites. We discussed such issues as the health requirements, quarantine, horse transportation, surgical facilities and expertise and the need for at least one horse ambulance, veterinary cover during the event, fodder and bedding, stabling and medication control.

Intensive construction was in progress into updating the park to the standard required for international jumping and dressage competitions and, of course, accommodation for the athletes. The beautiful undulating parkland of some 740 hectares, situated eight km from the airport was beautifully landscaped with lakes, streams, palm trees and bougainvillaea. There was no eventing scheduled, largely due to the Cuban's self-acknowledged lack of experience of this discipline. The construction of the athletes' village was interesting in that the locals were invited to assist in its development in return for free accommodation when the games were finished.

Joe O'Dea and AA consulting in Cocoyoc prior to visiting Cuba.

'You have mail' – the daily fax from Bern.

The following year, six months prior to the start of the games, a repeat visit was made with the same personnel but also including Mr Leopoldo Palacios, the

Venezuelan Course Designer. The purpose of this visit was to double check that all was on target for the games in August. Dr Raul Armandariz undertook to run a veterinary course in April specifically for the Cuban veterinarians who would be working at the games. The state of farriery was a cause for concern. I was able to arrange through my son-in-law, a past team farrier for the USA jumping team and based in Florida, to recommend a colleague to visit, run a farriery course and to bring a Cuban farrier back to work with him in Florida for a few weeks prior to the games.

In addition, it was anticipated that many of the visiting teams would have their own team veterinarian and often their own farrier in attendance and that they would also assist in providing cover for any visiting horses in need of care and attention. A mini-hospital was planned which would include facilities for X-ray and emergency surgery, by visiting team veterinarians. The event itself proved to be a great success with 31 competitors from Argentina, Brazil, Canada, Columbia, Cuba, the Virgin Islands, Mexica and USA participating.

In September 1990, Lord Hartington (now Duke of Devonshire), Senior Steward of the Jockey Club of Great Britain, organised an international forum, in Windsor UK, to discuss the many problems relating to inconsistent quarantine requirements which had been acute and numerous in the past. I was invited to attend this meeting, as the FEI had already established contacts with the World Animal Health Organisation (OIE) and was instrumental in having the subject 'Movement of Sport Horses within Europe' to be considered by the conference of its Regional Commission for Europe in Sophia, Bulgaria, which was scheduled to take place during the week after the Windsor meeting.

OIE Regional Meeting in Sofia

The FEI had recognised the problems facing the international movement of sport horses within Europe for some time. I raised this issue with the general session of OIE in 1989, which referred it to the Regional Commission for Europe to be considered at its meeting in Sofia, Bulgaria in October. H.R.H. The Princess Royal, then President of the FEI, attended the meeting and her physical presence and her presentation to the meeting had a significant impact on the delegates.

Shortly after I arrived in Sofia, on the day before the conference, I received a telephone call from the British Military Attaché asking me to meet him to discuss the security arrangements for the President. At the time, it seemed strange to me to ask an Irishman, who was a national of the Irish Republic, to discuss the security arrangements for a high-ranking member of the British Royal Family. We had a good laugh over this later when he collected Dr Peter Cronau, Chairman of the FEI Veterinary Committee and me to take us to the airport to meet the incoming flight bringing The Princess Royal to Bulgaria for the meeting. No doubt assisted by the contribution from the FEI President to the meeting this resulted in the formal approval by the OIE, in 1992, of a suitably modified Horse Passport. This had been produced following detailed discussion with representatives of the European Union (EU). Clearly, this was only part of the story and the approval of common health certification for movement of horses within the EU member states followed later.

A few days after the Sofia meeting, the International Conference (now Federation) of Racing Authorities, at their meeting in Paris, appointed a five member Working Group to consider adverse factors to which racehorses are exposed on their international travels and to make recommendations on how these may be overcome. I was co-opted to the group to enable the problems of the non-thoroughbred competition horse to be considered in parallel. The group which met on a number of occasions during the following 12 months comprised representatives of the Jockey Club of Great Britain (Dr Andrew Higgins), the Societe d'Encouragement, France (Dr Roland Devolz), the United States Department of Agriculture (Dr Karen James), the Australian Government Veterinary Service (Dr Bill Hetherington, later succeeded by Dr Kevin Dunn) and me (FEI). One year later, in September 2001 and having made considerable progress in a number of areas but especially concerning quarantine problems with the USA, Australia and South Africa, the Working Group reported back favourably to the International Conference.

Excellent relationships evolved over the years, both with the European Union (EU) and with the World Organisation for Animal Health (OIE). A close watch is maintained on disease situations worldwide and extensive negotiations take place with national veterinary authorities on health regulations and all relevant matters relating to the international movement of horses for competition purposes.

I next initiated a meeting, which took place in Cyprus in September 1992, to consider the difficulties surrounding the international movement of sport horses in the Middle East and the Arabian Peninsula, which wished to compete in Europe and elsewhere. This meeting, which had the considerable support of H.R.H. Prince Faisal Ibn Abdullah Al Saud, Saudi Arabia (Chairman of FEI Group VII – which was the region under consideration) and of H.R.H. Princess Haya Bint Al Hussein of Jordan and was kindly hosted by Dr Michael Akis Petris, Chairman of the Cyprus Equestrian Federation and a veterinary colleague. Michael had, in fact, graduated from the Veterinary College of Ireland just a few years before me. The gathering benefited enormously thanks to the participation of Dr Thierry Chillaud (OIE) and Dr Alf-Ekbert Fussel (EU). The following countries were represented by a member of their veterinary authority and/or National Federation: Bahrain, Cyprus, Jordan, Lebanon, Oman, Qatar, Saudi Arabia and the United Arab Emirates.

Shortly after the meeting and resulting from it, the EU organised inspection visits to many of the above countries, which resulted in horses from these countries being able to compete, both in Europe and several other countries within the region in the ensuing years. A few weeks after the Cyprus meeting, I received a call from Alf Fussel, who was planning to visit Jordan the following day. He could get no confirmation of acceptance of the visit from the Jordanian Veterinary Authorities and sought my help. I called Princess Haya who, at the time, was studying at Oxford University in the UK. She told me that she would resolve the problem. 30 minutes later, she called me back to say that everything was arranged and that Alf would be welcomed on arrival. Needless to say, Alf was suitably impressed and the visit went ahead successfully and as planned.

The Equestrian Olympic Games in Barcelona in 1992 had its own mega problems prior to the Games. The Games were severely threatened by reoccurring outbreaks of African Horse Sickness (AHS) in the Iberian Peninsula in the preceding years. AHS is an insect borne disease of equines causing high mortality. It is endemic in southern and equatorial Africa but for many years rarely crossed the Sahara, although there was an outbreak in the Middle East some years previously. However, due largely to climate change, making conditions more favourable for the insect vectors, AHS had started to make incursions across the Sahara, which may well become more frequent in the future, making Europe and other northerly regions more susceptible to infection.

The first outbreak of AHS in Spain occurred in a zebra at a zoo in Madrid in 1986, and in subsequent years, there were fresh outbreaks in the south of Spain, Portugal and Morocco. At their invitation, I joined several of the OIE/EU inspection visits to the affected areas in Spain. On one occasion, we flew to Madrid where we met with top-level representatives of the government's veterinary service to discuss the issues prior to flying on to Huelva in the south of Spain for a late lunch. There were some 20 of us in the party including Spanish officials, OIE and EU representatives and myself.

After lunch, we set off in convoy to inspect a recent outbreak of AHS in a farm some one hour's drive away. After 45 minutes, the convoy drew to a halt while our hosts consulted a map to ascertain where exactly we were supposed to be going. Full of confidence, we proceeded and soon turned off the highway and up a narrow lane. We could see a farmhouse in the distance on the side of a hill. The potholes were so bad on the lane that at one stage we all had to disembark from our vehicles and walk.

We finally reached the farmyard and watched while our hosts met with the farmer. This resulted in much gesticulating and pointing towards another farm in the distance. We had come to the wrong farm! We all re-boarded our transport, performed a U-turn in the yard and proceeded back down the lane, vacating the vehicles to walk around the potholes, until finally reaching the main road and proceeding to the next laneway, where we eventually found the infected farm. This episode did not increase our confidence in how the authorities were coping with the disease situation in Spain at the time.

During one of these trips and to emphasise the seriousness of the situation, a Moroccan veterinarian explained to me that the donkey in Morocco is the equivalent of the working man's Mercedes and hence highly important to the family. Their livelihood will depend on this one small animal; hence, the loss of one man's donkey will have a devastating effect on the owner.

Dr Brian Marchant, an EU veterinarian, kindly came to Lausanne during this period to present his professional advice on the AHS situation at a meeting convened with Juan Antonio Samaranch, President of the International Olympic Committee (IOC) and the FEI. The Swiss tend to dine early in the evening and, having met Brian at the airport, I had great difficulty in finding a restaurant still open to receive and feed us.

Two weeks later, Brian came to a further meeting in Barcelona. He arrived at approximately the same time as he had in Bern, following which, we had related difficulties in finding a restaurant already open, as the Spanish tend to eat late.

This was a worrying time for all, but as a result of recommendations made by the OIE, subsequently ratified by the EU, the concept of regionalisation (an area free of any indigenous equines) of Spain was adopted. This came into force officially on 1st January 1992. As Barcelona was in the disease free zone of Catalunia, the FEI

Bureau recommended to the International Olympic Committee (IOC) that it would be safe to proceed with the equestrian Olympic Games in Barcelona as planned.

An unrelated crisis was averted when, in the days immediately prior to the start of the games and as a result of an equine health scare in the USA, the EU closed its borders to that continent. Knowing in advance that this was going to happen, and at my request, the EU kindly delayed implementing this action until the last plane carrying American horses, scheduled to compete in the Olympic Games, had safely landed on Spanish soil. We all sighed with relief when I received the call advising that the flight had touched down, which meant that all expected horses had now landed and the EU could safely close the border.

Finally, we keep talking about horse welfare and I make no apology for this. What about the horse from a northern European nation, which did its best for his connections competing at the Sydney Olympic Games in 2000 Following the games, it was flown back to Europe, presumably looking forward to a little peace and relaxation in its home environment. Not so. It disembarked, following the long haul flight from Australia and was immediately loaded onto its lorry to be transported to Rome to compete at another international event.

Think of the indoor events, particularly during the winter months. These take place in large arenas adapted for whatever entertainment it will next provide. It could be a circus, a motor show or a trade exhibition. If it is a horse event, jumping or dressage, temporary stables, which are often too small for the larger horses, are erected but as soon as the event finishes all must be dismantled to prepare for the next scheduled event in the stadium. This often means that horses competing in the final event, normally on a Sunday night, have no stable to which it can return at the end of competition. So, having given its all over three to four days and nights its reward is to be loaded straight onto its lorry for a long drive home or off to more temporary stables for the next event at which it is scheduled to compete. It's tough at the top but do the above examples reflect care for the horses' welfare – I think not.

Chapter 9

TACKLING WELFARE

Ethics Committee – Negative Publicity – Welfare Joint Committee and Sub-Committee

It is generally accepted that equines benefit from their association with man. Their use is beneficial. Their abuse is not. Similarly, stress is largely beneficial but distress is to be avoided. The welfare of all animals has become increasingly topical. This varies from public rejection of animal experimentation, through factory farming to the stresses imposed by long journeys. These are often under deplorable conditions with little, if any, rest, food or water, which many horses (and other animals) must endure on their final travels, mostly from Eastern Europe or from South America initially, to the slaughter houses in Belgium, France and Italy but now almost entirely to Italy.

In 2007, the remaining two USA based horse slaughter plants, one in Texas and the other in Illinois, were ordered closed. These were the last horsemeat abattoirs in the USA. So, what happens to US horses destined for slaughter now? They must travel excessively long journeys to the slaughterhouses of either Canada or Mexico. Is this looking after their welfare? I think not. There is absolutely no reason why horsemeat should not be available for human consumption, while the demand is there, but surely they and other animals destined for slaughter deserve to be shown a modicum of care and respect. There can be no justification for not slaughtering horses (and other animals) close to home and so avoiding these horrendous journeys. It would be infinitely more preferable to have them transported 'on the hook' rather than 'on the hoof'.

Increasingly, equestrian sport is coming under attack. Much of this is from the uninformed public often fed by the equally uninformed media – but not all. The specialist equestrian press publish what they see. It is up to us to ensure that what they see is acceptable. A smile and a pat on the neck are infinitely preferable to a scowl and a jab on the reins from a rider following an unsuccessful round.

There are many more injuries and deaths in the racing world but, with limited exceptions, they do not stir up the same amount of controversy or emotion. TV cameras tend to concentrate on the leaders, and even if there is a faller amongst them, on which the camera may briefly dwell, it quickly reverts to those in the front. An exception to this being the fracture of a foreleg of Mr Brooks in the 1992 Breeders Cup, to which we have already referred, and which received high media attention.

In sport horse competition, the camera tends to dwell on the competitor throughout its round. If it refuses a fence, falls, becomes exhausted or gets into any sort of trouble, this is liable to be highlighted, played and replayed for the benefit of the viewing audience, while the commentator analyses what has gone wrong. A brilliant clear round is quickly forgotten but several refusals and the over pressing of an exhausted horse lingers on in the memory.

The FEI recognised that there was a need to define more accurately the FEI's responsibilities and roles in monitoring and supervising welfare, and hence the Ethics Committee, which, following the agreement of the FEI General Assembly in 1989 in Budapest, was established.

This committee was chaired by Professor Vittorio de Sanctis, FEI's 1st Vice-President and was composed of riders from each of the three Olympic disciplines, veterinarians, medication experts and a representative of the (events) Organising Committee. It subsequently co-opted Colonel George Stephen, chief executive of World Horse Welfare, to membership. This was a significant appointment.

In the course of several meetings in 1990, attention was focused on the newly launched Medication Control Programme (MCP), stable security, stewarding and measures to be taken to avoid any form of horse abuse, which was reflected in the production of the Code of Conduct for the Welfare of the Horse (Annex 11).

This newly formed committee was responsible for:

- The production and introduction of the Code of Conduct for the Welfare of the Horse, initially in English and French and subsequently translated into Arabic, German and Spanish, with further languages to follow. The Code was launched in 1991 thanks to Colonel Stephen, World Horse Welfare, who generously funded the costs for its printing and publishing. It was widely circulated through all national federations; the equestrian community and Organising Committees were requested to include the text in their event schedules and programmes. The Code was continually updated over the following years,

- The appointment of the widely experienced Paul Weier as FEI Honorary Steward General. Many federations then appointed their own chief steward and an appropriate number of assistant stewards. Several stewards' seminars took place and an illustrated Aide Memoire for the stewards was produced,

- Yellow Warning Cards (as in football) were introduced. These were intended to be used in cases of physical abuse to a horse or verbal (or physical) abuse to an official – the rider could either accept or reject the card. If accepted no further action would be taken, unless he/she received two further Warning Cards in the same year, in which case the normal procedures foreseen in the Legal System would be instituted. If rejected, the Legal System procedures would be immediately instigated,

- Risk management for both horse and rider was kept continually under review. A survey conducted in the early 1990s showed that out of 1,554 rider injuries more than one-third involved head and face. Over time, the FEI Eventing Risk Management Policy and Action Plan placed the ultimate decision for protection against injury on the rider, with head protection (up-to-date crash helmets) becoming compulsory in most disciplines and these were described as, "A properly fastened protective headgear with a three-point retention harness at all times when mounted." At a later stage, body protection followed suit,

- The appointments of Dr Andrew Higgins as Honorary Scientific Advisor and Dr John Lloyd-Parry as Honorary Medical Advisor were welcome additions to the Ethics Committee. John also joined the Veterinary Committee, as being the nearest appropriate body in the FEI to the medical profession. This was a peculiar situation, but given the need for flexibility in those days, it worked well. John was President of the British Institute of Sports Medicine and was awarded his MBE in 2006, for services to sports medicine.

Dr Andrew Higgins

Dr Andrew Higgins is a graduate of the Royal Veterinary College, London where he also acquired his PhD in the role of *Inflammation in Horses*. He also holds a Master's degree in *Tropical Animal Health and Production* from the University of Edinburgh. After leaving the Army, he joined the Welcome Foundation before becoming scientific director and chief executive of the Animal Health Trust in Newmarket. He has a particular interest in doping and medication control in animal sport and, for over 25 years, was a regulator with the FEI. He chaired an anti-doping and medication review for the Greyhound Board of Great Britain and is a member of the Board's Impartiality and Disciplinary Committees. He is a trustee of the Kennel Club Charitable Trust and has been a trustee of many other charities working with animals, including World Horse Welfare, SPANA, Dogs Trust and the Animals in War Memorial Fund. After 25 years as editor, he is now honorary editor-in-chief of the Veterinary Journal and has co-edited two textbooks: *The Equine Manual* and *The Camel in Health and Disease*. He has also written *With the S.A.S. and Other Animals* based on his veterinary experiences during the Dhofar War in 1974.

AA and Andrew Higgins in discussion with two wallabies at time of ICRAV conference, Gold Coast, Australia, 1996.

119

When we think of negative publicity, we can look back as far as 1972 (10 years before I commenced duty with the FEI) when a British rider competing in the Olympic Games in Munich was suspended for 3 years, when sharp plastic strips were found under his horse's boots. Let us also remember the alleged abuse of training methods by a German rider in the lead up to the first World Equestrian Games in Stockholm in 1990, which accelerated the setting up of an Ethics Committee. Take a look back to 1992. First, there were the three fatal falls during the cross country phase of Badminton's, UK, three-day-event, next there was NBC's one-sided coverage of the three-day-event at the Olympic Games in Barcelona, which appeared to concentrate primarily on horses falling and which caused the subsequent media and public outrage. Then there was the fatal injury sustained by the eight-year-old gelding, Sir Arkay, when he broke a hind leg on the steep, newly built, bank at Wembley (jumping) Stadium in London, UK and finally Mr Brook's broken leg in the six-furlong Sprint at the Breeders Cup in Hallandale, Florida, to which we have already referred. This is not to mention the USA's Sports Illustrated story on fraud, whereby horses were killed to claim the insurance money. None of this did much good for the image of equestrian sport.

To add insult to injury, Animals International, the publication for the World Society for the Protection of Animals, in its winter edition of 1992, grouped together photographs and accompanying texts of, "Clubbing seals to death in Canada; bear-baiting using bull terriers in Pakistan and a horse falling at the three-day-event at the Olympic Games in Barcelona, Spain." The caption referring to the latter read *Cross country cruelty at the Olympics* and went on to state how horses collapsed from exhaustion and numerous horses were withdrawn or eliminated due to fatigue.

In response to this, readers of Animal International were urged to write to the Canadian Minister of Fisheries, requesting a cessation to seal hunting; to the Pakistan Embassy expressing their outrage at bear baiting, which incidentally contravened the Nations Prevention of Cruelty to Animals Act (1890) and the Wildlife Protection Act (1974) and to Etienne Allard, secretary general of the FEI, urging action to prevent a repetition of the exhaustion and injury to horses at the next Olympic Games in Atlanta in four years' time.

In fact, according to the FEI's Annual Report of 1992, 82 horses representing 18 countries took part in the three day event at the Barcelona Olympic Games, 72 horses completed the endurance phase including all 18 teams, and 62 horses completed the whole event including 15 teams. Only two horses (two, too many?) presented symptoms of extreme exhaustion. An American horse finished but required intensive therapy and was immediately disqualified. A Russian horse collapsed from exhaustion at fence 23, near the end of the phase, and following concentrated and prolonged therapy had to be anaesthetised and unceremoniously (but very publicly) hoisted by crane from the fence and transported to the equine hospital where it remained for several days prior to making a full recovery. All horses, including the two referred to, returned to their home countries none the worse for their experiences. The Report concluded: *This has to be the most satisfactory result in the history of the Olympic Games three-day-event. There were no serious injuries to horses or competitors. The competitors rode with responsibility and respect for their horses.*

Any negative publicity for any segment of equestrian sport has a rub off effect on other, but totally unrelated, elements. From time to time, the FEI received complaints regarding the Pardubice, a demanding steeplechase in Czechoslovakia, the English Grand National, the sport of Polo and the plight of the Tennessee Walking Horse and more.

In addition to the formation of the Ethics Committee, it was considered that further collaboration with World Horse Welfare would provide a forceful tool for improving both organisations' approaches to dealing with important welfare issues in equestrian sport.

As you will read later, World Horse Welfare was founded in 1927 to prevent the ill treatment of horses being exported from the United Kingdom to the continent of Europe for slaughter for human consumption. World Horse Welfare saw itself as an independent body, which could act as a buffer between the sport and other organisations, which may not have the best interests of the sport at heart. A further solid link between the two organisations was provided with the appointment in 1999 of Dr Andrew Higgins as a Trustee of the charity. In addition, Andrew was also a member of the FEI's Veterinary and Ethics Committee and of the Medication Sub-Committee. In fact, Andrew was a member of FEI committees for over 25 years, up to 2010, when he retired at his own volition. This was always in a voluntary capacity. One wonders if anyone else ever served as long and who was not a paid member of staff?

Welfare Sub-Committees/Committees

I had been Head of the FEI Veterinary Department from 1982 until 1995, when I retired of my own volition and joined the United Arab Equestrian and Racing Federation as Veterinary Officer and Consultant. I next moved to a consultancy position with World Horse Welfare. During this latter period, I felt immensely grateful and privileged when my good friend and colleague, Andrew Higgins, continually drew me back into the fold to become secretary of the various FEI/World Horse Welfare Sub-committees/committees, of which he was chairman.

An initial meeting of a Working Group, comprising Michael Stone, assistant secretary general, and Frits Sluyter, my successor as Head of the Veterinary Department, representing the FEI and Douglas Munroe and I, representing World Horse Welfare, to investigate potential areas for future collaboration. This meeting took place at Badminton Horse Trials, in May 1999. Arising from this, several further meetings largely instigated by Dr Andrew Higgins and Captain The Hon. Gerald Maitland-Carew, Chairman of the World Horse Welfare, took place.

It was announced, in May 2001, that the Bureau of the FEI and the Council of World Horse Welfare had agreed on the formation of the FEI/World Horse Welfare Joint Committee on Equine Welfare, with Andrew appointed Chairman and me as secretary. The members appointed to the new Joint Committee were Michael Stone and Frits Sluyter, of the FEI and Dr Douglas Munroe and me, representing World Horse Welfare.

We met with Professor Leo Jeffcott, Chairman of the FEI Veterinary Committee, and past dean of Cambridge University Veterinary School, who had officiated at five Olympic Games and four World Equestrian Games. Leo subsequently became dean of the veterinary faculty at the University of Sydney. We identified a number of issues as currently in need of consideration, including the need to review the Code of Conduct for the Welfare of the Horse, the use and abuse of horses, welfare issues in the discipline of 'reining', welfare of retired sport horses, medication abuse, disease dissemination, difficulties and delays for horses crossing national borders and to identify any specific problems in emerging countries.

We needed: to ensure that World Horse Welfare was recognised as the Welfare Arm of the FEI;

- To consider areas in need of research e.g., hypersensitisation, use/abuse of altrenogist (a drug used to suppress oestrus in the mare);
- To maintain and develop existing contacts with the Humane Society of the United States (HSUS) and the Royal Society for the Protection of Cruelty to Animals (RSPCA);
- To broaden the base of FEI and World Horse Welfare in developing countries and to exchange information between both organisations on Development Programmes (FEI > World Horse Welfare) and Training Programmes (World Horse Welfare > FEI).

There was much to be done.

A small working group met a few weeks later to set in motion another *International Workshop on Equine Transport* to be held in 2002 and to look at opportunities for collaboration in developing countries. It ascertained that the former Soviet Bloc countries had experience but little money, the Arab countries had the money but little experience and the African countries had neither.

The group recommended that World Horse Welfare should continue to expand its presence at major equestrian and other events. It already had an established presence at FEI General Assemblies and at the last World Equine Veterinary Association (WEVA) congress in Paris, France in 1999 and was scheduled to have the same presence at the next conference in Sorrento, Italy later in the year.

In addition, plans were afoot to have a promotional stand at the next World Equestrian Games (WEG) in Jerez de la Frontera in Spain, in 2002. I attended this latter event throughout in an attempt to spread the word. Leo Jeffcott, Foreign Veterinary Delegate, kindly allowed me the use of the veterinary office on site and invited me to attend relevant meetings during the games.

The Working Group next concentrated on specific concerns in the different disciplines. These amounted to:

Jumping: Primarily wear and tear, locomotion problems, pain management, frequency of competition and transport between events. It was currently thought that the average top horse jumps on some 80–100 days per annum in competition. The FEI was currently producing a data system, which was finalised later in the year following which more detailed information became available;

Dressage: Dressage competition was not considered as stressful as jumping although the indications were that training methods may well be more so (e.g. Rollkur/Hyperflexion);

Eventing: Recent tragic deaths of both horses and riders resulted in the Hartington Report, and considerable emphasis was now placed on improved safety measures. Most rider deaths had been caused by slow somersaults. Proposals were considered as to how to modify various elements of the discipline.

Summary of the Recommendations of the Hartington Report 2000

The Marquess of Hartington CBE chaired a committee comprising a wide range of experts in the sporting world (not only equestrian) to review the causes (sometimes fatal, particularly in eventing) and to make recommendations. The committee was composed of Christopher Bartle, David O'Connor, Dr Gerit Matthesen, Lt Col Gerry Mullins, Professor Inggar Lereim, Michael Tucker and Jackie Stewart OBE.

In its conclusion, the committee recognised that the Sport of Eventing was a great all-round test of horse and rider and a tremendous examination of horsemanship, but it is also, and will remain, a risk sport. The final decision and the ultimate responsibility for participation must continue to rest absolutely with the rider. The rider alone has to decide upon the limits in performance and the ability of his or her horse.

The Committee believed that the FEI should re-evaluate its own internal and external communications and examine its organisational structures to ensure that these recommendations are examined and if deemed sensible and practical put in place promptly. The Committee expected the FEI to ensure that an internal annual audit be established to continue to monitor the risks inherent in the sport.

The Committee hoped that it had some success in drawing the fine line between recommending changes to reduce risks, yet enabling the FEI and National Federations to continue to manage a sport that maintains its distinctive, traditional and thrilling character.

The Chairman of the Committee, as a self-confessed outsider from the sport, expressed his boundless admiration for the participants, both equine and human, in this remarkable sport. The selflessness, enthusiasm and sporting attitude shown by all those who wrote and spoke to the committee was a revelation and augured very well for the sport of Eventing. The report had the unanimous support of all the members of the committee.

Driving: No specific problems were reported.

Endurance: This was recognised to be a rapidly growing discipline, particularly in the Middle East, where, at the time, it had comparatively little FEI presence. Although this was the only discipline, in which the judges are the veterinarians, it tended to be the latter that caused the major problems through lack of consistency. The United Arab Emirates (UAE) led this discipline in the Middle East. It promoted and encouraged other countries in the region to organise rides. These countries saw the UAE riders on good, expensive horses travelling much more quickly than they themselves could ever hope to replicate. They considered this to be the norm and this inevitably resulted in over-ridden and exhausted horses, or worse, but without having sufficiently experienced veterinary expertise to cope and care for these horses after the ride. Once the ride was finished the experienced veterinarians, imported to manage the ride, were normally on the next flight home leaving the unfortunate animals in less experienced hands. It was considered to be essential to effectively monitor this discipline very carefully as it continues to grow, often in countries with little concern for the welfare aspects of their horses. In saying this, it is necessary to remember the hugely varied culture between countries with competition horses. Religions, history, tribal rivalries, acute poverty, and extreme wealth can all influence attitudes to animals and in some countries the concept of 'animal rights' or even 'animal welfare' may not be recognised.

Reining: This was a new discipline and many members of the Joint Committee registered their concern at the potential welfare aspects involved. The discipline, which was widely practised in many countries, was being monitored closely although training facilities, as in all other disciplines (and where most abuses occur) were outside the remit of the FEI.

Vaulting: Although the level of soundness of the horses concerned often left much to be desired, the demands on the horse were not excessive and no specific welfare problems were known other than the continuous circle on one rein.

The Joint Committee held many more meetings, under the chairmanship of Dr Andrew Higgins, which often included inviting relevant equestrian experts to attend and contribute to the subject under discussion. Terms of reference, which had been established shortly after the instigation of the Joint Committee and the Code of Conduct were kept continually under review and up-dated from time to time, as the need arose.

In 2005, the Bureau of the FEI decided that the Veterinary Committee needed its own sub-Committee dealing specifically with welfare issues relating to the sport horse. Andrew Higgins discussed this new issue with Captain Gerald Maitland-Carew, Chairman of World Horse Welfare, who wholeheartedly endorsed the establishment of the Sub-Committee but with the membership restricted to four (two experienced veterinarians and two non-veterinarians) with the possibility to co-opt others as and when necessary.

Andrew was appointed chairman and the members comprised: Dr Michael Düe (GER), former member of the FEI Veterinary Committee and veterinarian to Deutsche Reiterliche Vereinigung (German Equestrian Federation) and Professor Catherine Kohn (USA) former Deputy Chairman of the FEI Veterinary Committee and Consulting Veterinarian to the United States Three Day Event Equestrian Team. The non-veterinary members appointed were The Right Hon. The Lord Carew, FEI Honorary Bureau Member and former Chairman FEI Three Day Event Committee (Patrick Carew had competed in this discipline as a member of the Irish team at the 1972 Olympic Games in Munich) and Tony Tyler (GBR), World Horse Welfare Director of Operations. I was again appointed secretary, based both on my previous role in the FEI and now as a World Horse Welfare consultant.

The first meeting of the FEI Welfare Sub-Committee was held in Badminton, UK, in May 2005, by kind permission of Hugh Thomas, Director. The meeting was joined by a wide selection of internationally recognised equestrians and other experts:

- Jim Wolf, United States Equestrian Team Manager;
- John McEwen, Director of Equine Sports Science and Medicine at the British Equestrian Federation and formerly team veterinarian to the British

Jumping and Dressage teams (subsequently Chairman of the FEI Veterinary Committee and first Vice-President of FEI);
- Paul Farrington, current member FEI Veterinary Committee and former veterinarian to the British Event Team;
- David Muir, Equine Consultant to the Royal Society for the Protection of Cruelty to Animals (RSPCA);
- Brigadier John Smales, now chief executive of World Horse Welfare.

Among the many achievements of the Welfare Sub-Committee had been the organisation of a number of workshops aimed at specific challenges facing the horse in competition.

The *Rollkur/Hyperflexion* Workshop took place in Lausanne, Switzerland, in February 2007. The Chairman of the Veterinary Committee had asked the Welfare Sub-Committee to comment on the use of Rollkur with regards to possible concerns for the welfare of the horse. The FEI Code of Conduct specifically prohibited any training methods of horses, which are abusive or cause fear.

A meeting of 50 invited representatives from all aspects of international dressage and equestrian sport was organised by the FEI Veterinary and Dressage Committee to review the training technique that has become known as Rollkur (in German) and Hyperflexion (in English). The meeting was addressed by some twelve speakers, including veterinarians, researchers and a leading international dressage trainer. Evidence was presented that indicated that in experienced hands there was no apparent abuse, improper welfare or clinical side effects associated from the use of hyper flexion.

However, if not practiced correctly, there are serious concerns for welfare and possible clinical injury that will affect a horse's well-being and performance. Horses must not be seen to be put under pressure. There must be a clear understanding and proper application of such training tools. Evidence was required to brief FEI Stewards adequately so that they can take action to prevent abuse in all disciplines. It was recommended that the Dressage Committee should carefully consider the findings from the Workshop with particular focus on stewarding and judging and the Veterinary and Welfare Sub-Committee should identify what research was required to confirm if there was a welfare issue involved in training using Rollkur and Rollkur like techniques. The Welfare Sub-Committee subsequently issued a Preliminary Report on the use of Rollkur as a Training Method for Dressage Horses.

Further issues tackled included a review and subsequent recommendations to update the *FEI Code of Conduct for the Welfare of the Horse.* This was subsequently kept continually under review and up-dated from time to time.

The Sub-Committee was asked to produce a *Report on the Use of Tongue Ties* (these are common in racing where they are only in situ for a short time against in eventing where prolonged use could cause damage to the tongue). Interestingly, when consulted, Dr Geoffrey Lane reported that some 50% of UK horses in which tongue-ties have been applied by presumably 'competent' stable staff, sustained damage to their tongues due to restriction of blood supply and pressure necrosis.

Dr Geoffrey Lane

Dr Geoff Lane BVetMed DESTS FRCVS came from farming stock near Ross-on-Wye where I was in practice back in the early 1960s. His father did not suffer fools (or veterinary assistants) gladly. I was one of the latter. Geoff recalls a time when he was on his tricycle in the farmyard, when I came to dehorn some cattle. When introducing me to an imminent colleague, at his mother's funeral many years later, he told him that "Alex made such a b...awful mess of the procedure that I thought there must be a better way and hence decided to become a veterinary surgeon." In fact, Geoff graduated from the Royal Veterinary College in 1969. After a period in mixed practice in Berkshire, he moved to Bristol University to undergo training as an ENT Surgeon gaining his Fellowship of the Royal College in 1974 and remaining at the University for 30 years. He is a recognised Royal College of Veterinary Surgeons (RCVS) Specialist in Soft Tissue Surgery and was a British Equine Veterinary Association (BEVA) President in 1989. Since 1998, he has carried out consulting work for private referral practices and performs several hundred upper respiratory tract procedures each year.

Dr Andrew Higgins summarised his report on tongue- ties by stating that, "careful stewarding would be essential to ensure that the tongue-ties were removed promptly and not applied excessively tightly or for too long. Stewards would require training in the application of a tongue-tie and welfare aspects relating to its use and abuse. In the meantime, it should remain a Prohibited Practice."

A number of other issues were considered by the Sub-Committee including *Competition Intensity* which had been a concern to the FEI for many years, although any earlier action was limited by poor database facilities. The WSC produced a Discussion Document listing factors that may contribute to the intensity of competition. It recommended to the Veterinary Committee that it should define what is meant by this condition and examine the frequency of competition in the three disciplines (dressage, jumping and three day event) using a representative sample of horses, anonymous, but balanced for age and sex and level of competition. Horses were followed initially for 12 months, recording entries to establish frequency of competition, seasonality, effect of age or sex and any other relevant factors.

The WSC was highly concerned at the state of the *Endurance Discipline* where, in a number of countries and particularly in the Middle East, the rules and regulations were not always adhered to thereby exposing horses to a variety of abuses and an unacceptably high mortality rate. The WSC posed a number of queries to the Veterinary Committee, which included:

- Identifying any FEI events where a horse's metabolic state is being manipulated pharmacologically where the recovery rate was abnormally fast at the Vet Gate;
- To ascertain if eventual lameness was masked by medication;
- Clarify if riders were in communication with their horses on the subject of fatigue;

- Ascertain if prohibited substances were ever used to stimulate the horse for the Best Conditioned Prize (awarded to the horse in the best condition, normally on the day following the completion of the ride);
- Identify if effective medication control procedures were in place and properly enforced.

It was generally felt that the FEI Code of Conduct for the Welfare of the Horse was often being ignored.

Cloning was another concern which merited investigation. Cloning is defined as making a genetically identical copy of another cell or organism through non-sexual means. Cloning a horse means using the genetic material (DNA) from a donor horse to produce a genetically identical foal. There was likely to be profound ethical concern if large numbers of clones were produced in the hope of producing a champion of which many might well be destroyed early in life, as they simply do not perform phenotypically as anticipated from a cloned sibling. The WSC felt that cloning was not a major relevant issue under the FEI's jurisdiction at the time, but felt that a watching brief must be maintained on the practice.

The WSC recommended the need to research *Footing and Surface Design* to evaluate training (horses and riders will normally spend more time training/warming up in the practice arena than they will in the actual competition) and competition surface and in addition the consequences for improved welfare and orthopaedic health of horses that use them. This would be a multi-disciplinary project to examine the effect of equestrian arena surfaces on the orthopaedic health of the horse.

A number of issues needed to be addressed, such as:

- Identifying and evaluating the properties of commonly used surfaces (indoor and outdoor);
- Investigating the relationships between surfaces, orthopaedic injury and competition intensity;
- Analysing the biomechanical properties of surfaces and how these may induce injury;
- Identifying surface type and conditions that lead to inappropriate loading and thereby cause injury;
- To prepare practical guidelines on competition surface types and make recommendations for maintenance;
- Develop a method to evaluate track surface properties for use in the field.

This resulted in a major project funded jointly by FEI and World Horse Welfare with some additional support from the British Equestrian Federation and was led by Professor Lars Roepstorff of the Swedish University of Agricultural Sciences. This is an ongoing project although an initial report was issued by the FEI in 2014.

Hypersensitisation (irritants applied to horse's legs to make them more sensitive), *Cosmetic glossectomy* (surgical removal of all or part of the tongue), *Prohibited Practices, Cribbing Rings* (rings inserted around the incisor teeth of a horse in an attempt to stop it 'crib biting') were other issues considered by the

Welfare Sub-Committee with the relevant reports submitted to the Veterinary Committee.

It was a sad day when those of us involved learnt, in 2007, that the FEI had decided to disband all Sub-Committees and make the parent committee responsible for its work in the future. For what it is worth, I and several others did make our feelings known to the authorities at the time and, on my behalf, John McEwen, Chairman of the Veterinary Committee, presented my case. However, as chairman of a number of committees and sub-committees within the FEI, Andrew Higgins was invited to address the Bureau at its meeting in Interlaken in April 2008 and to review the work and achievements of the Sub-Committee and its predecessor, the FEI/World Horse Welfare Joint -Committee on Equine Welfare.

Referring to the imminent demise of the Welfare Sub-Committee, Andrew drew the Bureau's attention to the fact the WSC had served the FEI diligently, thoughtfully and appropriately, but will shortly cease to function with the removal of all FEI Sub-Committees. In accordance with its Terms of Reference, the WSC had reported to the Veterinary Committee, but its work and impact appeared to have been largely limited to that Committee.

He considered that the WSC should be replaced without delay with a similar group or panel of educated and knowledgeable individuals who can take a responsible, but internationally respected view on equine welfare issues. Independence of this group input would be vital and there needs to be 'buy in' to the work of any FEI Welfare Group by the entire Federation.

Andrew concluded his presentation by drawing attention to the amazing support and funding obtained from the World Horse Welfare, which should remain firmly bound to the FEI as the 'objective voice' in all discussions on horse welfare in the FEI disciplines in the future.

A HISTORY OF INTERNATIONAL HORSE WELFARE

My Friend the Horse

Photo Credit: UAE Equestrian and Racing Federation Media Department

Alex Atock

MY FRIEND THE HORSE

ALEX ATOCK

Autobiography and Memoir

A HISTORY OF INTERNATIONAL HORSE WELFARE

My **Friend** the **Horse**

Photo Credit: UAE Equestrian and Racing Federation Media Department

Alex Atock

PB £10.99   9781786937933
HB £14.99   9781786937940
EB £3.50   9781786937957

Alex Atock was born in Dublin in 1932 and graduated from the Veterinary College of Ireland in 1958. His love for all things equine commenced as a small child and continued throughout his life. This book will take the reader through his veterinary life, from his initial years in general practice, to veterinary officer of the Irish Turf Club, head of the Veterinary Department of the International Equestrian Federation (FEI), consultant to the UAE Equestrian and Racing Federation, and, finally, consultant to World Horse Welfare. The latter took him from the elite world of thoroughbred horse racing and international equestrian sport to assisting underprivileged working equines and their owners in developing countries.

Throughout his time with the FEI, Alex worked closely with the European Union and was actively involved with the conception of FEI relations with World Horse Welfare, the World Organisation for Animal Health (OIE), and the International Federation of Racing Authorities.

If you would like to review or order this book please visit www.austinmacauley.com and if you would like to book the author for an event please email: marketing@austinmacauley.com

---

Please send me ...... copy/ies of

MY FRIEND THE HORSE

Alex Atock

Please add the following postage per book:
United Kingdom £3.00 / Europe £7.50 /
Rest of World £12.00

Delivery and Payment Details

Format		Price	Qty	Total
Hardback ☐ Paperback ☐				
Subtotal				
Postage				
Total				

Full name: ....

Street Address ....

City:.. County:..

Postcode: .... Country: ....

Phone number (inc. area code): .... Email: ....

I enclose a cheque for £................... payable to Austin Macauley Publishers Limited

Please send to: Austin Macauley, CGC-33-01, 25 Canada Square, Canary Wharf, London E14 5LQ

Tel: +44 (0) 207 038 8212
Fax: +44 (0) 207 038 8100
orders@austinmacauley.com
www.austinmacauley.com

AUSTIN MACAULEY PUBLISHERS™
LONDON · CAMBRIDGE · NEW YORK · SHARJAH

Chapter 10

OLYMPIC RESEARCH
Heat and Humidity – Atlanta 1996 – Hong Kong 2008

Following the Olympic Games in Barcelona in 1992 the FEI turned its attention to Atlanta in four years' time and to the far more extreme adverse climatic conditions, which the horses were expected to face there. It was essential that the FEI would be in a position to fully brief all those involved as to how best to prepare their horses to cope with the high heat and humidity, which would be the norm in Atlanta at the time of the Games in July 1996.

There was much public criticism voiced at the state of some of the horses following the cross-country phase of the three day event at the World Equestrian Games (WEG) in Stockholm in 1990 and also after the Barcelona Olympic Games in 1992. The Three-Day Event and Veterinary Committees had been meeting to consider this and other issues concerning the welfare of horses and the stress of the endurance (cross-country) phase of this competition.

The Veterinary Committee had all the necessary resources to set in motion relevant research studies to tackle the issue. Although, at the time, we were unaware of the fact that Hong Kong would be awarded the 2008 Olympic Games and face similar problems, the research instigated for Atlanta was subsequently further embellished in preparation for Hong Kong.

I believe that the focus on these two Olympic Games, both facing similar problems with adverse climatic condition, highlighted not only the specific problems of heat and humidity, but also on the enormous amount of work, effort and detail put in by international veterinary and other experts, into protecting the health and welfare of the equine athletes at the highest level of competition. It is expected that less privileged horses will eventually benefit from this work by default.

In March 1994, the FEI Samsung International Sports Medicine Conference took place in Atlanta, Georgia. As indicated in the name, the conference was generously sponsored by the Samsung Group, which had been excellent supporters of the FEI since the time of the Seoul Olympic Games in 1988. There were 120 delegates in attendance in Atlanta and 31 papers were presented by recognised experts on topics relating to horses competing in three day eventing, particularly the endurance phase, and the other disciplines at the Olympic Games.

The conference was opened by H.R.H. The Princess Royal, President of the FEI and key representatives were present from the FEI, National Federations and other interested parties from the sport.

The objectives of the meeting were:

- To consider the current situation in equine sports medicine relating to thermoregulation and its control;
- To review the challenge for horses competing in hot and humid conditions;
- To provide a forum for scientific discussion so that clear guidelines for planning the Olympic equestrian events can be formulated;
- To resolve the issue of the tick borne disease, piroplasmosis, which was not currently found in continental USA;
- To publish a comprehensive report of the conference.

In his introduction to the Atlanta conference, Professor Leo Jeffcott, Foreign Veterinary Delegate for the Games and later to become Chairman of the FEI Veterinary Committee, informed the meeting that considerable concerns had been expressed in the media about horses being exposed to heat stress in competition.

Since the decision to nominate Atlanta as the venue for the 1996 Olympic Games, the concerns about horses competing in temperatures of 30–35 °C and relative humidity of 70–90% had dramatically increased. Of course, one would not chose to stage an Olympic Event under these conditions but, for the equestrian competitions to remain as part of the Olympic movement, there did not appear to be any alternative. It was therefore a difficult situation, which confronted the veterinary profession and those involved with exercise physiology. It was also an enormous challenge with very little time to undertake studies that would determine whether it would be safe for horses to compete under these very hot and humid conditions.

The FEI's contribution to the overall expense of the subsequent research was in the region of a mere US$500,000. Even the scientists who contributed to the Atlanta conference paid their own expenses. The publication *On to Atlanta '96* became the proceedings of this conference.

Abstracts from the 42 presentations from worldwide veterinary experts were provided to all 120 delegates from around the globe. Dr David Marlin, who presented at Atlanta, performed much high profile research investigating the response of the competition horse to prolonged air travel and subsequent performance in hot and humid conditions.

The research identified fluid and electrolyte losses via sweating (which can be monitored by daily weighing) as factors determining the period for flight recovery and acclimatisation. Equipment to assist rapid cooling for horses with heat accumulation was implemented. These included horses being housed in air-conditioned stabling.

Immediately after completing the cross-country phase in eventing, they were walked through misting fans, while at the same time undergoing aggressive cooling with iced water rapidly applied and reapplied by four attendants (one at each corner of the horse). As a result of this work, the games were completed without any horse being seriously compromised by heat overload.

Resulting from this research, a number of additional recommendations were made, one of which was that horses would need a significant amount of time to acclimatise following travel to the USA. European based horses traveling to the USA normally travel on temporary health certificates allowing them to remain for no more than 30 days.

However, due to the necessity to acclimatise in Atlanta the EU, following a request from the FEI, exceptionally extended the validity of the certification to 90 days, thereby facilitating these horses. The FEI recommended that horses should arrive in Georgia around three weeks before the start of competition and in the early morning to avoid the excessive heat. This advice was followed by most federations. The air-conditioned quarantine facilities had been brought up to date and no complaints were received during the Games.

An impressive clinic, equipped with the latest technology for diagnostic imaging and a fully equipped laboratory were available during the Games. All the competitions took place at the Horse Park, approximately one hour's driving time from downtown Atlanta.

On endurance day of the Three Day Event, an abundance of horse ambulances, horse trailers and a 'rapid response' team were continuously on stand-by. Effectively, every obstacle on the course was under visual control of a veterinarian, with a fully equipped medical van available.

The endurance phase had already been reduced by 20% to 30% and no further modifications were necessary during the competition. In contrast to what was reported by the press in several countries, no horses suffered significantly from the heat and humidity or were seriously injured during the competition. The cooling stations provided with misting fans, ice, water and well-trained crews functioned very well and some 61.5% of horses completed phase D (cross-country). From the group of horses, which did not complete the course, numerous combinations decided to withdraw because the possibility of a good result was no more feasible, rather than to veterinary related reasons.

The jumping competitions were characterised by fair and sporting course designs. The surface and footing conditions were most adequate and no major injuries to horses' legs occurred. Horses did not show problems due to the expected adverse weather conditions. The standard of competition in the dressage discipline was very high. The competitions were also characterised by the participation of representatives of 'lower level' horse countries – an example of the increasing worldwide acceptance and universality of the discipline.

Due to the expected adverse climatic conditions and the huge amount of information, which was distributed to national federations and riders in advance, preventive and therapeutic care for the horses reached an unprecedented level. All competitions were extremely successful from a veterinary point of view. This result confirmed the interpretation of the research data and provided a safe, but exciting competition with not a single horse being seriously compromised by dehydration.

Although not strictly 'research', the piroplasmosis issue raised its ugly head prior to Atlanta. On behalf of its member National Federations (NFs), FEI pressure had, for some years, been exerted on the National Veterinary Authorities of the USA to grant a waiver for horses testing sero-positive to piroplasmosis prior to these games.

Piroplasmosis is a tick-born disease primarily transmitted to equines by ticks, which are often found in deep undergrowth. Piroplasmosis was one of several diseases that all horses would be tested for prior to entering pre-export quarantine. Infected animals may remain carriers of these blood parasites for long periods and act as sources of infection for other ticks.

The introduction of carrier animals into areas where competent tick vectors are prevalent can lead to spread of the disease. Failure to obtain a waiver would have had serious repercussions on the participation of horses from a number of major NFs. Again, considerable interest and assistance had been obtained from the OIE and EU. The International Olympic Committee (IOC) was also stimulated into taking action to have the matter resolved. Eventually, it was agreed that, on arrival in post-import quarantine, all horses would be re-tested for piroplasmosis and any failing this re-test would then be immediately sent back to its country of origin without having the possibility to compete.

American Horse Council

> The role of the American Horse Council was:
> * To promote and protect the equine industry by representing its interests in Congress and in federal regulatory agencies on national issues of importance;
> * To unify the equine industry by informing industry members of regulations and pending legislation, and by serving as a forum for all member organisations and individuals;
> * To advise and inform government and the industry itself of the equine industry's important role in the United States economy.
>
> The American Horse Council's representative at the Atlanta Conference was Dr Amy Mann, who I had not met before, but with whom I had correspondence prior to the meeting. On one evening of the conference, there was a social event at a stud farm on the outskirts of Atlanta. Amy had a car and drove three other veterinarians, including myself, to the farm. She parked her car, along with many others, at the side of the long twisting avenue leading down to the venue. We all disembarked and walked down to the site through woodland from where we could see lights and hear the sound of music. We all had a good evening and duly returned to our hotel in Amy's car.
>
> A few days later, when I was back in Switzerland, we exchanged 'thank you' faxes. This was long after the day of carrier pigeons and before the internet was invented. In her fax Amy wrote, "…you will not believe it but on returning to the hotel after the party, I found a tick on my thigh which I must have picked up as we walked through the woods…" Anybody can read faxes and some in the FEI secretariat did. I subsequently took ribald comments as to what else we had got up to when walking in the woods.

In the event four horses actually did test positive to piroplasmosis, and these were immediately assigned to a special isolation facility, rather than being sent back to their country of origin as originally planned. An around the clock surveillance system ensured that these horses did not become a threat to any other competing horses. After the games, all horses returned to their home countries as scheduled and without further problems.

While all this discussion on piroplasmosis in the USA was ongoing, Dr Kevin Doyle, Australian Government Veterinary Service, kindly contacted me to say that although the disease was already endemic in Australia the government would be willing to grant waivers for any sero-positive visiting horses for the 2000 Olympic Games in Sydney – this was a great relief.

While the Sydney Olympic Games did not face such adverse climatic conditions, Athens, four years later, dealt with hot and dry conditions but not the humidity experienced in Atlanta and to be later experienced in Hong Kong.

Change of Eventing Format

The traditional endurance test in Three-Day Eventing, known as the 'classic format', included roads and tracks (Phase A and C), steeplechase (Phase B) and cross-country (Phase D). Subsequently at the 2004 Olympics in Athens, the 'short format' was introduced, removing phases A, B and C from the endurance day.

These changes were intended to reduce the amount of space needed to hold an Olympic-level competition, thereby helping to ensure that the sport was not ousted by the IOC from the Olympics. This new short format drew criticism from various members of the discipline, but is now considered to be the 'standard' competition format at all levels. In summary, the discipline of Three Day Eventing was substantially modified to become Eventing prior to the Athens Olympic Games.

Following the success of the Atlanta Olympic Games, it was decided to capitalise on the research results and to build on that experience and hold a further Workshop prior to Hong Kong, which would face similar conditions.

There were many difficulties encountered in attempting to create a Disease Free Zone for horses in China after Beijing originally won the Olympic bid. No international equestrian event had ever taken place in China before and hence no health protocols were then in place. Hence, the subsequent decision to stage the equestrian events in Hong Kong due to its long-established sound equine health status and to the expertise available from within the Hong Kong Jockey Club.

Following the Hong Kong Olympic Games and due to the above difficulties subsequent negotiations took place with China which enabled the country to host the Asian Games in Guangzhou in 2010 and the Global Champions Tour in Shanghai in 2012 and other major events in the country.

The introduction or spread of disease, especially the highly-contagious equine influenza (EI) virus, was of major concern in Hong Kong. A panel of international experts to advice on equine quarantine and biosecurity management was established.

The On to Hong Kong Pre Olympic Workshop on Heat and Humidity took place in Lausanne, Switzerland in February 2008. This meeting largely built on the excellent work undertaken 12–15 years earlier in the lead up to the 1996 Atlanta Olympic Games.

The goal of this Workshop was to share information and to help National Federations, veterinarians, riders, Chefs d'Equipe, owners, members of the press and others to understand the science and reasoning behind the rules and recommendations that would be in place to protect the equine athletes at the Olympic Games in 2008. The Workshop, which was sponsored by the FEI, World Horse

Welfare and Peden Bloodstock, provided a unique opportunity to listen to the collective wisdom and advice from the best veterinary team in this field in the world.

The day's programme was comprehensive and had been designed to blend relevant science with applied knowledge to benefit all stakeholders. The Chairman of the FEI's Veterinary Committee, John McEwen, set the scene. Then, Mr Lam Woon-kwong, chief executive officer of the Olympic Equestrian Company, outlined how Hong Kong had prepared itself for the equestrian events. Also from Hong Kong, Dr Keith Watkins, on behalf of a team of distinguished co-authors, spoke on quarantine and biosecurity management, and Dr Chris Riggs, Head of Veterinary Clinical Services for the Hong Kong Jockey Club, and Beijing Organising Committee BOCOG's Veterinary Services Manager, explained the local arrangements for veterinary care and attention at the Games. Martin H. Atock, Managing Director, Peden Bloodstock, outlined the logistics of transporting the equine athletes to Hong Kong.

In August 2007, the Test Event, named the Good Luck Beijing – Hong Kong SAR 10th Anniversary Cup had been held and this enabled a number of the procedures and facilities to be tested. Dr David Marlin, who (with many others) did considerable work to help understand the impact and control of heat and humidity on equine athletic performance before the 1996 Atlanta Olympics, advised on air-conditioned facilities and cooling stations at the Games. Professor Leo Jeffcott, Foreign Veterinary Delegate to the 2008 Games and for the past eight years Chairman of the FEI Veterinary Committee, reported on an extensive, highly relevant and important two-year study undertaken with Mr Wing-Mo Leung, Senior Scientific Officer, Hong Kong Observatory, to understand the likely weather conditions in August and September 2008. Dr Catherine Kohn, President of the Veterinary Commission of the 1996 Olympic Games in Atlanta, and intimately involved with horse sports throughout most of her working life, presented the results of the horse monitoring work undertaken in August 2007 and explained their significance.

The second part of the programme comprised a Panel Discussion with all speakers, which allowed an opportunity for the delegates to ask questions of concern about the health and welfare of the horses due to compete in Hong Kong.

When the proposal for the meeting was first discussed by the Welfare Sub-Committee, Andrew Higgins commented that the FEI must be proactive in providing the necessary information to ensure that National Federations were fully informed to enable them to prepare their horses optimally for the challenging climatic conditions that they will face in Hong Kong.

The Workshop enabled the leading scientists and veterinarians in the field to share all available information with stakeholders. This was therefore an important and timely meeting. Andrew was particularly pleased that the FEI decided that this Workshop should be run under the auspices of the Welfare Sub-Committee. Welfare can be an emotive subject and it is essential that the FEI is perceived to be a responsible body that does not shirk its responsibilities when it comes to ensuring that every effort is made to protect the health and welfare of horses competing under its rules and regulations.

Peden Bloodstock had arranged Pre-Export Quarantine (PEQ) at Aachen showgrounds in Germany for all horses based in Central Europe. Horses from many other competing countries based themselves in Central Europe for the months prior to travelling to Hong Kong as this enabled them to be treated as EU horses, having undergone PEG in Aachen. I was employed by Peden Bloodstock to check that all the documentation (passports, laboratory test reports etc.) for each horse were present, correct and in order. The facilities and procedures in the quarantine were conducted throughout under the watchful and kindly eye of two Chinese colleagues and by Dr Barry Bousfield, a veterinarian from South Africa who was a part-time lecturer at City University of Hong Kong and part-time senior veterinarian at Hong Kong Agriculture, Fisheries and Conservation Department (AFCD). I was kept very much on my toes by these eminent veterinarians although we developed an excellent working relationship during our time spent together in Aachen.

Dr Hormeyer, the German State Veterinarian, who visited the quarantine facility regularly, had the final say to authorise all these horses to leave the quarantine premises and proceed directly to Amsterdam Airport to embark for Hong Kong. Other quarantine facilities were used to accommodate horses travelling from London Stansted, New York, Los Angeles and Sydney. All horses were in their stables at Sha Tin within 1 hour 50 minutes of arrival in Hong Kong, which was an impressive achievement.

Business Class Passengers

Combi aircraft, which carry both passengers and cargo, normally deliver their passengers directly to the Arrivals area at an airport and then transfer their cargo to the Freight Terminal. In view of the excessive heat and humidity, expected on arrival on the tarmac in Hong Kong, Peden Bloodstock negotiated with the authorities that the aircraft would proceed directly on arrival to the Freight Terminal, to enable the horses to off-load and then proceed by horse lorry to their final destination with minimum delay. This left the (human) passengers to be bussed to the Passenger Terminal. History does not relate the reaction of the business and other passengers when this information was relayed to them following touch down after their long haul flight. Most importantly, the horses' welfare was not compromised.

For the most intensive, short format eventing, the cross country phase was overseen by a core team of 11 international veterinary surgeons, which were augmented by others from mainland China and from the Hong Kong Jockey Club (HKJC) Department of Veterinary Clinical Services.

These were supported by a group of eight senior students/graduates in the Olympic Veterinary Clinic with technical back up from HKJC staff. In addition, a six-strong group of farriers provided extra support to team farriers. The purpose-built Olympic Veterinary Clinic constructed at the core venue in Sha Tin was equipped with a range of diagnostic and treatment facilities including two examination rooms, two holding stables, a wash/cooling bay, a breezeway, dispensary and main office/reception area. Emergency services were available 24 hours daily. Cooling facilities, which were available during training and competition included misting tents capable of holding several horses simultaneously, which were chilled by rows of misting fans. Chilled water and ice were available in each tent and all stables were air-conditioned with the temperature set at the optimum (around 23 °C) to assist recovery after exercise.

In most horses, acclimatisation was complete some 10–14 days post arrival. The Test Event in Hong Kong in the previous year, run on the same dates as the actual Games, had provided a great deal of valuable information about air quality and dust control with air-quality in the indoor and outdoor arenas remaining extremely good, even by human standards.

In conclusion, approximately 300 horses from more than 40 nations accompanied by 140 attendants and 96,000 kg of equipment travelled to Hong Kong on an estimated 56 flights. There were no significant injuries to horses or riders throughout the Games.

The Atlanta and Hong Kong research projects and the information obtained from them were vital to the success of both these Olympic Games and to future major events facing similar adverse weather conditions. It was gratifying that as a result of all this work there were no significant injuries to horse or rider other than the normal cuts and bruises which are to be expected by any sporting athletes.

The vast majority of the research individuals and institutions involved in the Atlanta project, brought together by Professor Leo Jeffcott (at the time a member and later Chairman of the FEI Veterinary Committee) and Dr Andrew Clarke, (Equine Research Centre, Canada) who had no direct connection with the FEI but generously gave willingly of their time and expertise. For the Hong Kong research project, it was Dr Andrew Higgins and his Welfare Sub-Committee, who initiated the programme.

In summary, these were two major and significant research projects, which established a blueprint for dealing with high heat and humidity facing the organisers, the relevant veterinarians, the competitors and their competition horses, wherever they may be asked to compete in the world in the future.

Chapter 11

BACK TO THE OFFICE

Change of Guard at HQ – Dinner at the Palace – Secretariat Move –
Australian Tour – World Horse Welfare Petition – Retirement from FEI

While we have been busy dealing with drugs, their control under the MCP, the international movement of horses, tackling welfare and heat and humidity there had been changes back in the secretariat in Bern and subsequently in Lausanne. So, what had been going on?

To start with, the General Assembly in London in 1986 was the last at which H.R.H. The Prince Philip, Duke of Edinburgh, presided. After 22 years in office, his daughter, H.R.H. The Princess Anne, was elected to the presidency unopposed. On the final evening of the meeting, Prince Philip left the assembly by horse drawn carriage having invited all the delegates to a reception and banquet at Buckingham Palace that night. This was a magnificent evening and thoroughly enjoyed by all.

H.R.H. The Princess Anne announced at the General Assembly in Paris in 1987, the first at which she was at the helm, that the time scale for General Assemblies in the future would be altered. There would be no assembly in 1988, and the next one would be in Budapest in March 1989 rather than in December of the previous year, as heretofore and this would be the cycle for the future.

Over the years, the relationship between the FEI, the World Organisation for Animal Health (OIE) and the International Conference of Racing Authorities (ICRA) continued to develop. Dr Louis Blajan, Director General of the OIE addressed the FEI General Assembly in Paris in December 1987, and the following May, H.R.H. The Princess Anne, President of the FEI, reciprocated by addressing the general session of OIE.

Her Royal Highness Princess Anne visits the Secretariat to meet the staff following her appointment as President of the FEI. Secretary general, Fritz Widmer, is shown fourth from right and looking to the right.

Prior to this, in August 1987, I had been invited to address the bi-annual conference of the World Equine Veterinary Association (WEVA) in Montreal, Canada, on the *International Movement of Horses*. The following month, I was back across the Atlantic for the Bureau meeting in Rio de Janeiro and was able to go straight from that meeting to Caracas in Venezuela where we ran a Veterinary Course focused specifically on Central and South American countries. Later that month, we ran a further Veterinary Course in Hong Kong aimed at those from predominantly Asian countries. As always, these courses were directed at those, not necessarily at the forefront of international equestrian sport, but to make them aware or how these events operate and what is expected of the officiating veterinarians.

Many people will tell you that travel sounds exciting, and it is, but going from one meeting to another, with little time to overcome jet lag or to do anything other than go from airport to hotel, to meeting and back to the airport, has its limitations. These were increasingly busy times and rather than go into detail about the various meetings with which I was involved over the years, I have listed those reoccurring on a regular basis in Annex 1. You will note that from 1996 onwards, when I was consultant successively to the UAE Equestrian and Racing Federation and then to World Horse Welfare, I continued to attend many more FEI General Assemblies as part of the delegation representing these two organisations.

In April 1988, I attended the Seventh International Conference of Racing Analysts and Veterinarians in Louisville, Kentucky. Two of the most important decisions, emerging from this conference were the need to closely monitor the introduction of new drugs, which could be used in illegal medication and secondly to encourage investigation into the actions and concentrations of endogenous and normal nutritional substances (such as the steroid hormone, cortisol, which can either be naturally produced by the body or administered) the presence of which could be regarded as natural to the horse and not evidence of illegal medication.

The FEI Secretary General, Fritz Widmer announced his decision to retire at the end of 1988. Dr Franz Pranter (Austria), later to become Treasurer of the FEI, generously stepped in to fill the gap until a new secretary general could be appointed. In the meantime, Brigadier Rene Ziegler, a Swiss army general, was appointed director. We viewed this latter appointment with some trepidation. The thought of an army general in charge was not our idea of ecstasy. In fact, the appointment turned out to be very much welcomed and Rene Ziegler exuded an aura of peace and calm in the office – not seen before in the FEI. He was a very welcome addition to the team, was well liked by all, and acted rather as a father figure.

To be fair, during my first few months with the FEI, Mr Widmer and his wife had been very kind and welcoming to Sherley and me. They often invited us to dinner either at a restaurant or in their home. I was always aware that there was some friction in the office, but it was not until our 'honeymoon period', as described by others, was over that I started to feel the full blast of his wrath. I believe that he was so dedicated to the FEI that absolutely nothing, but the very best would please. This was, of course, highly commendable and we all tried to do our best, but for many it became intolerable and it was his dictatorial manner and his use of the 'stick rather than the carrot' (equivalent to beating a donkey rather than encouraging it) that made life so difficult. As a result, there was continuous rotation of staff, which was unsettling for all.

At Mr Widmer's retirement lunch, I had the dubious task of proposing his health and wishing him well. This was a balancing act between genuinely wishing him well for the future, while still letting him know how difficult it had been to work for him. At the same time, I conveyed to him that we appreciated that he was striving to do his utmost for the good of the FEI and its membership. He took it all in good faith, thanked us for our support and appeared to recognise the difficulties we had experienced.

In 1989, Etienne Allard, a Belgian national, was appointed secretary general to succeed Franz Pranter. Mr Allard was totally different to his predecessor with a much more relaxed style of management. While his appointment was generally welcomed, his lack of equestrian background and knowledge did, at times, create its own difficulties.

In the following year, 1990, the OIE Regional Commission for Europe met in Sofia in Bulgaria in October. The subject of official government approval of Horse Passports was on the agenda. The Director of the Bulgarian Government Veterinary Service was Dr Belev. I had always liked Dr Belev. He was a large imposing gentle giant of a veterinarian. Having shaken his hand, it normally took some time before the blood supply in the relevant appendix returned to normal.

One day in May, I received a phone call from the Bulgarian Embassy in Bern saying that "Dr Belev would like to call on you".

I said that he would be most welcome and when would he like to come – thinking maybe next week, next month…? "In 20 minutes," came the reply. Duly, a short time later, a knock on the door of my office heralded the arrival of Dr Belev and several of his colleagues. After pleasantries and the refusal of a seat or a cup of coffee, he came straight to the point, "We would like your President, H.R.H. The Princess Anne, to attend our conference in Sofia – can you arrange it?"

Normally, such requests to Buckingham Palace need to be submitted a year or more in advance of the event. In this case we had less than 5 months. I told him that I would do what I could and he and his team departed.

I went straight to the Secretary General who took the request on board, registered it through the appropriate channels and very shortly afterwards we had a positive answer. There is no doubt that the Princess's presence in Sofia played a significant role in having horse passports officially accepted by the OIE and the veterinary services of its member countries.

The following month, we held a Veterinary Course in Varna, a lovely Black Sea Resort in Bulgaria. This was shortly after the uprising against the President in Romania and one of the veterinarians who came to Varna was from Romania. Dr Lucian Blaga had arrived a day late and it transpired that he had spent the previous night sleeping on a bench in the railway station not knowing where the meeting would take place. He turned up at our meeting the following morning bearing a large cardboard box containing a beautiful Romanian glass bowl as a present for me. This was extremely thoughtful of him as he had been through enormous trauma in Bucharest in the previous few weeks, having to sleep in a metal bath in his apartment, which protected him from incoming bullets and other missiles.

In June 1991, I attended an Executive Board meeting, which took place in the dining room of the President's apartment in Buckingham Palace.

On one occasion during the meeting, a query arose and I had to call the FEI secretariat in Bern for the answer. The princess told me to go into her sitting room next door and use her phone.

I picked up the receiver and the telephonist immediately answered with, "Good morning, Your Royal Highness, what number can I get you?" With great credit to her, she never flinched when a strange man with a Dublin accent, calling from the Princess's sitting room, asked her to put through a call to the FEI telephone number in Switzerland.

Pam Walker, secretary general of the Australian Equestrian Federation (AEF), was well liked and a good friend to all the FEI staff when we met at various general assemblies around the world on a regular basis. .

In Australia, each state has its own equestrian federation under the overall umbrella of the AEF. While chatting to Pam one day, she said that Australia, being so far away, felt isolated from the HQ of equestrian sport in Switzerland although many of the Australian international horses and riders were based in Europe, as indeed were horses and riders from their New Zealand neighbours.

She asked if I would come to Australia to meet and talk to their member federations. I was delighted with the invitation, obtained the necessary permission, and a couple of weeks after the Executive Board meeting in London was on my way to Perth, Western Australia.

I was met at the airport by a young Australian veterinarian, Warwick Vale, who chauffeured me around and generally made me feel welcome. The following evening I gave a talk to a group of some 20–30 veterinarians and others involved in the sport in their region, explaining what the FEI was, how it operated and then went into some detail of the veterinary input expected from those planning and officiating at events.

All the time, during such meetings, I continued to stress the essential need to protect the health and welfare of the horses participating, and to have firm plans in place to care for those injured during competition. This, of course, included emergency plans to evacuate those horses in need of specialist care, including surgery, to an appropriate equine hospital facility. I stayed for two or three days in Perth during which, I was shown around the state's equestrian facilities. I then proceeded with the same basic itinerary to Adelaide, Melbourne, Sydney, Canberra, Brisbane and then across to Wellington and Auckland in New Zealand.

Pam Walker met me on arrival in Adelaide, where she lived and where the AEF had its headquarters, and travelled with me to the other states as far as Brisbane, where we met with her charming parents. I believe that the trip was a success and I certainly met (and re-met) with many interesting and knowledgeable equestrians in the southern hemisphere at all points of call.

Just before Christmas 1991, the FEI secretariat moved from Bern to Lausanne. At this time, many international sports federations were encouraged to establish their HQ's in Lausanne, where the International Olympic Committee (IOC) had its base. While Swiss-German speaking Bern was a very beautiful city, French speaking Lausanne had a more relaxed ambiance. Having spent my early life close to the sea in Ireland, it was good to be back close to the water of the stunning Lake of Geneva.

Water is a great calmer. As you will already have noticed, several significant FEI workshops and conferences took place in the Olympic Museum, which was within walking distance of our new office and next door to the headquarters of the Court of Arbitration for Sport (CAS), with which everybody with an interest in sport will be familiar.

The following year, 1992, the FEI President visited the secretariat and later attended a reception at the Villa Mon-Repos, the previous residence of the Baron Pierre de Coubertin, the first President of the International Olympic Committee (IOC). In 1993, the International Olympic Committee proclaimed Lausanne as the Olympic Capital of the World.

At about the same time, the FEI, with the support of the International Conference of Racing Authorities (ICRA), called for a ban on the trade of live horses for slaughter. This is a matter for which World Horse Welfare, which funded the Transport Stress Research Project and which was the unofficial welfare arm of the FEI, had been fighting for long and hard and for which it raised a petition of an incredible 3,000,000 signatures, which was presented to the European Parliament, seeking improved conditions for horses destined for slaughter. We will go into more detail on this whole contentious issue in a future chapter.

Later, in December 1992, our son Martin married Inez van Tienhoven, in Hamburg. In addition to the many guests, some family members from Ireland also attended. On the day after the wedding, we bade farewell to them, as we were under the impression that they were leaving to travel home. Not so, as we were to later discover.

Two days after the wedding was my 60th birthday and generously Inez's parents, Joop and Chrystal, invited us to dine with them. They duly collected us from our hotel and we drove down to Hamburg Harbour. It was a miserably wet night, but

Joop insisted that we get out of the car and walk down a pier. As we did so, we could hear, in the distance, the sound of a bagpipe and it was playing the lovely tune *When Irish eyes are smiling*. We all looked surprised and Joop suggested that we should investigate. We continued down the pier coming closer to the music and then started climbing up the gangplank of an old sailing ship, the Rickmer Rickmers. As we reached the top, all our family and friends, who had attended the wedding and whom we thought had gone home the previous day, cheered.

Some 20 of us proceeded to have the most wonderful reception and dinner in the boardroom of this magnificent ship, all kindly organised by Joop and Chrystal. There were various impromptu speeches during which Peter Cronau, Chairman of the FEI Veterinary Committee, read a fax from H.R.H. The Princess Royal, President of the FEI, wishing me well on my birthday. When writing to thank her, I was pleased to be able to wish her well for her forthcoming marriage to Commander Timothy Laurence, just a few days later.

During 1993, I let it be known that, although only 63, I would like to take early retirement. I enjoyed my work but felt that all the pressures that kept building up were engulfing me and preventing me from giving of my best and doing full justice to the many responsibilities under my control. I felt the position really required a younger man with more energy and drive. My request was taken on board and the Secretary General appointed my old friends and colleagues, Leo Jeffcott, Andrew Higgins and Marty Simensen, an FEI Veterinary Committee member from the USA, who became known as the 'Visitors', to assess my position and responsibilities and to make proposals to find a successor. Leo and Andrew made a three-day investigative visit to the secretariat in September, discussed how my department fitted into the whole FEI operation and considered the issues with other department heads and reported back to Marty. They also kept Peter Cronau, in his capacity as chairman of the FEI Veterinary Committee, in the loop.

The Visitors, in their subsequent report on the future of the Veterinary Department, listed the current duties of the department as:

- Organisation of veterinary coverage for Events;
- Management of the Medication Control Programme;
- Supervision, liaison and follow up on health regulations, quarantine matters and outbreaks of disease;
- Administration of the horse registration system and revision of the FEI passport design and health certification;
- Compilation and updating of the Veterinary Regulations, in association with the Veterinary Committee and Medication Subcommittee (MSC);
- Organisation of all Veterinary Committee and MSC meetings, veterinary courses and seminars and MCP debriefing sessions;
- Liaison with the Legal Department particularly in connection with the MCP, MSC and horse registration matters;
- Veterinary aspects of general FEI work associated with Bureau meetings and General Assembly;
- Produce relevant articles for insertion in FEI monthly Bulletins, Annual Report and Directory;

- Other consultative activities with outside organisations (e.g., OIE, ICRA, EU, international veterinary associations etc.,)
- To maintain a high FEI profile
- To act as a point of contact for Contact and Event Veterinarians in member federations.

Until I saw all this in writing, I had not fully realised the full extent of my responsibilities – was it any wonder that I found it all too much? Among the Visitors' recommendations, following their meetings in Lausanne, were that the position of Head of the Veterinary Department should be replaced by an official veterinary officer (OVO), to be assisted by a part time veterinary liaison officer (VLO) as and from 1st April 1994— in fact this did not take effect until one year later.

It was suggested that I could fill this latter support role, which I was pleased to accept. The position of OVO was advertised. Following an interview procedure, Dr Frits Sluyter (Netherlands) was appointed. We developed a good relationship and worked together for a couple of months until finally, on 1st June 1995, I stepped down to become the VLO, keeping in touch with the office and visiting for two or three days each month.

In November 1993, the 3rd Congress of the World Equine Veterinary Association (WEVA) was held in conjunction with the Congress of Medicine and Equine Surgery in Geneva, Switzerland. The first two days of the five-day congress were devoted to WEVA. This immediately preceded an FEI Veterinary Seminar, also in Geneva. This high profile event, chaired by Dr Peter Cronau, Chairman of the FEI Veterinary Committee was attended by 32 veterinarians from 20 different countries, who heard presentations from Paul Weier, FEI Honorary Steward General, Dr Thierry Chillaud (OIE), Dr Bernard Van Goethem (EU), Dr David Baker (World Horse Welfare, Europe) and others.

The ties between the International Olympic Committee (IOC) and the FEI were further strengthened by the presence of IOC President, Juan Antonio Samaranch, at the FEI General Assembly in Rome in 1995.

This was my last assembly as Head of the Veterinary Department. Etienne Allard, FEI Secretary General, resigned following the assembly and was succeeded by Dr Bo Helander.

Bo was well known in equestrian circles and liked by us all in the secretariat, both as a former President of the Swedish Equestrian Federation, but also as Head of the FEI Legal Department, having succeeded Robert Hoffstetter in this role some years earlier. Dr Helander was successful in jumping and was still active in racing, training and breeding, including owning a stud farm in Co. Wicklow in Ireland. He was also an FEI Course Designer and an International Official Judge.

The General Assembly at its meeting in Tampa, Florida, in March 1994 had elected H.R.H. The Infanta Doña Pilar de Borbòn as President of the FEI to succeed the Princess Royal, as by then, the latter had completed her maximum eight-year term in office.

We can get a true indication of the Princess Royal's love and respect for horses from the Forword to her last Annual Report, in 1993, in which she wrote: *We enjoy our sport because of the horse. We are extremely fortunate that this animal is not only prepared to put up with our substitutes of their working life, but makes every appearance of enjoying the challenge almost as much as we do. We must not abuse their trust and enthusiasm. We have a responsibility to them and for them and the environment in which they live and work. They can choose not to co-operate, but they have no choice about where they live, how they are looked after or what medications they are given. At the risk of being obvious – without the healthy, happy horse, we have no sport.*

The Infanta Doña Pilar de Borbòn was the daughter of Their Royal Highnesses the Count and Countess of Barcelona and sister of King Juan Carlos I of Spain. She had resided in Italy, Switzerland and Portugal. In Portugal, she obtained her nursing diploma and practised her profession for three years in various hospitals.

Not long after her election, the President visited Lausanne to view the secretariat and to meet the staff. We then adjourned to the Olympic Museum for lunch. Being the most senior staff member, in age, I was seated next to the new President.

During lunch, the conversation flowed to others, initially, across the table and in French. My heart sank as my knowledge of French, or any other language, was decidedly limited. After a while, she turned to me and, in perfect English, said, "Well, Alex, I understand that your French is a little rusty, so let's talk in English."

That gesture was much appreciated and she went on to chat about herself. She told me that she had trained as a nurse, as had my wife, and went on to ask me about my family. It was a very pleasant and friendly conversation.

I was still in post at the time of the 1995 Veterinary Committee meeting, which took place in Cambridge. Both Frits and I attended. This was hosted by Leo Jeffcott, although Peter Cronau was chairman at the time.

On the final evening, we had dinner in a private room in one of the historic colleges in Cambridge University. Towards the end of the meal, Andrew Higgins turned to me and said, "What are you going to do next? This Veterinary Liaison Officer job will be fine in the short term, but you will need a bigger challenge? How would you fancy a stint in Dubai?"

At the time Andrew, Roland Devolz and Michael Lambert, all members of the FEI Medication Subcommittee, were advising the Dubai Royal family and Andrew knew that an opening would soon occur as an advisor to the chief veterinary officer of their Ministry of Agriculture. This would be to replace Dr Neil Farr, a retired British Ministry of Agriculture veterinarian, who I vaguely knew and who would be leaving at the end of the year. My immediate reaction was that I had never been employed in any governmental role and would not have the required qualification. We left it at that.

I continued to commute to Lausanne monthly as arranged and kept in regular contact with Frits in the interim. A few weeks later, in early June, Andrew called me on a Thursday evening and asked me if I could be in Epsom, where the English Derby would be run, on the following Saturday.

I flew to London on the Friday night, met Andrew and Roland Devolz the next morning and we drove to Epsom. On the way they explained to me that the United Arab Emirates Equestrian and Racing Federation were looking for a veterinary advisor and that this would suit me better than the Dubai job.

It was anticipated that we would meet some of the Royal family at Epsom where Sheikh Mohammed bin Rashid Al Maktoum, Vice President and Prime Minister of the United Arab Emirates, had a runner in the Derby. His horse, Lammtara not only won the Epsom Derby in record time, but also went on to win the King George VI and Queen Elizabeth Stakes at Royal Ascot and the Prix de l'Arc de Triomphe in Paris later in the year.

We did not meet any of the members of the Royal family but we did meet several of his advisors, including significantly, Dr A. H. Billah, Veterinary Consultant to Sheikh Mohammed. He became a great support subsequently during my time in the UAE. At the time, Sheikh Mohammed's world-renowned Godolphin racing operation was still in its infancy. I subsequently met Faisal Siddiq M. Samea Al Mutawa, Secretary General of the UAE Equestrian and Racing Federation, at the Prix de l'Arc de Triomphe racemeeting in Longchamps, Paris in October.

By coincidence, the FEI Bureau meeting was due to take place in Abu Dhabi early in November and I was scheduled to attend this anyway as part of the FEI delegation. Effectively I went to Abu Dhabi as FEI Veterinary Liaison Officer and left the meeting as Official Veterinary Officer and Consultant to the United Arab Emirates Equestrian and Racing Federation. An amicable severance of my relationship with the FEI was agreed with Bo Helander and Conor Crowley, FEI treasurer, in Abu Dhabi although, thanks to Andrew Higgins, I continued for several more years to act as secretary to various FEI/ILPH welfare committees. This was to be the end of a privileged and highly exciting era for me although I really looked forward to the new challenge of living and working in the Middle East.

I would like to pay tribute here to my successors, Frits Sluyter (1995–2008), Graeme Cooke (2009–2015) and Göran Akerström (2015–present), who undoubtedly drove forward many of the issues with which I had been initially involved in addition to initiating their own.

Chapter 12

UNITED ARAB EMIRATES EQUESTRIAN AND RACING FEDERATION

Official Veterinary Officer UAE Equestrian and Racing Federation – Endurance in the Middle East – International Movement of Horses in the Region

I commenced my new role as official veterinary officer and Consultant to the United Arab Emirates Equestrian and Racing Federation, based in Abu Dhabi, in December 1995.

On my way to Australia in 1991, the plane had refuelled in Abu Dhabi, which, at that time, was just a few lights in the middle of a vast desert, but clearly much had happened since, as I was soon to discover. On the drive into the modern city following arrival, I was fascinated to discover areas of manicured green grass interspersed with floral beds – it was not all sand and it was quite beautiful.

When shown into my new office, I found an envelope addressed to me on my desk. This was a most welcoming letter from the resident federation veterinarian, Dr B.L. Surendra Babu, known to all as Dr Bobby. He became a great friend and colleague from the very beginning and guided me through all I needed to know in the federation and out in the field (or, rather, the desert).

I found some of it a little confusing as, regardless of the name of the federation – UAE Equestrian and Racing Federation – it was the Emirates Racing Authority (ERA) in Dubai, which was the internationally recognised governing body for the United Arab Emirates horse racing industry.

The ERA, of course, had absolutely nothing to do with the discipline of endurance riding, which came under the umbrella of the federation regardless of in which emirate the event actually took place. Often rides would be sprung on us with little notice in which to prepare. This effected the smaller owner, whose horses would sometimes not be adequately fit. Racehorses were trained over weeks/months in preparation for racing, with the calendar of race meetings announced well in advance, so why were endurance horses not trained in a similar way with an equivalent calendar of rides published?

The President of the Abu Dhabi based, UAE Equestrian and Racing Federation, was His Excellency Dr. Sheikh Sultan bin Khalifa bin Zayed Al Nahyan and the secretary general was Faisal Seddiq Al Mutawa. Faisal and I quickly moved on to first name terms and we had a good relationship, with very limited exceptions, throughout my tenure in the UAE.

Among others I met in the first few days in the federation offices were Fritz Burkhardt (ERA Steward), Neil Abrahams (Arabian Racing Handicapper), Vijay Murthy (one of the Thoroughbred Racing Handicappers and sometime judge at the racetrack) and quite a few others.

Fritz Burkhardt and AA share a joke at an endurance ride.

I quickly learnt that I would have two main functions to fulfil. One was to work as official veterinary officer of the ERA along with Dr Neil Farr and the other was to assist with organising and officiating with the management and veterinary coverage of endurance events throughout the UAE. Endurance was a highly popular and rapidly growing sport with a long tradition throughout the Emirates, the entire Middle East and other parts of the world.

Before discussing the Endurance Rides/Races, let us first review the FEI website, which describes endurance as a *long-distance competition, against the clock, testing the speed and endurance of a horse and challenging the rider over their effective use of pace, thorough knowledge of their horse's capabilities and ability to cross all kinds of terrain.* Although the rides are timed, the emphasis is on finishing in good condition rather than necessarily coming in first.

Each rider is responsible to safely manage the stamina and fitness of their horse and each course is divided into phases – in principle at least every 40km – with a compulsory halt for a veterinary inspection, or 'vet gate', after each segment. Each horse must be presented for inspection by a veterinarian within a set time of reaching each 'vet gate'. The veterinarian determines whether the horse is fit to continue in the ride, remain longer in the vet gate to further recover or be eliminated.

The horse that finishes first is adjudged the winner, provided it is subsequently considered fit to continue by the examining veterinarians. If this is not the case, the next finisher, which meets the necessary criteria, will be judged the winner. There is normally a Best Conditioned Horse Award on the day following the competition for the first 10 horses to complete and again this is judged on the basis that they are 'fit to continue'.

The classical endurance riding championship distance is 100 miles (160 km) in one day although other rides may be considerably shorter. Up to 80 km are often loosely referred to as Marathons or Races. Because the relatively short races are run at a much faster pace, they are therefore more prone to cause distress and injury to horses. Naturally the rider's aim is to get through each vet gate as quickly as possible, which the more experienced will normally achieve by pacing the speed between one gate and the next, thereby ensuring that the horse is not overstressed and can meet the necessary physiological criteria when presented to the veterinarian in the gate.

As has been mentioned elsewhere, and to its credit, endurance is the only FEI discipline that never permitted the use of any prohibited substance, including the non-steroidal anti-inflammatory drug, phenylbutazone, (which was, of course, historically permitted in other disciplines in the past) at time of competition.

The racing duties in the UAE were very much the same as those undertaken when working for the Turf Club in Ireland. Admittedly, the racetracks and their facilities were a little more salubrious than in the Emerald Isle and consisted of, during my tenure, Nad Al Sheba in Dubai, although this was later replaced by the new track, Meydan, Jebel Ali also in Dubai, and Abu Dhabi close to the city of the same name. There was also occasional racing in Al Asayl, Ghantoot and Sharjah. Some 50 race meetings took place during the season with normally two per week in Nad Al Sheba, Sundays in Abu Dhabi and Fridays in Jebil Ali. I was expected to attend all of these.

Racing took place from November through March, when it featured the Dubai World Cup, which, in March 1996, was worth £2,580,645 (approximately US$2 million) to the American owner of Cigar, the inaugural winner. Subsequently the Dubai Racing Carnival over several months in the spring was introduced, which culminated with the World Cup. 20 years later, in 2016, the World Cup carried a prize fund of US$30 million in addition to other high value races. Horses from the European Union in addition to other countries, including Hong Kong, Japan, USA and South Africa competed with UAE trained horses for the valuable races. Jockeys from all parts of the world rode there during the winter months and foreign trainers often sent their horses to race in this warmer climate.

You will recall the meeting in Cyprus in 1992, when I was still with the FEI, which considered how we could facilitate the international movement of horses in the Middle East and Arabian Peninsula. Following that meeting, Alf Fussel (EU) and his team had quickly undertaken a number of inspection visits to countries in the region, which had been represented in Cyprus. This was to assess and advise them on actions to take to fulfil requirements to open up the region to horses from other countries, based on a sound and acceptable health status. Prior to this and on the initiative of Neil Farr, in Dubai and Australian veterinarian, Patricia Ellis, my predecessor in Abu Dhabi, they had already surveyed the health status of equines in the UAE with satisfactory results.

As the UAE was organising equestrian sport (racing and endurance) at an increasingly high level, it was vital that no risks were taken in allowing horses from other countries to enter the Emirates to compete with any suggestion of health problems, which could be passed on to the resident population. The chief veterinary officer (CVO) of the UAE Ministry for Agriculture was Dr Ali Abdullah Arab, who was later to be advised by Dr Tom Morton, after Neil Farr retired, and they were responsible to ensure that all animal imports met these high standards.

It was decided in 1996 that the UAE should establish a *Higher Technical Committee for the Import and Export of Horses (HTC)* to confirm that the countries in the region met the standards expected, as already pertained in the Emirates, and to monitor the ongoing situation. The committee comprised Dr Ali Arab, Faisal Siddiq, secretary general of the Federation, Dr A. H. Billah, Veterinary Consultant to Sheikh Mohammed, Dr Tom Morton and I, as veterinary officer to the Federation.

Following initial preparatory meetings, Dr Ali, Tom and I commenced our own fact-finding missions over the succeeding nine months. We went to Amman (JOR), Damascus (SYR), Cairo (EGY), Beirut (LEB) and Casablanca (MAR) where we met with the relevant authorities and discussed the situation in their country. This was all with a view to developing health conditions, which would be acceptable to the UAE. Not all of those countries visited met the high standards required.

However, with certain modifications to procedures and additional compulsory testing in their own country and confirmed when re-tested in quarantine following arrival in the UAE, conditions were created, which enabled movement of competition horses between many of these countries. In some cases, the conditions also became acceptable to permit entry into European Union member states. The Cyprus meeting had undoubtedly motivated a reaction, which resulted in more free movement of horses for competition purposes throughout the Middle East and Arabian Peninsula.

The concept of the Dubai World Cup proceeded by a racing carnival, had been on the initiative of Sheikh Mohammed bin Rashid Al Maktoum, vice president and prime minister of the United Arab Emirates.

When I arrived in the UAE in late 1995, Lord John Fitzgerald was the Director of the Emirates Racing Authority (ERA). He was succeeded shortly afterwards by Irishman, Michael Osborne, a fellow student at the Veterinary College or Ireland many years earlier, and it was these two and others that followed who were responsible for driving the project forward to fulfil Sheikh Mohammed's vision.

Many of the multinational veterinarians working in the UAE were employed by various members of the Royal family both in Dubai and in Abu Dhabi. During my time in the UAE, the magnificent Dubai Equine Hospital, was under the direction of USA veterinarian, Dr Michael Hauser and employed a number of mostly North and South American veterinarians. He kindly allowed some of these to assist with officiating at endurance rides. Most notable of these was Dr Martha Misheff who, over time, developed hospital facilities at the ride site, which became essential at the majority of these competitions.

Left to right: Neil Farr, AA and Lord John Fitzgerald at Jebel Ali Racecourse.

Left to right: AA, UAE-based Andrew Dalglish and Frits Sluyter, my successor as head of the FEI veterinary department, at Nad Al Sheba Racecourse at time of FEI bureau meeting, October 1995.

Instead of rides going directly from A to B across the desert, which required vet gates to be manned every 20–40 km, we organised them to revolve around one central vet gate, which was used as the fully equipped base and from which horse and rider could go off onto several different loops, but always return to the one centralised vet gate at the end of each loop. This had the distinct advantage that the treating veterinarians (i.e. Martha and her team) were based centrally and the other veterinarians could split between monitoring the rides from their vehicles and caring for distressed or injured horses, with others remaining to man the vet gates.

Of these veterinarians, Dr Bobby was dual purpose as he acted both as veterinarian to Al Asayl Stables, which was owned by the President of the UAE Equestrian and Racing Federation, and to the Federation itself. He spent the mornings tending to the racehorses based at Al Asayl and then worked with me in the Federation in the afternoons.

Dr Andrew Dalglish, a highly experienced Scottish veterinarian, was in the employment of the Abu Dhabi Royal Family. I had known Andrew for some time before I came to the UAE and it was good to have a friend and colleague to work with. Others included Dr Kamaal Pasha, who had attended the Cyprus conference and many others, mostly employed by the major stables. Dr Jim Bryant, Canada, joined later in preparation for the World Endurance Championship in 1998.

My first impressions of endurance riding were that the enjoyment of riding and winning often took precedent over the needs and welfare of the horses involved but, on one occasion, following the deaths of several horses, when I raised my concern with the authorities, I was told: "What is the problem? – 10 horses died at Cheltenham (races) last week – is that acceptable?" Not an easy question to answer.

The letters received following one of my first races, rather than rides, at Al Wathba camel racing track, contained such highly charged comments as (Senior Veterinary Official): *There were a lot of injuries in this race and the Higher Council will want to do everything to ensure that endurance racing can take place in future without abuse to the horses involved. I see this as an important test case for the authorities to demonstrate that rules must be enforced and the welfare of the horse protected.* (Horse ambulance provider) *...the scenes at the last race (Al Wathba) were totally unacceptable to us. The writer's career has hardened him to most livestock incidents and brutality thus, unless we are guaranteed drastic changes and become part of their planning, we will not offer our services again.*

My initial reaction after these first experiences was to get on a plane out of the Emirates and return home. On the day after the Al Wathba race, I went to see Faisal Siddiq, secretary general, and told him that unless the situation improved immediately, I would not stay. I tore up the UAE Endurance Rule Book in front of him as nobody seemed to respect it. Understandably, he was not pleased and I have to admit that it was an insulting act, but I believe that he took my message to heart. Shortly afterwards, I began to feel that it would be cowardly to abandon these unfortunate animals and that it was just possible that if I stayed on we might be able to improve the situation.

In my report to the Higher Council, which was the ruling authority for each ride/race, following this particular race I made a number of recommendations, which included:

- The need to encourage the planning of endurance rides/races as far in advance as possible to give maximum time for preparation for horse and rider;

- Each season's rides should be planned and published well before the first ride/race takes place;
- Not to organise races of less than 80km at the start of the season but encourage all rides to be over distances in excess of 80km (which will be run at a slower pace and hence cause fewer injuries than those over shorter distances);
- Gradually increase the distances as the season progresses and ensure that internationally accepted standards to protect the health and welfare of competing horses are enforced;
- Establish an endurance department within the federation and form an endurance committee composed of, at least, two internationally experienced veterinarians and two internationally experienced riders;
- Be highly conscious at all times of the effects of adverse public opinion if the welfare of horses continues to be compromised.

I will spare you any further details of experiences at races, but which were rarely seen in rides in excess of 80 km. If these were examples of endurance racing, I certainly did not wish to be part of the discipline. This also stimulated me into having the FEI Code of Conduct for the Welfare of the Horse translated into Arabic, although I am not sure how many may have actually read and digested its contents. The Federation's Media Department brilliantly illustrated the various points in the text, an example of which is shown overleaf.

On reflection, I am pleased that I did stay in the UAE as gradually the situation started to improve. I was consulted more by the Higher Council and helped by a number of willing and concerned veterinarians, who were also distressed with what they had to witness at each race over less than 80 km.

National Federations are responsible for providing rules and facilities for training and education in all aspects of horse care and equestrian sports. Through the FEI's Development Assistance Programme, National Federations are encouraged to seek help from other Federations who may be able to provide particular expertise. In conjunction with its member Federations and other organisations (like the ILPH), the FEI promotes scientific studies in equine health. Results are available to National Federations who are responsible for their distribution as appropriate.

FEI code of conduct: English (example page).

Neil Farr was very supportive, although he occupied a ministry position, as was his successor, Dr Tom Morton and, of course, so was Dr Bobby, Dr Andrew Dalglish and many others. We needed their support but it was often difficult for them as the majority were employed by the major stables, which were also providing most of the horses and riders which were competing and naturally, their first loyalty had to be to their employers.

Regardless of the negative comments I must say that UAE teams, which travelled abroad to compete, mostly in rides in excess of 80 km and admittedly with the best horses and riders, acquitted themselves well and had significant success in major events around the world.

During my first season in 1996, in addition to national rides/races, we also travelled to international rides/races in other counties. We travelled to Riyadh, Saudi Arabia in March, Kansas in the USA for the World Championship (160 km ride) in September and to Amman in Jordan the following month. The situation did not appear to be greatly different in these other countries with the exception of the USA, where much more concern for the horses' welfare was evident.

Although international races had taken place in the Emirates long before I arrived, we organised more rides, rather than races, in the UAE as we progressed. In addition to the 'home' veterinary team, we also invited many internationally acclaimed veterinarians from other countries to officiate at these rides. Amongst these were Drs Jim Bryant (CAN), Rod Fisher, Kieran O'Brien and Tony Pavord (GBR), Frans Arts (NED), Hallvard Sommerseth (NOR who later succeeded me in my role in the Federation), Fred Barrelet and Dominick Burger (SUI), Jerry Gillespie, Ray Randall and Kerry Ridgeway (USA). Effectively, when we organised an international ride, we had the top endurance veterinarians and other internationally well-recognised officials, as Technical Delegates, Ground Jury members and others, supervising them.

Also from 1996 onwards, we commenced organising a number of educational veterinary symposia in Abu Dhabi and Dubai, with international speakers. Their main purpose was to assist in increasing the knowledge of those in the UAE, involved in endurance riding, with the ultimate aim of making them more aware of the health and challenging aspects of welfare in this discipline and how it is perceived elsewhere in the equestrian world.

Amongst those who addressed these symposia were veterinarians: Fred Barrelet (SUI), Colin Vogel (GBR), Reuben Rose (AUS) and Joe Pagan (USA). In addition, we obtained a lot of shared knowledge from David Marlin (GBR whose work on heat and humidity was so valued prior to both the Atlanta and Hong Kong Olympic Games) and Peter Pike, Australian endurance rider, whose ethos was *to finish first you first have to finish* and who was now based and riding competitively in the UAE.

In March 1997, we had a welcome visit to the Federation office from the President of the Federation, H.H. Sheikh Sultan bin Khalifa Al Nayan, who met with several of the staff in response to our concerns on a number of issues, which had been raised at our regular weekly meetings.

I believe that we were all striving to do our best for the Federation and we were delighted to have this opportunity to speak directly and individually to the President who seemed to be genuinely interested in our concerns. I subsequently drafted the report, which contained a number of recommendations addressed to the President and Members of the Board of the Federation.

In the following spring of 1998, I returned from a visit to Warsaw, Poland having attended the European Long Distance Riding International Conference (ELDRIC), where I had promoted the forthcoming World Endurance Championship in Abu Dhabi. It had been bitterly cold in Warsaw and on arrival back to the UAE, I went straight from the airport to officiate at an endurance ride on a beautifully warm sunny day. I became ill during the ride and was hospitalised with a severe chest infection for ten days. During this time, I decided that I should finish in the UAE after the World Championship and during my subsequent summer leave, I wrote a letter of resignation to Faisal Seddiq, secretary general of the Federation.

A few months later, as part of the UAE delegation, I attended the FEI General Assembly in Hong Kong. By this time, George Stephen, chief executive of World Horse Welfare, was ill and unable to attend to make his annual presentation to the assembly. Jeremy James, World Horse Welfare consultant, made the presentation on his behalf. I had dinner with Jeremy one night and intimated to him that I would be leaving the UAE at the end of the year and hoped to pick up some form of consultancy on returning to the UK. He immediately suggested that there might be such a vacancy in World Horse Welfare and he would make enquiries.

Following on from this, during my summer leave, Dr Douglas Munro, now CEO of the charity, called me, we subsequently met in London and a new challenge was offered to me. This was to take over the position previously held by Major Noel Carding, although I did not know who he was at the time, to lead the overseas training programme in developing countries, with the aim of getting these projects onto a more professional and sustainable basis in each country. I commenced my new role with World Horse Welfare in January 1999.

However, let us first return to the UAE where we continued to organise international rides. This culminated in December 1998 when the Federation hosted the largest ever FEI World Endurance Championship. It started and finished in Ghantoot, Abu Dhabi, although the course also covered large areas of Dubai. It was wisely decided that for the preparations for the World Championship we really did need a highly experienced internationally acclaimed veterinarian at the helm of the organising committee. Following FEI advice and deliberation of potential candidates, it was decided to invite Dr Jim Bryant (CAN) to fill this role. I telephoned him on my mobile phone from the stables at Nad Al Sheba racetrack one night. He seemed interested in my proposal and, as he would be in Qatar officiating at an endurance ride the following month, he agreed to come to Abu Dhabi afterwards to discuss the issue.

Resulting from this meeting, Jim accepted the offer and commenced duty a few months later.

Organisation for the World Championship was a massive task. We contacted and interviewed several horse shipping agents and naturally, I was delighted when Peden Bloodstock was appointed.

Mike Bullen, Managing Director (MD) and our son, Martin, later to succeed Mike as MD, visited to set the wheels in motion and eventually arranged all aspects of the shipping of some 170 horses from 42 countries to this Championship.

Jim Bryant and AA in discussion

The 'Irish Volunteer Team' for the World Championship – Left to right Sherley and her sisters, Diana Gilna and Mary McCann.

Dr Martha Mischeff and her team, from the Dubai Equine Hospital, had brilliantly organised the hospital facility with some 50–60 stables and at some stages of the ride, all were fully occupied. This was a ride, a sporting occasion and yet we needed a hospital facility for so many horses – why? I cannot believe that there is any other sport anywhere in the world that has to cater for so many injured and/or metabolically compromised equine (or human) athletes during or following an international event.

Before I departed the UAE, after the World Championship at the end of the year, I presented Faisal Siddiq, secretary general, with a document in English but also translated into Arabic, which we called 'The Plan'. This was based on the views of those of us working in the Federation, as to what we felt needed to be done if the Federation wished to join the select band of FEI member National Federations and serve equestrianism in the UAE as it should. These views were largely based on our concerns, as registered during our weekly meetings in the office, and were presented in the form of a SWOT (Strengths, Weakness, Opportunities and Threats) analyses. In the document, we expanded on the following:

Strengths: The UAE is already a major player in World Endurance, with a good basic infrastructure, but needs to modernise to develop equestrian sport in the country;

Weakness: There is no current Vision **(1)** or Mission **(2)** statement. There is a real need to review organisational/management structure in the Federation and to centralise decision-making;

Opportunities: Promote other equestrian disciplines, such as riding schools, leisure riding, riding for the disabled etc., which will lead to further educating the youth of the country in equestrianism. Involve industry stakeholders to help to set goals, discuss industry needs and promote equine welfare;

Threats: The authority of the Federation needs to strengthen and avoid being superseded by Organising Committees, Clubs etc. there is a real threat that worldwide public opinion of endurance in the UAE could become disastrous for the sport in the country and in the region. Remedial action needs to be taken urgently.

1 Proposed Vision Statement: *Our vision is of a federation which promotes all aspects of equestrianism in a manner where participation in leisure riding or competition brings distinction to our country and enjoyment to both horses and riders;*

2 Proposed Mission Statement: *Our mission is to promote equestrianism by guiding, encouraging and educating while fully respecting the capacity and welfare of the individual horse and rider.*

Following much persuasion, I did eventually return to the UAE Equestrian and Racing Federation for the 2003/2004 season. I had very much hoped that I would be able to assist in pushing the reforms mentioned in 'The Plan' forward, but this was not to be.

So, now let us move on and read about experiences with World Horse Welfare and its work for the underprivileged equine in developing countries.

Chapter 13

WORLD HORSE WELFARE

History of the Charity – Appointment as Veterinary Consultant –
Training in Developing Countries

At the time that I joined the charity as Veterinary Consultant, in January 1999, it was known as the International League for the Protection of Horses (ILPH) but it was subsequently re-branded in 2008 as World Horse Welfare and it has been referred to as such throughout this book.

The President of the charity was H.R.H. The Princess Royal who still holds the position to-day. The Chairman was Lord Allenby who, shortly after my appointment, kindly invited Douglas Munro, chief executive and I to lunch in the House of Lords in London. He was followed as chairman later that year by The Hon Gerald (Bunny) Maitland-Carew (1999–2006), brother of Lord Carew, one time Chairman of the FEI's Eventing Committee. Bunny was then succeeded by Christopher Hall (2006–2011), under whose chairmanship, ILPH was rebranded World Horse Welfare and who himself was succeeded five years later by veterinarian, Barry Johnson.

However, first let us look back to see how the connection between FEI and World Horse Welfare all started. Early in 1985, Charles Frank, a well-known Lambourn veterinary surgeon and at the time Deputy Chairman of the FEI Veterinary Committee, called me to say that he had been in touch with the, then, Honorary Director of World Horse Welfare, Captain Charles Bennington, regarding the possible awarding of funds to support the FEI's Transport Stress Project. On my next visit to the UK, Charles and I drove to the charity's headquarters at Snetterton in Norfolk to meet with Captain Bennington and discuss our plans.

The meeting went well and shortly afterwards, he advised us that the Board of World Horse Welfare was impressed with our ideas and had agreed to grant us funds.

Following a selection process, the Irish Equine Centre and the University of California were appointed to conduct the relevant research. Charles established a small committee comprised of himself as chairman, Lucinda Green (international event rider), Eric Wauters (international jumping rider), Brigadier A. D. Seton (veterinary advisor to World Horse Welfare) and Professor H. J. Breukink (member FEI Veterinary Committee) as members with me as secretary to oversee the project.

Clearly, the FEI was concerned with the stress imposed on competition horses while World Horse Welfare's interest was to ascertain the adverse effects on horses destined for slaughter that often travel vast distances by road mostly from Eastern Europe to the slaughter houses of Belgium, France, and Italy.

A similar trade is also in operation in many other regions of the world. These often diseased, work-worn and wretched horses often travel for days on end, without adequate rest periods, food or water.

Thanks to the work of organisations such as World Horse Welfare, EU legislation has been positively influenced (although enforcing the legislation has often proved difficult), significant welfare improvements have been achieved and the numbers dropped from 165,000 horses in 2001 to around 54,000 in 2012.

However, despite enormous efforts to bring about a carcase-only trade, the practice continues to this very day. Dr Des Leadon, who led the project on behalf of the Irish Equine Centre, has also been very active in lobbying the European Commission for changes to legislation.

Des focused his work on monitoring equine movements ranging from ponies travelling for a few hours in a trailer behind a car, to race-horses, travelling in rather more comfortable road transport, and also short aircraft flights in addition to long haul to Australia and all areas in between. He initially monitored the Royal Canadian Mounted Police horses during their ten-week tour of Europe in the summer of 1988 for which our son, Martin, was Road Manager. This was an invaluable opportunity to assess these horses under wide conditions similar to that experienced by competition horses.

In 1990, I arranged for Des, who was a long-time friend and colleague, to present the results of his initial findings to the FEI General Assembly at its meeting in Bern in Switzerland. This was well received.

In addition to numerous eloquent scientifically based presentations by Des to various organisations, his work eventually became the subject of a practical booklet *Recommendations to Horse Owners on the Transportation of Horses,* which was published by the FEI in 1990. As a result of World Horse Welfare's support for this project, I persuaded the FEI secretary general to invite Colonel George Stephen, who was by then chief executive of the charity, following Captain Bennington's retirement, to attend FEI general assemblies. The first assembly he attended took place in Berlin in 1992, where he made a short presentation on the work of World Horse Welfare. These presentations continued annually in subsequent years until 1998 when illness prevented George from attending the Hong Kong General Assembly and Jeremy James represented him.

Later in the year, I flew up to Edinburgh to visit The Royal (Dick) School of Veterinary Studies, who were undertaking a research project into Grass Sickness in horses on behalf of World Horse Welfare. I was met at the airport by Hamish Lochore, World Horse Welfare's consultant in Scotland, who drove me to the university.

We next visited George Stephen and his wife, Roxy, at their lovely home on the Scottish Borders. Clearly, George was not well but, after exchanging pleasantries, he picked up a bottle of his best Scotch whisky and he and I retired to his study where we put the (horse) world to rights, accompanied by a few drams of the 'hard stuff'. That was the last time I was to see him. A few months later, in November, a delegation from World Horse Welfare, in which I was included, made the sad journey back to Edinburgh to attend George's memorial service. H.R.H. The Princess Royal was represented at the service and his old army friend and work colleague at World Horse Welfare, Lt Col John Sharples, delivered a magnificent eulogy. John kindly sent me a copy of this, which I still retain. Following is an obituary which appeared in The Herald, Scotland, October 1999:

Colonel George Stephen

During his army career, George Stephen served in many parts of the world, but from the early days of his service, he developed a great interest and affection for the Arab world. He did tours in Aden, Jordan, Oman, Sharjah and the UAE. As Brigade Major of the Trucial Oman Scouts, he relished the description of him by a visiting journalist as a 'modern Tyrone Power'.

He was an affluent Arabic speaker and was trusted by many Arabs. He was a confidant of Sheikh Mohammed bin Rashid Al Maktoum of the UAE and trusted by King Hussein of Jordan, whose son Prince Abdullah was an officer in the 13th/18th Royal Hussars under Colonel Stephen's command.

He took early retirement from the Army in 1988 as a full colonel, having been an instructor at the Australian Staff College and on the Defence Sales staff at the MoD. He was immediately invited to be the first chief executive of World Horse Welfare and then a little-known charity centred in Norfolk. With his customary enthusiasm and leadership, he set about developing this organisation into a formidable and effective force within the horse world. He believed passionately in the debt mankind owed to the horse, and was determined to improve the lot of equines around the world, be they for sport or at work.

He was not a sentimentalist, but took a pragmatic, although compassionate, view on equine welfare, which was respected by horse people, as well as by politicians whom he lobbied regularly. His slogan was, "The use, not the abuse, of the horse." His vision was that World Horse Welfare should be international, so he set up branches in New Zealand, Australia, Israel, and established a European branch in Paris with sub branches throughout Europe. He organised teams that now work in 20 countries, training people who depend on equines for their livelihood to look after their animals.

One of his campaigns was to end the appalling treatment of horses transported from the Soviet Bloc to Western Europe for slaughter. He mobilised the efforts of most equine charities, not only in Britain, but around the world, to raise a petition to the European Parliament to legislate against the trade. As a result, 3.2 million signatures supported the petition, the largest ever to be submitted to the parliament.

He established World Horse Welfare as the welfare arm of the Federation Equestre International (FEI) and was a driving force behind the research into the effects of heat stress on horses participating in the Olympics. He chaired the working group set up by the Jockey Club and the British Horse Racing Board to look into welfare issues related to failed racehorses. He was president of the Percheron Society in 1992 and was also appointed Haute Dignitaire d'Honneur, Grande Chancellerie Internationale de l'Ordre Equestre de Sainte Georges de France.

To return to the Berlin General Assembly, following the meeting, I received a charming hand-written letter from George in which he thanked me for opening up a whole new range of FEI contacts, many of which would be invaluable to World Horse Welfare. He ended the letter by saying that he hoped we would meet at Badminton (Three-Day Event) in May, "Where perhaps we can sort out what I have forgotten to do!"

We did meet at Badminton and he had not forgotten anything. There is no doubt in my mind that without George Stephen's enthusiasm and commitment, back in the 1980s, FEI and World Horse Welfare might not now have the solid relationship that it has today.

Now let us take a look at the charity itself. World Horse Welfare was founded in 1927 as a campaigning organisation to prevent the export of live British horses for slaughter. The charity's founder, Ada Cole, was spurred into action after witnessing a procession of British work horses being unloaded and whipped for four miles to slaughter in Belgium. From the beginning, she defined the charity's approach as, '*combining practicality with passion.*'

Today, as a leading international equine charity, World Horse Welfare has fifteen training programmes in place in 13 countries and continues to work to change legislation and attitudes to horse welfare, including through its campaign to end the long distance transportation of live horses across Europe to slaughter.

World Horse Welfare's UK-wide network of Field Officers, who were historically nearly all ex-mounted police, but today come from a variety of backgrounds, armed with consummate equine welfare knowledge and who investigate and resolve welfare problems.

The charity runs four Rescue and Rehoming Centres where horses in need can be rehabilitated and find loving new homes through its rehoming scheme – the largest of its kind in the UK.

Internationally, World Horse Welfare runs practical international training programmes in some of the world's poorest countries, often in conjunction with other welfare charities and always in partnership with local organisations and governments to ensure that their impact is sustainable, to combat the major causes of equine suffering and thereby helping the owners to help themselves.

The aim is to improve the well-being of the equine, be it horse, mule or donkey and thus improve its working capacity to the benefit of its owner and his/her family. World Horse Welfare believes in using locally available materials to establish sustainable and permanent solutions to problems in the world where needed.

As part of my preparation to become a cog in the administrative wheel of World Horse Welfare's overseas training programmes, I found Jeremy James's excellent book *Debt of Honour*[9], with the Foreword written by its President, H.R.H. The Princess Royal, to be a fountain of knowledge on the workings of the charity.

On my first 'getting to know you' visit to the charity, I met and addressed the staff, several of whom I already knew, the idea being to inform them of my background and let them know that I would be venturing into unknown territory in taking on responsibility for its overseas training programmes (later to be re-named *International Training Programmes)* and would need all the help and support they would give me. Following our meeting, I was able to tell Douglas that in the early 1950s I was part of a delegation that had ridden through the streets of Dublin to

---

[9] Jeremy James, Debt of Honour, Macmillan London, 1994

present a petition to the Dail (Irish Houses of Parliament) campaigning for the end of exportation of live horses for slaughter from Ireland.

It was agreed with Douglas Munro that in addition to international training I would continue with my long time goal of encouraging and assisting closer ongoing collaboration between World Horse Welfare and FEI.

Most importantly, at this initial meeting, I met Andre Bubear, Master Saddler, whom I had known by name for some time but had never met before and renewed my acquaintance with Jeremy James, who were the two key personnel at the time working on international training.

Andre and Jeremy had known each other for many years and, in fact, in 1990 had ridden on horses, through Eastern Europe into Romania. It was seeing the horses on that journey that got Andre to start thinking of equine welfare, which led to the job with World Horse Welfare. Jeremy had previously ridden from Eastern Europe back to Wales in 1987 and both these journeys were commemorated in two of several books written by Jeremy.

My understanding of international training was that it all started with Working Together for Equines (WTFE), which was established by Walt Taylor, the American President at the time of the World Farriers Association and Dr Tina McGregor, a well-known and highly respected Scottish veterinarian. These two initiated the concept and hired themselves out to various equine charities, who wished to have a presence in a country in need to assist working equines. Captain Bennington engaged WTFE to operate on behalf of World Horse Welfare in a number of such countries.

However, shortly after Colonel George Stephen succeeded Captain Bennington as chief executive he recommended to the Board of Trustees of World Horse Welfare that it should establish its own international training programme. Lt. Colonel John Sharples who, at the time, was in charge of overseas training, invited Andre Bubear, Master Saddler, who had been part of WTFE, to find a farrier to join the team and he selected Tom Burch with whom he had worked in the Metropolitan Police. They took over from WTFE in Mexico and elsewhere. Jeremy James joined the team later bringing his nutrition and equine management expertise to the group. Other nutritionists, saddlers/harness makers and farriers were soon appointed to work alongside Andre, who became the Team Leader.

Andre Bubear had trained as a saddler with the Household Cavalry Regiment in London before moving to the Metropolitan Police Mounted Branch as master saddler, responsible for all horse tack and leather accoutrements. He designed specialist equipment for other sections of the Metropolitan Police including the dog group. Andre also worked part-time for WTFE and later moved on to become the first saddler trainer for World Horse Welfare working on its international training programmes. This involved teaching people saddlery/leather work skills which were badly needed to help working equines in these countries.

Jeremy James had spent his life working in developing countries with cattle and horses, and once, with Rendili, Masai, Samburu and Somali drovers walked a herd of 86 camels from Somalia to Tanzania.

In the 1990s, during the last stages of the Balkan Wars, he ran the State Lipizzaner Stud in Bosnia. He had worked with horses of burden in economically deprived communities across the world: from the rubbish dumps of Mexico City to the gharry horses of Ethiopia, from the horses of the Hmong people of Northern

Vietnam, the working horses of the Fijian tropical interior, the *tonga* horses of Lahore, to the village horses of Eastern Turkey and of Morocco.

He had travelled on horseback, written about horses, although from a different perspective from the norm. He had contributed material to broadsheets, magazines, television, film and radio embracing within his interests, art, history, vernacular architecture and more abstract matters, usually with some rural slant. Having had the great good fortune to have been born and brought up in Kenya and having worked with rural peoples and their animals all around the world, he had developed his own outlook on man's association with the natural world, which both informed and is reflected in his work.

In 1997/98 Major Noel Carding, recently retired veterinary officer to the Household Cavalry, was appointed to oversee the new World Horse Welfare international training programmes.

Major Carding, Sefton and the London Bombings 1982

On 20th July 1982 at 10:40 am, Cavalry horse, Sefton, was en route to the traditional Changing of the Guard in London with 15 other horses from his regiment. A car-mounted nail bomb planted by the Irish Republican Army (IRA) detonated on South Carriage Drive in Hyde Park, hitting the formation of horses and riders from the Blues and Royals.

The explosions killed 11 military personnel: four soldiers of the Blues and Royals at Hyde Park and seven bandsmen of the Royal Green Jackets at Regent's Park. Seven of the Blues and Royals' horses also died in the attack. Sefton survived but suffered serious injuries and was subsequently featured on television programmes and was awarded 'Horse of the Year.'

Due to the severity of his wounds, Sefton was led in to the first horsebox to arrive on scene, in which he was driven to the barracks along with Major Noel Carding, Farrier-Major Brian Smith and three other troopers holding Sefton. Carding ordered the horsebox to the forge, rather than the stables, due to its proximity. Here, Carding began 90 minutes of emergency operation to save Sefton's life – the first of the British Army's veterinary officers to operate on war-like wounds to a cavalry horse in more than half a century – whilst also directing care of the other wounded horses prior to the arrival of civilian vets to assist.

During this first visit to World Horse Welfare headquarters in 1999, I had learnt that World Horse Welfare currently had training programmes operating in Ethiopia, Fiji, Kenya and Mexico. These programmes were later extended during my time to cover El Salvador, Egypt and Ukraine.

My first overseas trip for World Horse Welfare was to Ethiopia with Jeremy James in March 1999. I was initially surprised to find that the UK based Donkey Sanctuary, already had a base in Debra Zeit, some two hours driving time northeast of Addis Ababa, the capital. Another UK based charity, The Brooke Hospital, was planning to join with a further base in the same town. I totally failed to understand why World Horse Welfare contemplated operating in this same small area; where there were already, two other UK based equine charities, in a country as large as

Ethiopia. There were some 400 gharry (horse drawn cab) horses working in the town and environs, all in poor condition.

We did set up an initial training visit to cover saddlery, farriery, equine management and nutrition but unfortunately it was not a great success, largely due to lack of genuine interest by the students and the overall bureaucracy faced in the country. We did not persevere with further work in Ethiopia.

Shortly after this trip, I met with Clive Woodham. Clive had spent much of his working life as a veterinary surgeon when he was employed, from 1970 to 1992, by the Inter-American Development Bank (IADB) in Latin America, including El Salvador.

IADB is the main source of financing for projects involving development and reduction of poverty in Latin America. Clive had established the World Association for Transport Animal and Welfare Studies (TAWS) – along with UK veterinary colleagues Carl Boyde and Roger Connan. TAWS operated in a number of countries and World Horse Welfare agreed to join up with them in El Salvador, where it already had a presence and where Dr Ernesto Calderon was their Project Co-ordinator.

Sometime later, when we visited the British Ambassador in El Salvador to discuss the proposed project we instantly recognised each other. The Ambassador had been Military Attaché in Dubai, where we had met and chatted at a function a few years earlier while we were both based in the UAE – a small world.

The Board of Trustees of World Horse Welfare established an Overseas Training Committee (OTC), which held its first meeting in January 2000, which Douglas Munro and I also attended. The object of this committee was to look at overseas training in depth, formulate what it should be doing and how best to do it. The OTC comprised Captain The Hon. G. Maitland-Carew (Chairman) and Trustees: Mary Gordon-Watson, Andrew Higgins (my FEI colleague), Lord Soulsby, Roderick Watt and Johnnie McIrvine as members.

One day in August, some months after the overseas training meeting, Andre Bubear and I met with Tom Burch, farrier, at the unlikely venue for a 'high level conference', namely Clacketts Service Station on the M25 south of London. Our discussions resulted in a paper containing a number of recommendations to the World Horse Welfare's Board of Trustees, which included:

- Careful selection of potential training projects;
- A detailed selection procedure to include an investigative visit prior to commitment;
- Establish Diplomatic links, both in the host country and in the UK;
- Wherever possible collaborate with another equine charity;
- Involve the FEI, as competition horses often end up as working horses in target countries when their competitive careers are over;
- Appoint a project co-ordinator in the host country;
- Produce Course Manuals on management and nutrition, farriery and foot care and saddlery and harness making;
- Seek approval from the World Horse Welfare's Overseas Training Committee (OTC) and General Purposes and Finance Committee, before proceeding with each project.

With regard to the actual courses to be run we recommended:

- That these should be planned well in advance (up to 12-18 months if possible) to give the trainers we would send to run courses adequate time to prepare and re-arrange their normal work schedules;
- Be of two to three weeks duration, with four courses per annum and the project in total should last for a minimum of five years to ensure a sustainable result;
- The subjects to be covered in the courses would be (1) Management and Nutrition, (2) Farriery and Foot Care and (3) Saddlery, Harness Making and repairs;
- Copies of the relevant manuals should be given to each student at the beginning of their course.

It was anticipated that at the end of the five-year term some of the better trainees would be identified as potential national trainers and competent to run their own national courses and hence expand relevant knowledge on the care of equines in their country. Once this was established World Horse Welfare trainers would make an annual visit for a year or two afterwards to monitor progress and assist and advice where needed.

Not long afterwards, after some two years in the job, I let it be known that I considered that with all this activity OST really required the full time commitment of one individual, rather than me working part time on a two days a week basis. When I broached this to Douglas, his immediate response was, "You have just talked your way out of a job."

However, shortly afterwards Richard Felton, charity secretary and overseas affairs, joined me and together we made several further overseas trips, including to Mexico, El Salvador and the Ukraine. Richard's contribution was a great help and eventually this led to the appointment of Major Ian Kelly in 2001 to succeed me in a permanent role as director of international training.

Before proceeding further, may I first introduce you to the circumstances in which World Horse Welfare became involved in Kiev, Ukraine.

Following a call for help from a British couple living in Kiev, Ukraine, I made a brief visit in May 1999 to meet with Zoe Stamper, her husband and their veterinarian, Dr Levitsky. They were all charming and persuasive and I attended the official opening of Dr Levitsky's new veterinary clinic during this visit. It became clear from our discussions that there was a real thirst for equine veterinary knowledge in the country.

On return, I reported to Douglas Munro and then set about finding a seat of learning in the UK, which would be willing to establish veterinary courses in the Ukraine. I received a very positive response from Dr Derek Knottenbelt of the University of Liverpool and he and his team set up a Veterinary Seminar, which took place with FEI participation in October 1999.

This was just a start but it made a really good impression and the teaching of the Liverpool veterinarians had a significant impact on the Ukrainian veterinarians and students and on the welfare of horses in the region. This course was repeated each year for several years. It was very much hoped that the Liverpool example could become a blueprint for similar seminars in other Eastern European or other countries in the world.

Not long after Ian Kelly's appointment, Lieutenant Colonel Richard Felton, ILPH charity secretary and overseas affairs, summed up international training in an excellent article, which was published in World Horse Welfare's Quarterly News. I take the liberty of quoting from this document as it gives a very clear account of work in several of the countries in which World Horse Welfare's International Training Teams were in operation:

Transcending political, economic and cultural boundaries, the ILPH's (note: understandably, in this article, Richard referred to the charity by its name at the time, ILPH rather than World Horse Welfare) *international equine welfare training programme is reaching out to more countries and equines than ever before. Last year, (2000) we conducted eight courses in six different developing countries while this year (2001) we shall be actively involved again in six different developing countries running nine courses. We shall be operating as far afield as East Africa – Kenya; Central America – El Salvador and Mexico; Pacific and Eastern Europe – Fiji, Ukraine and Romania.*

In addition, we are supplying consultant trainers for the Brooke Hospital for Animals (BHA) projects in Pakistan and Egypt and with the Donkey Sanctuary in Mexico providing Mobile Treatment Teams.

Our training, carried out by highly skilled and dedicated experts led by Master Saddler, Andre Bubear, is holistic and based on the 'whole horse' concept covering management and nutrition, farriery, and foot care and saddlery and harness making and repairs. By providing the relevant education and practical training for farriers, horse owners (working and sports horses) and tradesmen, we are equipping these people with the necessary knowledge and skills to enable them to look after their equines properly and in return improve their own livelihood through improved health and performance of their animals.

In addition to this training, we also run veterinary training seminars whose purpose is primarily to assist with the continuing professional development of veterinarians specialising in horses. We are now planning our third seminar at Kiev in the Ukraine, which once again will be led by Professor Derek Knottenbelt and his team from the University of Liverpool Veterinary School.

However, results are not achieved overnight. It takes both time and money to train farriers and saddlers and harness makers to an acceptable standard. In each country, we currently allocate nine weeks (note: Andre's and my recommendations had not yet been taken on board at this time) *of intensive horse-training by both ILPH and local specialist trainers spaced over two years to this task. During the intervening period, students continue to improve their skills and their progress is monitored by our in country co-ordinators. Although costs vary between countries, the cost of training a farrier, for example, in El Salvador is presently some £9,000.* (Note: today, in 2016, it costs in the region of £5,000 to run each module).

Readers will be interested to learn of our activities in three of the countries in which we are presently working—the Ukraine, Mexico and Kenya. Although no two countries are the same the horse's basic needs are common throughout.

Run by the ILPH with assistance from the National Agricultural University of the Ukraine (NAUU), the Federation Equestre Internationale (FEI) and eminent veterinarians from the Equine Division of the University of Liverpool including Professor Barrie Edwards and Dr Derek Knottenbelt, the seminars have been an outstanding success. This year's programme (2001) in addition to covering farriery, orthopaedics, respiratory medicine and surgery, radiography and intestinal procedures and suture patterns will also have new topics—dentistry and nutrition, transport, welfare care and saddle fitting.

Last year's (2000) seminar was attended by fifty veterinarians, mostly engaged in teaching or working with sports horses in the Ukraine, Russia, Belarus and Lithuania together with some nineteen veterinary students from the National University of the Ukraine (NAUU). This year we shall be encouraging more veterinarians dealing with the working horse to attend.

The enthusiasm among the delegates for the programme was overwhelming as they are starved of educational opportunities and have no access to current journals, books, or clinical meetings. Our seminars represent the most significant education and equine welfare event in this region for many years. The veterinary profession in the newly independent Eastern European States is desperate for help and we have a duty to provide this. It is also a privilege to meet and help such lovely people who appreciate very deeply what we are trying to do. This is a real contribution to real people with a real return in the improved welfare of horses in real need.

Our activities in Kenya have involved our working in close collaboration with the Kenya Mounted Police, the Kenya Society for the Protection and Care of Animals (KSPCA) and the racing and sports horse community. Kenya has some ten thousand horses but two million donkeys.

Here, as in other countries, we have been training based on the 'whole horse' concept. While there have traditionally been problems with donkey's welfare resulting from the lack of adequate foot care or nasty sores resulting from poorly fitting harness and pack saddles, the welfare of many horses is now of concern. Ownership of ex-racehorses has become fashionable and many of their new owners either lack the knowledge or sadly, sometimes the inclination, to look after them properly.

Many, in an appalling physical condition, have had to be taken into care by Jean Gilchrist, Director of the KSPCA. However, we have also been able to help the donkeys by developing suitable, inexpensive harness for those pulling carts. It is not uncommon to see three donkeys harnessed to a cart with a load weighing a quarter of a tonne urged on by a young boy driver, or worse – a large man, wielding and using a whip or stick goad with considerable force.

Unfortunately, because of their extremely ineffective harness system only one donkey is actually doing the pulling and then taking all the strain on its neck and withers resulting in horrific sores. The task is now to encourage their owners to use the new pattern harness, based on ILPH training, which are all made from local materials by Kenyans.

Our joint programme with the UK-based Donkey Sanctuary, led by June Evers and Dr Andrew Trawford, the latter a veterinary friend and colleague and the School of Veterinary Medicine and Zootechnics of the National University of Mexico (UNAM) aims to improve the health and general conditions of working equines owned by people of limited resources in Mexico. The animals receive free veterinary care and the owners are educated on the importance of good hoof care and proper nutrition for their animals. In order to reduce the incidence of different lesions, they are taught how to fit their tack and harness correctly for carrying loads or pulling carts or ploughs. By easing the work burden on the animals and by helping them to carry out their daily tasks under satisfactory conditions, they are likely to be of more use to their owners.

With vehicles donated by the ILPH and the Donkey Sanctuary, three mobile treatment teams each equipped with the necessary medicines and instruments and staffed by a veterinarian, a farrier, a fourth year veterinary student and a student carrying out social service operate throughout ten of Mexico's thirty-one states. The service, which is free of charge, deals with some 15,000 equines annually. In addition to the treatment of wounds and worming, vaccines are administered where necessary, mainly against rabies and encephalitis. Surgical cases are referred to the equine clinics at the School of Veterinary Medicine.

Left to right: Jean Gilchrist (KSPCA), Andre Bubear (WHW) and Sherley Atock, with her World Horse Welfare Mobile Unit at an event at Hartpury College in the UK.

Lectures are also given in the communities directed both to children and adults detailing the minimum care that animals require in order to do good work. It is explained to the owners that maintaining their animals in good condition will enable them to work more effectively and consequently improve their own livelihood.

A most serious problem is encountered on the rubbish dumps on the outskirts of Mexico City where equines are used to transport garbage, old iron and mattresses. The majority of the people who work with these animals, up to 400 equines at the Neza dump, do not have any experience with this sort of activity. They have no knowledge of the nutritional requirements, the working hours, or maximum loads for their animals, nor are they skilled in the proper construction of harness and carts. They make them trot and gallop along busy streets, amongst heavy traffic for many hours.

The horses they use are either bought at an animal market or at riding clubs or even at racetracks and have never done this kind of work before. The food they receive is totally insufficient being inadequate in quantity and quality. Under these conditions, the animals become exhausted, lame, weak, often develop fistulous withers and other serious lesions. They are then sold to slaughter houses, which operate under the most horrific conditions. Those with a broken leg, for example, will be strapped to the side of the lorry to prevent it falling and being trampled by others. Donkeys, some alive and some dead will be crammed onto the back of the same truck. Any foals will be discarded over the side of the truck prior to setting off to the slaughter house leaving their distraught mothers on the lorry.

The Donkey Sanctuary – ILPH – UNAM teams assist these animals as best they can and organise courses for their handlers to show them what animals require enabling them to work. However, the foremost difficulty one encounters in any attempt to improve the life of animals in general, is the lack of federal legislation governing the welfare of animals. The authorities of these peripheral areas of Mexico City have been approached and a draft has been submitted to control the use of working animals and we have been assured that the problem will be studied.

Public animal markets are another one of our targets. Conditions at the one held every Monday at the Puente de San Bernabe in the state of Mexico, are particularly cruel. The majority of equines there are sold for slaughter and are old, weak and often severely injured and it is not uncommon to see horses with compound fractures being led around the market, their eyes dull with excruciating pain.

Many are definitely unfit for travel and it is common practice to transport dead horses with live ones destined for the abattoir. Little food or water is available (although ILPH and the Donkey Sanctuary installed water troughs, which are often not filled on market day or are left out of reach of the animals). The way in which they are loaded, often without using the ramps also installed by ILPH and the Donkey Sanctuary, to be viewed by potential buyers, is beyond description. Jointly both charities' treatment teams have been assisting these miserable animals in any possible way they can and try to euthanize those that are not in any condition to continue to travel.

However, they have met with great resistance often with the argument that the live animal is more valuable than the dead one. All authorities have been visited and urged to enforce existing regulations with limited success. However, the new President has promised to improve conditions at the market. With the aim of *preventing injury to working equines, we are working with UNAM and the team members to design suitable, inexpensive harness and carts to replace those on the rubbish dumps around Mexico City. We are also conducting regular farrier and saddlery courses in Mexico.*

When one views the abject misery and pain that many working equines frequently have to endure in silence in many of the countries where the ILPH works, one cannot be faulted for wondering if we are ever going to improve their general well-being. Given the poverty that exists among their owners and their often-dispassionate attitude towards these animals – 'they were sent to suffer as we do' – is a common sentiment of the working community.

It was from the Mexican project that we were able to select World Horse Welfare's first 'in-house' trainers to join teams working in other countries. These included Marco Torres Sevilla who had trained as a farrier and Carlos Zuniga, who had trained as a saddler/harness maker in Mexico in 1989 and 1994 respectively. These were the first two Mexicans who went through World Horse Welfare training, to assistant trainers and full trainers in their own country and now work internationally.

In addition, I understand that Marco has translated the farriery manual into Spanish and may have arranged the same for the other manuals.

While Douglas Munro and I were attending the FEI General Assembly in Doha, Qatar, in 1999 we were in discussion one night on the highly emotive subject of the ghastly long distance travel of horses from Eastern Europe to slaughter in the west. After all, this was the issue on which World Horse Welfare was originally founded back in 1927. Douglas explained to me how the charity campaigned through Members of the European Parliament (MEPs) to the EU in Brussels to have the conditions for these animals significantly improved, or preferably, the trade ceased altogether. It suddenly occurred to me that it would be of great benefit to World Horse Welfare if it had its own campaigner 'in house'.

The hell that is San Bernabe.

Live and dead donkeys in the back of a pick-up truck at San Bernabe Market.

Live horse for sale with hind leg missing below hock.

Keith Meldrum, recently retired chief veterinary officer of the British Ministry of Agriculture, Fisheries and Food (MAFF, but now re-branded DEFRA) and a good friend and colleague, would be the ideal choice. I suggested this to Douglas who liked the idea and asked me to contact Keith. As a result Douglas, Jeremy James and I met Keith in London and shortly afterwards he was appointed Veterinary Consultant to the charity, a position which he still holds today.

I understand that Keith's experience and knowledge of the corridors of political power in Brussels and elsewhere has been invaluable to the organisation, not to mention his contribution to other issues on World Horse Welfare's agenda.

Early the following year, Andre Bubear and I met Ric Butson, veterinary officer to the Brooke Hospital for Animals, at its headquarters in London. Resulting from our discussions, Andre and I joined Ric in a visit, in July 2000, to view the Brooke's hospitals in Cairo, Luxor, Aswan, Edfu, Mersa Matruh (we did not visit the hospital in Alexandria)and the Nile Delta and witness how they operate.

We were highly impressed with the work that their veterinarians were performing in each of their well-equipped hospitals. Life is hard for both animals and their owners in Egypt. Access to affordable quality veterinary services for working horses, donkeys and mules remains a challenge, which the Brooke provides free of charge. The World Horse Welfare's philosophy is based very much on prevention rather than cure. We therefore arranged for a Jordanian saddler/harness maker, who World Horse Welfare had trained some years earlier, to visit these hospitals and to assist with training the Brooke's students. This worked well, much being due to the fact that Arabic was the mother tongue of both trainer and trainee.

In 2001, Douglas Munro retired as chief executive of World Horse Welfare. Johnnie McIrvine, a member of the Board of Trustees, took over in an interim capacity prior to the appointment of Brigadier John Smales who held the position of CEO until his retirement in 2007. Roly Owers, a veterinary colleague, who had previously been World Horse Welfare's Support Director from 1999 to 2003 returned to the charity as chief executive, a position he still holds today.

Let us next take a look back at, what I consider to be, the most significant highlights of my almost 60 years working with horses, from the privileged for most of this time, to the horrors of the exceptionally underprivileged towards the end. We often refer to man's inhumanity to man, but what about man's inhumanity to animals? Most particularly when that animal's owner and his family are utterly dependant on its working capacity to put food on their table each night.

Chapter 14

SUMMING UP

Review the Past and Look to the Future

I have been extremely privileged to have been given the opportunity to devote so much of my working life to the care and welfare of animals. This has ranged, in the early stages, through veterinary practice, from farm animals to small animals, mostly dogs and cats and a miscellaneous collection of small creatures that tended to arrive at my surgery in cardboard boxes, which I would open, often in trepidation as to what I would find.

However, horses were always of the greatest interest, although I never actually worked in a high-powered equine veterinary practice. Presumably, I would have equated to a general practitioner, or a GP, in human terms.

I would now like to look back and sum up the positives, relating to the benefits for the horse in the various roles with which I was associated and to review those that gave the greatest satisfaction. I will not dwell on the years in veterinary practice other than to say that I did my best for the living and for those who were tired of life, helped them to slip peacefully away at the end of their days with dignity. I then moved on to become veterinary officer to the Irish Turf Club, head of the Veterinary Department of the Federation Equestre Internationale (International Equestrian Federation – FEI), veterinary consultant to the United Arab Emirates Equestrian and Racing Federation and finally to a similar role with World Horse Welfare.

Irish Turf Club (1972–1981): The early beginnings in veterinary practice and interest in racing led me to being offered the position of veterinary officer (although the actual title was 'stewards secretary, veterinary') to the Irish Turf (Jockey) Club and into the world of this intriguing sport. What a privilege this was – to be actually paid to go racing. How good could that be? If I had not undertaken my years with the Turf Club, and been responsible for the doping control in Irish racing, I would not have met M. Jean Romanet, Director of France Galop, and other directors of international racing jurisdictions who became such a significant influence in my future career with the FEI. I would not have been in a position to recommend to the President of the FEI, a few years later, what needed to be done to upgrade the FEI's own medication control programme, which was to become so important to these controls in international equestrian sport for the future.

In retrospect, I realise that at least some of the items of concern highlighted in my presentation to the Melbourne racing conference in 1981 on *Welfare of the Horse*, are still relevant to this day. I have always had the highest regard for racehorses, jockeys and particularly national hunt jockeys (steeplechase and hurdle racing). These are the bravest of the brave. In what other sport does an ambulance, or two or three, follow the runners throughout a race, ready to pick up the pieces of an injured jockey whose chances of a fall are in the order of one in every 8–10 rides?

The convoy of ambulances are accompanied by one or more veterinary teams fully equipped to deal with horse's injuries and where necessary to have the injured horse transported to the nearest equine veterinary facility of excellence for further assessment, if deemed necessary. Yes, horses do fall and yes, horses do get injured and occasionally, these injuries prove to be fatal but, at all times, the care and attention horse and jockey receive in their time of need is, on the whole, exemplary.

And what about the trainers and stable staff? They are up and about feeding and exercising their horses, often in foul weather, while the majority of the rest of us are still tucked up in a warm bed. Not only that, but jockeys will regularly be called in to 'ride out' or school horses over fences, before both trainer and jockey head off to the day's racing.

This will often involve a return journey of well in excess of 100 or more miles. This will be repeated day in day out during the season, which is effectively 11 ½ months per year. Oh, I nearly forgot – the trainer will have to entertain his/her horses' owners during racing, regardless of whether the horse wins, loses or falls so that he must be prepared to celebrate or commiserate depending on the result.

As with all major sports, there is also a 'pyramid' effect in racing. A small number of trainers and jockeys make a very good living, but spare a thought for the vast majority who struggle to make the grade and eventually, many fall by the wayside and must turn to an alternative source of income.

However, I do have a grouse, or two. Racing is doing all it can to encourage more of the general public to come and watch racing. Publicity is ongoing. TV advertisements, banners and promotional leaflets invariably show horses fighting out the finish of a race with jockeys encouraging them on with raised whips. How often do we hear complaints from non-regular race goers saying, "Why do they have to beat the horses so much?"

The invariable answer is to say that, "The horses don't feel it in the heat of the moment." Think of rugby players. Most of the time they emerge from the scrum or the maul, looking certain to have been injured but just shrug it off and get on with the game. "It's the same with horses."

Much has been done to reduce whip 'abuse' by enforcing rules on how many times the whip can be used in a race and where, but I cannot help feeling that racing would be a much more pleasant spectacle for both man (and beast) and particularly the non-regulars who need to be encouraged, if jockeys rode out their horses with hands and heels and maybe a slap down the shoulder for encouragement. If a solution is not found, the major races, in particular, will continue to be marred by whip bans for jockeys who are often encouraged by the larger percentage pay cheque on offer to the winning jockey in the more valuable races.

In a close finish, with whips flaying and reins loose and flapping, jockeys are often seen to bump in the saddle or onto the horse's loins, which surely must impede its forward momentum instead of encouraging it? Hands, heels and an odd slap down the shoulder would spare us this unsightly spectacle, however effective it may or may not be. Enough said, jockeys do a really great job on the whole and I trust that the one or two who might stoop to read this book will not take offence at these comments.

Federation Equestre International (FEI): The difficulties incurred dealing with the restrictions on the international movement of horses had been a significant issue throughout my racing, FEI and sport horse career.

From my perspective, being sent to Seoul in 1984, four years prior to the Olympic Games in the city, to resolve the problems to enable horses from around the world to compete, and most importantly returning home again after the games, was a good result and a valuable exercise for me.

The approval of Horse Passports by the OIE was a major breakthrough. This was adopted, first, by the OIE European Commission at its meeting in Sofia in October 1989 and was formally ratified in 1992 by the General Session in Paris. The Cyprus meeting, which also took place in 1992, proved to be the catalyst to successfully focus attention on facilitating horse movements throughout the Middle East.

Within months of commencing my role as Head of the FEI's Veterinary Department in 1982, I was appalled at the length of time it took from receiving the laboratory report of the presence of a prohibited substance in samples collected from a horse after competing, until the case could be heard by the Judicial Committee. This could often run to 6–8 months, which was much too long. I put together a proposal based on placing time limits on the length of time any particular segment of the procedure must take. Following receipt of this proposal, Eric Rundle, Australian lawyer and member of the FEI's Judicial Committee, informed the secretary general that as soon as this proposal was adopted, this would assist greatly in speeding up the handling of cases, and it did.

In 1984, two years after tightening up the medication control procedures, I was in a position to present my concept to the President of the FEI, on the upper deck of a cruise boat on the River Nile in Egypt, of how the control of doping could be modernised and introduced as an efficient Medication Control Programme (MCP) of which the FEI would be proud. Prince Philip liked the idea and the Bureau of the FEI approved it in principle at the following day's meeting, but it then suffered an incredibly long gestation period before it was launched prior to the first World Equestrian Games (WEG) in Stockholm, six years later, in 1990, but it was worth the wait.

Allied to this, in 1991, the General Assembly meeting in Rio de Janeiro, Brazil finally accepted that the highly popular and much used non-steroidal anti-inflammatory drug (NSAID), phenylbutazone, should join the FEI List of Prohibited Substances at time of competition. While fully accepting the value of this medication in the treatment regime of the stiff or sore competition horse, the FEI Veterinary Committee took much pleasure in presenting to the then President, H.R.H. The Princess Royal, a framed empty sachet of 'bute', symbolising that this was not for use in a horse at time of competition.

Early in 1990, due to the scandal involving alleged abusive schooling methods of jumping horses in Germany just prior to the first World Equestrian Games in Stockholm, led to the rapid response of the FEI in establishing an Ethics Committee to protect horse welfare. In July, representatives of FEI and World Horse Welfare met in London to consider the establishment of a Joint Committee on Equine Welfare, which held its first meeting, chaired by Andrew Higgins, shortly afterwards. In addition to many other initiatives over the years, this joint-committee organised the *Second International Conference on Transportation of Horses by Land, Sea and Air* which took place at Hartpury College, Gloucestershire, UK in July 2003. This meeting focused very much on the practical issues of horse movements although a scientific meeting ran concurrently with it.

In 2005, the FEI and World Horse Welfare decided to abandon the joint committee and in its place the FEI established its own welfare sub-committee. It was under the umbrella of this group and following the request of the FEI Dressage Committee that the workshop on Rollkur (over bending or hyperflexion of the neck in training) took place in Lausanne in January 2006.

The results of the research projects into the effects on horses competing in conditions of high heat and humidity proved invaluable into ensuring safe competition at the Atlanta (1996) and Hong Kong (2008) Olympic Games and other events taking place under similar adverse climatic conditions.

Sadly, in 2008 and despite appeals from Andrew Higgins, John McEwen and me, the FEI decided to abandon all sub-committees, welfare included, and place the responsibility for such on the parent committee, which, in the case of welfare, was the Veterinary Committee. Finally, I was made redundant and no longer actively involved with the FEI after some 26 rewarding years.

United Arab Emirates Equestrian and Racing Federation: Despite the difficulties experienced, I very much enjoyed my time spent with the UAE Equestrian and Racing Federation, where thoroughbred and Arabian racing are world class.

I attended the International Conference on Emerging Infectious Diseases (ICEID) when it was first convened in Dubai in February 1998. The conference brought together public health professionals to encourage the exchange of scientific and public health information on global emerging infectious disease issues. Major topics included current work on surveillance, epidemiology, research, communication and training, bioterrorism, and prevention and control of emerging infectious diseases.

Many years later, I was honoured to be invited by my long time Irish friend and colleague, Dr Peter Timoney, to attend this conference, as his guest, when it took place in Lexington, Kentucky in October 2012. The knowledge exchanged at such conferences is, of course, integral to the identification and control of relevant diseases to ensure minimum interference to the international movement of horses.

May I touch on just one of the many achievements of H.R.H. Princess Haya Bint Al Hussein, FEI President (2006–2014) one of her greatest of which is surely her FEI Clean Sport initiative? This was established in 2010 to safeguard the integrity of equestrian sport and guarantee a level playing field for all. It got its greatest endorsement at the London 2012 Olympic and Paralympic Games where all equestrian human and equine dope samples tested negative. With rigorous testing alongside a comprehensive education programme, FEI Clean Sport has ensured that current and future generations of athletes and their support teams are fully aware of their commitments to protect their own health, the health of their horses and fair play in the sport. Sadly, this does not appear to be true for all athletes competing in other sports.

Several years after I retired, the FEI and a number of international organisations, all bound together by a common interest in the horse and its welfare, gradually came together to form alliances. I had been privileged to be party to the FEI's initial contact with each of these organisations:

FEI and OIE: In 1982, just after I first joined the FEI, Dr Paul Benazet invited me to join him at the annual session of the World Organisation for Animal Health (OIE) in Paris, which enabled me, and eventually my successors, to meet and get to know senior members of the government veterinary services of the major countries of the world. I attended every year subsequently until I retired in 1995. This association provided a major forum for discussing and overcoming difficult situations relating to disease issues, which could, and often did, interfere with horses travelling to and from international events.

During this period, Dr Louis Blajan, director general of the OIE (1980–1990), addressed the FEI General Assembly in Paris in 1987 on *The Modern Horse Industry and the Problems Posed by Infectious Diseases.* The following year H.R.H. The Princess Royal, President of the FEI, reciprocated by addressing the general session of the OIE on the *FEI's role in equestrian sport.* Dr Blajan was succeeded by Dr Jean Blancou (1990–2000), with whom I also worked and then by Dr Bernard Vallat (elected in May 2000). It was during Dr Blancou's time that he invited me to write an article on *Welfare in the Competition Horse,* which appeared in the *OIE's Scientific Review* dated March 1994.

FEI and World Horse Welfare: You will recall that Charles Frank and I visited the headquarters of World Horse Welfare in 1985. This was the beginning of FEI's association with the charity, which proved to be of great benefit to both organisations and which led to the various chief executives and/or chairmen of the charity attending and addressing the FEI General Assembly from 1992 to the present day. It also paved the way for me, sometime later, to become a consultant to World Horse Welfare, responsible for its international training programmes in developing countries.

IFRA and OIE: In July 2013, an official agreement between the International Federation of Horseracing Authorities (IFHA) and the World Animal Health Organisation (OIE) was signed at the OIE Headquarters in Paris by Louis Romanet, Chairman of IFHA and son of M. Jean Romanet, my benefactor many years earlier, and Dr Bernard Vallat, director general of OIE. The Agreement signalled the affiliation of the horseracing industry to the world animal health standard-setting body and the formalisation of the collaborative process by which the IFHA and the OIE have been working together to improve the international movement of racehorses.

The IFHA shared the view of the OIE, and believed strongly, that the import requirements for international competition horses should be based on scientific principles. By basing the requirements for international movement of horses on science, it established a high degree of harmonisation between Government regulations governing temporary importation of such horses, which facilitated their movements worldwide.

Such facilitation could only be achieved through a high level public-private partnership, in which the Government, through its Veterinary Services, worked hand in hand with the event organisers, to implement agreed biosecurity protocols, assure clear identification and traceability of the horse and high health standards to ensure the safety and welfare of these high level, high performance horses (HHP horses).

The HHP concept is built on the precondition that competition horses are under continuous veterinary supervision and of general high health status in order to be fit to compete in top-level international competitions, and therefore pose a very low risk of transmitting infectious diseases.

Although I was in no way involved, the FEI had already elaborated solutions with the OIE to address similar concerns regarding the international movement of their high-level sports horses. This fortuitously provided a first and very welcome opportunity for all high-level sports horses, both competition and racing, to join the OIE on a united and coordinated front to develop guidelines and international standards to facilitate the international movement of all HHP sports horses.

This agreement marked another significant milestone in the history of the IFHA and the horseracing industry. The IFHA was delighted to be able to join with the OIE and FEI on this exciting project to the benefit of both the HHP horse and the industry, and looked forward to a long and mutually beneficial working relationship with the OIE.

FEI and IFHA = IHSC: In 2014, the FEI and the International Federation of Horse Racing Authorities (IFHA) joined forces by the creation of the International Horse Sports Confederation (IHSC) and agreed on the priority to work together in the following fields, always with the aim of ensuring the highest standards for welfare of the horse:

- The continued commitment to fight against doping and any abuse of horses;
- The cooperation with the OIE to facilitate the international movement of horses through the adoption of the concept of the High Health High Performance Horse (HHP);
- Assist the industry by surveillance of and reporting of diseases;
- The creation of a Fund for joint initiatives to support the horse sports industry.

Attendees at First Meeting of IHSC

FEI President, H.R.H. Princess Haya, was appointed President of the International Horse Sports Confederation (IHSC) at its first meeting. Louis Romanet, Chairman of the International Federation of Horseracing Authorities (IFHA), was appointed IHSC Vice President.

Other attendees at the first meeting of the newly formed group were Graeme Cooke, FEI veterinary director; Ingmar De Vos, FEI secretary general, who later succeeded H.R.H. Princess Haya as president; John McEwen, FEI 1st vice president and chair of the FEI Veterinary Committee; Pablo Mayorga, FEI 2nd vice president; Winfried Engelbrecht-Bresges, CEO of the Hong Kong Jockey Club (HKJC) and vice chairman of the IFHA; Andrew Harding, secretary general of the Asian Racing Federation, IFHA regional technical adviser (Asia) and director of racing development HKJC; Dr Roland Devolz, IFHA technical advisor; Dr Anthony Kettle, secretary of IFHA International Movement of Horses Committee (IMHC) and head of Veterinary Department at Dubai racing club.

FEI Meeting Hong Kong. Left to right: Dr Reiner Klimke, German dressage Olympian, AA, Winfried Engelbrecht-Bresges, listening in, watched by Dr Hanfried Haring, Secretary General, German Equestrian Federation

Dr Klimke was a German equestrian, who won six gold and two bronze medals in dressage at Summer Olympic Games — a record for equestrian events. He appeared in six Olympics from 1960 to 1988, excluding the 1980 Games in Moscow that were boycotted by West Germany and a number of other countries.

World Horse Welfare: Finally, working in the developing world was an amazing experience. To go from top-level sport horses to witness the lives of appalling poverty and depredation endured by working equines, their owners and their families was truly horrific. The work undertaken by the many equine charities

179

into providing knowledge, education, help and assistance to those so desperately in need is to be applauded and requires all the help we can give them.

I believe it is now time for me to retire and be 'put out to grass.' It is my pleasure to thank those many organisations for whom I have had the privilege to have worked in over the years. My heartfelt thanks go to them for giving me the opportunity to contribute in some small way to care for the health and welfare of our great friend, the horse. May he continue to be *USED BUT NEVER ABUSED*.

Annex 1

MEETINGS/CONFERENCES ATTENDED

Year	FEI Bureau	FEI Bur / Gen. Ass.	OIE	IFRA	WEVA	Vet Comm	ICRAV
1981	Joined FEI	Vienna, (AUS)					Dublin
1982	Los Angeles, (USA)	Geneva, (SUI)	Paris			Cambridge	
1983	Regensdorf, (SUI)	Amsterdam, (HOL)				Bern	Toronto
1984	Luxor, (EGY)	Bern, (SUI)	Paris			Bern	
1985	Seoul, (KOR)	Lisbon, (POR)	Paris			Newmarket	Hong Kong
1986	Tokyo, (JPN)	London, (GBR)	Paris			Leningrad	
1987	Rio de Janeiro, (BRA)	Paris, (FRA)	Paris		Montreal	Bern	
1988	Bern, (SUI)	No Bur/Gen Ass	Paris			Bern	Louisville
1989	Barcelona, (ESP)	Budapest, (HUN)	Paris and Sofia	Paris	Essen	Bern	
1990	Barcelona, (ESP)	Bern, (SUI)	Paris	Paris		Paris	
1991	Istanbul, (TUR)	Tokyo, (JPN)	Paris	Paris	Rio de Janeiro	Bern	
1992	Florence, (ITA)	Berlin, (GER)	Paris	Paris		Warendorf	
1993	Hong Kong, (HKG)	Rio de Janeiro, (BRA)	Paris	Paris	Geneva	Newmarket	

Year	FEI Bureau	FEI Bur / Gen. Ass.	OIE	IFRA	WEVA	Vet Comm	ICRAV
1994	Vienna, (AUS)	Tampa, (USA)	Paris	Paris		Bochum	Stockholm
1995	Abu Dhabi, UAE	Rome, (ITA)		Paris	Yokohama	Cambridge	
1996	Consultant UAE						Gold Coast
1997	Consultant UAE				Padua		
1998	Consultant UAE	Hong Kong, (HKG)					
1999	Consultant WHW	Doha, (QAT)			Paris		
2000	Consultant WHW	Mainz, (GER)		Paris			
2001	Consultant WHW	San Francisco (USA)					
2002	Consultant WHW	Rabat, (MAR)					
2003	Consultant WHW	GA Cancelled					
2004	Consultant WHW	Paris, (FRA)					Dubai
2005	Consultant WHW	London (GRB)					
2006	Consultant WHW	Kuala Lumpur (MAL)					
2007	Consultant WHW	Estoril, (POR)					

Annex II

CODE OF CONDUCT FOR THE WELFARE OF THE HORSE

The FEI requires all those involved in international equestrian sport to adhere to the FEI Code of Conduct and to acknowledge and accept that at all times the welfare of the Horse must be paramount. Welfare of the horse must never be subordinated to competitive or commercial influences. The following points must be particularly adhered to:

1. General Welfare:
a) Good Horse management
Stabling and feeding must be compatible with the best Horse management practices. Clean and good quality hay, feed and water must always be available.
b) Training methods
Horses must only undergo training that matches their physical capabilities and level of maturity for their respective disciplines. They must not be subjected to methods which are abusive or cause fear.
c) Farriery and tack
Foot care and shoeing must be of a high standard. Tack must be designed and fitted to avoid the risk of pain or injury.
d) Transport
During transportation, horses must be fully protected against injuries and other health risks. Vehicles must be safe, well ventilated, maintained to a high standard, disinfected regularly and driven by competent personnel. Competent handlers must always be available to manage the Horses.
e) Transit
All journeys must be planned carefully, and horses allowed regular rest periods with access to food and water in line with current FEI guidelines.

2. Fitness to compete:
a) Fitness and competence
Participation in Competition must be restricted to fit Horses and Athletes of proven competence. Horses must be allowed suitable rest period between training and competitions; additional rest periods should be allowed following travelling.
b) Health status
No Horse deemed unfit to compete may compete or continue to compete, veterinary advice must be sought whenever there is any doubt.

c) Doping and Medication

Any action or intent of doping and illicit use of medication constitute a serious welfare issue and will not be tolerated. After any veterinary treatment, sufficient time must be allowed for full recovery before Competition.

d) Surgical procedures

Any surgical procedures that threaten a competing Horse's welfare or the safety of other Horses and/or Athletes must not be allowed.

e) Pregnant/recently foaled mares

Mares must not compete after their fourth month of pregnancy or with foal at foot.

f) Misuse of aids

Abuse of a Horse using natural riding aids or artificial aids (e.g. whips, spurs, etc.) will not be tolerated.

3. Events must not prejudice Horse welfare:

a) Competition areas

Horses must be trained and compete on suitable and safe surfaces. All obstacles and competition conditions must be designed with the safety of the Horse in mind.

b) Ground surfaces

All ground surfaces on which Horses walk, train or compete must be designed and maintained to reduce factors that could lead to injury.

c) Extreme weather

Competitions must not take place in extreme weather conditions that may compromise welfare or safety of the Horse. Provision must be made for cooling conditions and equipment for Horses after competing.

d) Stabling at Events

Stables must be safe, hygienic, comfortable, well ventilated and of sufficient size for the type and disposition of the Horse. Washing-down areas and water must always be available.

4. Humane treatment of horses:

a) Veterinary treatment

Veterinary expertise must always be available at an Event. If a Horse is injured or exhausted during a Competition, the Athlete must stop competing and a veterinary evaluation must be performed.

b) Referral centres

Wherever necessary, Horses should be collected by ambulance and transported to the nearest relevant treatment centre for further assessment and therapy. Injured Horses must be given full supportive treatment before being transported.

c) Competition injuries

The incidence of injuries sustained in Competition should be monitored. Ground surface conditions, frequency of Competitions and any other risk factors should be examined carefully to indicate ways to minimise injuries.

d) Euthanasia

If injuries are sufficiently severe a Horse may need to be euthanized on humane grounds by a veterinarian as soon as possible, with the sole aim of minimising suffering.

e) Retirement
Horses must be treated sympathetically and humanely when they retire from Competition.

5. Education:
The FEI urges all those involved in equestrian sport to attain the highest possible levels of education in areas of expertise relevant to the care and management of the Competition Horse. This Code of Conduct for the Welfare of the Horse may be modified from time to time and the views of all are welcomed. Particular attention will be paid to new research findings and the FEI encourages further funding and support for welfare studies.

Annex III
ABBREVIATIONS/GLOSSARY

National Federation Members (1995)	
ALG	Algeria
ARG	Argentina
AUS	Australia
AUT	Austria
BAH	Bahamas
BRN	Bahrain
BAR	Barbados
BLR	Belarus
BEL	Belgium
BER	Bermuda
BOL	Bolivia
BOT	Botswana
BRA	Brazil
BUL	Bulgaria
CAN	Canada
CHI	Chili
CHN	China – People's Republic
TPE	Chinese Taipei
COL	Columbia
CRC	Costa Rica
CRO	Croatia
CUB	Cuba
CYP	Cyprus
CZE	Czech Republic
DEN	Denmark
DOM	Dominican Republic

ECU	Ecuador
EGY	Egypt
ESA	El Salvador
EST	Estonia
ETH	Ethiopia
FIN	Finland
FRA	France
GER	Germany
GBR	Great Britain
GRE	Greece
GUA	Guatemala
HON	Honduras
HKG	Hong Kong
HUN	Hungary
IND	India
INA	Indonesia
IRN	Iran
IRQ	Iraq
IRL	Ireland
ISR	Israel
ITA	Italy
JAM	Jamaica
JPN	Japan
JOR	Jordan
KAZ	Kazakhstan
KOR	Korea
KUW	Kuwait
KGZ	Kyrgyzstan
LAT	Latvia
LIB	Lebanon
LBA	Libya
LIE	Liechtenstein
LYU	Lithuania
LUX	Luxemburg
MAS	Malaysia

MAR	Morocco
MRI	Mauritius
MEX	Mexico
MDA	Moldova
MON	Monaco
NAM	Namibia
NED	Netherlands
NZL	New Zealand
NOR	Norway
OMA	Oman
PAK	Pakistan
PAN	Panama
PNG	Papua New Guinea
PAR	Paraguay
PER	Peru
PHI	Philippines
POL	Poland
POR	Portugal
PUR	Puerto Rico
QAT	Qatar
ROM	Romania
RUS	Russia
SMR	San Marino
KSA	Kingdom of Saudi Arabia
SEN	Senegal
SIN	Singapore
SVK	Slovakia
SLO	Slovenia
RSA	Republic of South Africa
ESP	Spain
SWE	Sweden
SUI	Switzerland
SYR	Syria
THA	Thailand
TUN	Tunisia

TUR	Turkey
UKR	Ukraine
UAE	United Arab Emirates
USA	United States of America
URU	Uruguay
UZB	Uzbekistan
VEN	Venezuela
ISV	Virgin Islands
ZAI	Zaire
ZAM	Zambia
ZIM	Zimbabwe
Other	
AAEP	American Association of Equine Practitioners
BEVA	British Equine Veterinary Association
CEO	Chief Executive Officer
CH	Championship
CHIO	Multiple Discipline Official International Event
CI*	(One star) International Event
CIO*	Official International Event
CVO	Chief Veterinary Officer
EU	European Union
ELDRIC	Endurance and Long Distance Riding International Conference (equestrian)
FEI	The Fédération Equestre Internationale
HHP	High Health High Horse Performance
HTC	Higher Technical Committee – Import and Export of Horses
ICEID	International Conference on Emerging Infectious Diseases
ICRA	International Conference of Racing Authorities (subsequently Federation)
ICRAV	International Conference Racing Analysts and Veterinarians
IFRA	International Federation of Racing Authorities (previously Conference)
IHSC	International Sports Horse Confederation
ILPH	International League for the Protection of Horses (subsequently WHW)
MAFF	Ministry of Agriculture and Fisheries (now DEFRA)
MCP	Medication Control Programme

MEP	Member of European Parliament
MOU	Memorandum of Understanding
MSC	Medication Sub-Committee
NSAID	Non-steroidal anti-inflammatory drugs
OG	Olympic Games
OIE	World Animal Health Organisation
OST	Overseas Training Programme
OTC	Overseas Training Committee
RDS	Royal Dublin Society
RCVS	Royal College of Veterinary Surgeons
SG	Secretary General
VC	Veterinary Committee
VO	Veterinary Officer (Steward's Secretary Veterinary – Irish Turf Club)
VR	Veterinary Regulations
WEG	World Equestrian Games
WEVA	World Equine Veterinary Association
WHW	World Horse Welfare (previously ILPH)
WVA	World Veterinary Association

*add (after C) D=Dressage; S=Jumping; C=Eventing; D=Driving, etc.

CPSIA information can be obtained
at www.ICGtesting.com
Printed in the USA
LVOW13*1830290518
578853LV00008B/186/P